D0744497

Prominent Visitors

to the

California Missions

Prominent Visitors
to the
California Missions
(1786-1842)

Compiled with Critical Annotations

by

Msgr. Francis J. Weber

Dawson's Book Shop

Los Angeles

1991

The Archival Center gratefully acknowledges the dedicated interest and generous support of the Fred and Mary Meier Foundation in the publication of this book.

Jacket Design by Anthony Kroll

Library of Congress Cataloging-in-Publication Data

Prominent visitors to the California missions: the provincial period (1786-1842) / compiled with critical annotations by Francis J. Weber.
  p.220 cm.
Includes bibliographical references.
ISBN 0-87461-933-5
1. California–History–To 1846.   2. Missions, Spanish–California –History.   3. Franciscans–Missions–California– History.   4. Indians of North America–California–Missions– History.   5. Travelers–California –History.   I. Weber, Francis J. F864.P96   1991
979.4 02–dc20   90-28492
                                                                CIP

This book was printed in a limited press run of 500 copies at the Kimberly Press in Santa Barbara.

"It is of prime significance for the life of America today that the first white men to settle on those western shores were Spaniards and Roman Catholics, representatives of a powerful nation that was the citadel of a united faith."

Herbert Ingram Priestley

Table of Contents

Foreword

The mercantilistic rigidity of Spanish officialdom effectively shielded Alta California from outside influences during its initial sixteen years as the world's most geographically isolated province. Gradually, in the years after 1776, the contagion engendered in European capitals by Captain James Cook's nautical feats along the Alaskan coast attracted ships flying the colors of other foreign nations to the rich blue waters along the Pacific Slope. Further penetration followed upon the fur trade in the great Northwest, when European and American vessels, as well as overland expeditions, began gravitating further south to the ports and population centers of California.

The published accounts of Provincial California's early visitors "are vitally important for a well-balanced view of the area's historical development."[1] Contemporary observations are now and always have been an excellent source of information and, "though frequently based on inadequate evidence, their combined worth contributes immeasurably to the overall historical pageant of a given area."[2]

This treatise chronologically examines the credibility and literary competence of twenty-four writers whose impressions of the Franciscan missions noticeably influenced later chroniclers and historians of the period.[3] The collection encompasses a wide spectrum of opinion concerning the missionary enterprise and the friars who implemented its program among what one writer described as a "heterogeneous lot of culturally destitute, peripheral peoples, among the most backward and abject of American red men."[4]

A number of commentators portray the 142 Franciscans whose investment of 2260 man-years brought nearly 100,000 aborigines into the Christian fold, as models of piety, simplicity and benevolence; others depict them as indifferent and unresponsive to their charges, while a minority represent the friars as debased drunkards and monsters. In fact, the *padres* were predominantly sincere, honest and devoted men who regulated their personal activities by the precepts of the religion they professed. As would be expected in any group of human personalities, there were a few who were more austere by nature and habit as well as a remnant whose excesses brought discredit to their cause. The final appraisal about that handful of "men who made of California a success story"[5] will be determined not by their worst or best representatives, but on the "larger number who, having consecrated their lives to a self-sacrificing employment, toiled on day by day according to the light that was in them."[6]

1

THE CALIFORNIA MISSIONS

Formal Title	Comenzada Date	Traditional Date	Engelhardt Date	Geiger Date	Popular Title
Mision de San Diego de Alcalá	July 16, 1769	July 16, 1769	July 16, 1769	July 16, 1769	San Diego
Mision de San Carlos del Puerto de Monterey	June 3, 1770	June 3, 1770	June 3, 1770	June 3, 1770	San Carlos
Mision de San Antonio de Padua	July 14, 1771	July 14, 1771	July 14, 1771	July 14, 1771	San Antonio
Mision del Santo Principe el Arcangel San Gabriel de los Temblores alias Proviscanza	Sept. 8, 1771	Sept. 8, 1771	Sept. 8, 1771	Sept. 8, 1771	San Gabriel
Mision de San Luis, Obispo de Tolosa	Sept. 1, 1772	Sept. 1, 1772	Sept. 1, 1772	Sept. 1, 1772	San Luis Obispo
Mision de Nuestro Padre San Francisco	Aug. 1, 1776	July 26, 1776	June 29, 1776	Oct. 9, 1776	San Francisco Mission Dolores
Mision de San Juan Capistrano de Sajivit	Nov. 1, 1776	Oct. 30, 1775	Nov. 1, 1776	Nov. 9, 1776	San Juan Capistrano
Mision de Nuestra Madre Santa Clara	Jan. 12, 1777	Jan. 12, 1777	Jan. 12, 1777	Jan. 12, 1777	Santa Clara
Mision de Glorioso Obispo Cardenal y Doctor Seráfico de Iglesia San Buenaventura	Mar. 31, 1782	Mar. 31, 1782	Mar. 31, 1782	Mar. 31, 1782	San Buenaventura
Mision de la Señora Santa Barbara Virgen y Martir	Dec. 4, 1786	Dec. 4, 1786	Dec. 4, 1786	Dec. 4, 1786	Santa Barbara
Mision de la Purisima Concepción de la Santisima Virgen Maria	Dec. 8, 1787	Dec. 8, 1787	Dec. 8, 1787	Dec. 7, 1787	Purisima Concepcíon
Mision de Santa Cruz	Sept. 25, 1791	Aug. 28, 1791	Aug. 28, 1791	Aug. 28, 1791	Santa Cruz
Mision de María Santísima Nuestra Señora de la Soledad	Oct. 9, 1791	Oct. 9, 1791	Oct. 9, 1791	Oct. 9, 1791	Soledad
Mision del Gloriosísimo Patriarca Señor San José	June 11, 1797	June 11, 1797	June 11, 1797	June 11, 1797	San Jose
Mision de San Juan Bautista, Precursor do Jesucristo	June 24, 1797	June 24, 1797	June 24, 1797	June 24, 1797	San Juan Bautista
Mision del Gloriosísimo Principe Arcangel Señor San Miguel	July 25, 1797	July 25, 1797	July 25, 1797	July 25, 1797	San Miguel
Mision de Señor San Fernando, Rey de España	Sept. 8, 1797	Sept. 8, 1797	Sept. 8, 1797	Sept. 8, 1797	San Fernando
Mision de San Luis, Rey de Francia	June 13, 1798	June 13, 1798	June 13, 1798	June 13, 1798	San Luis Rey
Mision de la Nuestra Santa Inés, Virgen y Martir	Sept. 17, 1804	Sept. 17, 1804	Sept. 17, 1804	Sept. 17, 1804	Santa Inés
Mision de el Gloriosísimo Principe San Rafael Arcangel (Asistencia de San Rafael Arcangel)	Dec. 14, 1817	Dec. 14, 1817	Dec. 14, 1817	Dec. 14, 1817	San Rafael
Mision de San Francisco Solano	lost	July 4, 1823	July 4, 1823	July 4, 1823	Sonoma

VISITORS TO THE CALIFORNIA MISSIONS

Author	Lifespan	Nationality	Visit to California	Year Published	Place Published	Order
1. Laperouse	1741-1788	French	1786	1797	Paris	1
2. Vancouver	1758-1798	English	1792-1793	1798	London	2
3. Menzies	1754-1842	Scotch	1792-1793	1924	San Francisco	22
4. Shaler	1773-1833	American	1803-1805	1808	Philadelphia	4
5. Langsdorff	1774-1852	German	1806	1812	Frankfurt	3
6. Kotzebue	1787-1846	Russian	1816, 1824	1821	London	5
7. Roquefeuil	1781-1831	French	1817-1818	1823	Paris	6
8. Bandini	1771-1841	Spanish	1819	1951	Berkeley	23
9. Beechey	1796-1856	English	1826-1827	1831	London	7
10. Rogers	-1828	American	1826-1827	1918	Cleveland	21
11. Duhaut-Cilly	1790-1848	French	1827-1828	1834-1835	Paris	9
12. Pattie	1804-c.1850	American	1828-1829	1831	Cincinnati	8
13. Green	1796-1878	American	1829	1915	New York	20
14. Robinson	1807-1895	American	1829-1845	1846	New York	16
15. Davis	1822-1909	American	1831-1833	1889	San Francisco	19
16. Reid	1811-1852	Scotch	1832-1852	1852	Los Angeles	18
17. Coulter	1778-1863	Irish	1835	1847	London	17
18. Forbes	1815-1882	English	1835	1839	London	10
19. Dana	1815-1882	American	1835-1836	1840	New York	11
20. Atherton	1815-1877	American	1836-1839	1964	San Francisco	24
21. Petit-Thouars	1793-1864	French	1837	1840-1855	Paris	12
22. Laplace	1793-1873	French	1839	1841-1854	Paris	13
23. Farnham	1804-1848	American	1840	1844	New York	14
24. Motras	1810-1884	French	1841-1842	1844	Paris	15

While there were undeniable shortcomings in the mission system as it evolved in Alta California, it should be recalled that such obvious deficiencies as excessive paternalism, inadequate health standards and lack of clerical personnel, cannot be separated or adequately appreciated apart from their historical milieu. For that reason, the statements of early visitors must be balanced against the individual author's preconceived sympathy with or innate rejection of the basic objectives underlying the Spanish colonial policy. Even the less enthusiastic observers probably would have endorsed Richard Henry Dana's view that "the dynasty of the priests was much more acceptable to the people of the country, and indeed to everyone concerned with the country, by trade or otherwise, that that of the *administradores*."[7]

Hubert Howe Bancroft singled out nine of the visitors for the merits of their productions, *viz.*, Beechey, Coulter, Dana, Duhaut-Cilly, Kotzebue, Laplace, Mofras, Petit-Thouars and Simpson, placing "Peit-Thouars at the head of the list, and Coulter at the foot."[8] Bancroft's ecclesiastical counterpart, Zephyrin Engelhardt, cited with differing degrees of favor, the works of Kotzebue, Vancouver, Langsdorff, Forbes, Beechey and Robinson. The Franciscan chronicler reserved his most complimentary remarks for Mofras whose work he considered "the most complete and trustworthy description of the California missions published in the early days."[9]

Opinions about historical credibility widen as authorities are multiplied. John Walton Caughey's "Classics," for example, emphasizing the matter presented, included Shaler, Pattie and Robinson, three works "distinguished for content more than for style."[10] Charles Franklin Carter felt that the French writings were the most far-reaching of all the accounts. In his opinion, the narrative of Petit-Thouars was "quite the most valuable of these from the historical point of view," while "Duhaut-Cilly is the most interesting, even entertaining, in his lively narrative."[11] In the public arena, Richard Henry Dana's opus has been and will probably remain the "most popular work on California ever written."[12]

A literary evaluation of the twenty-four authors here cited reveals their generally impressive stature in the general field of Californiana. Among the titles of "the twenty rarest and most important books dealing with the history of California," compiled in 1931, can be found the works of Duhaut-Cilly, Pattie, Mofras and Robinson.[13] That list, expanded by Phil Townsend Hanna to embrace works showing a "thorough and fundamental understanding of California and its diverse aspects," included Davis and Dana.[14]

Another appraisal, drawn up in 1945 by a panel of six Californiana experts[15] under the auspices of The Zamorano Club, enumerated the accounts of Laperouse, Vancouver, Kotzebue, Beechey, Duhaut-Cilly, Pattie, Davis, Forbes, Laplace, Farnham and Robinson among eighty of the most "distinguished California books."[16] In the more general listing of 11,620 titles of "uncommon and significant books relating to the continental portion of the United States," Wright Howes included all but three of the twenty-four narratives.[17] Any completely objective evaluation of the published recollections here treated must presume the basic affirmation that "opinion and education often cause the same things to be looked at under very different aspects."[18]

This writer is inclined to think that the earliest outside observers, apart from their endorsement or condemnation of the mission system, would rather uniformly admit, some perhaps a bit grudgingly, that "there are few events in history more remarkable on the whole, or more interesting, than the transformation, on the great scale, wrought by the Jesuits and Franciscans in Paraguay and California."[19]

Prologomena

A critical introduction, containing a descriptive appraisal of the particular author and the esteem his work occupies in the overall field of Californiana precedes each entry. Documentary notes augment the text only in those cases where factual elaboration seems appropriate or useful.

From a mechanical point of view, it might be pointed out that, in all instances, the spelling, grammar, and punctuation and italization used in the acknowledged source has been retained. For purposes of reference, the reader would be well-advised to disregard the various listings of missionary foundations in favor of the chart compiled herein.

In 1968, portions of the critical introduction to these twenty-four selections were extracted for an article which appeared in *The Americas*.[20] Four years later, that essay was re-published, with some minor alterations, in monograph form.[21] The hope of issuing the whole of the original treatise, complete with annotations, has only now been realized, some twenty-three years after the study was inaugurated.

The writer is grateful to the late Miss Lucille V. Miller, Curator for the Estelle Doheny Collection of Rare Books, Manuscripts and Works of Art, for her patience and kindness in making available the sources wherein these selections initially appeared. He is additionally indebted to the late Reverend Maynard J. Geiger, O.F.M., Archivist for the Santa Barbara

Mission Archives and Dr. Doyce B. Nunis, Jr., Professor Emeritus of History at the University of Southern California, for their encouragement and advice during the long years this volume was in preparation.

Msgr. Francis J. Weber
Archivist
Archdiocese of Los Angeles

References

1. Francis J. Weber, "The 'High Spots' of Californiana Historical Literature to 1835," *California Librarian* XXIV (July, 1968), 202.
2. Francis J. Weber, "Book Review," *American Ecclesiastical Review* CLIII (August, 1965), 135.
3. Though the "mission period" or Provincial Era technically ended on April 27, 1840, with the erection by Pope Gregory XVI of the Diocese of Both Californias, this survey extends the treatment an additional two years to include Eugene Duflot de Mofras and Alfred Robinson, both of whom commented on the change in ecclesiastical government. Such an extension seems all the more justified in view of the fact that the newly consecrated prelate, the Right Reverend Francisco Garcia Diego y Moreno, O.F.M., did not arrive at Santa Barbara until 1842.
4. Clark Wissler, *The American Indian* (New York, 1922), pp. 225-226.
5. Maynard J. Geiger, O.F.M., "Biographical Data on the California Missionaries (1769–1848)," *California Historical Society Quarterly* XLIV (December, 1965), 296.
6. Zoeth Skinner Eldredge (Ed.), *History of California* (New York, 1915), II, 99.
7. *Two Years Before the Mast* (New York, 1840), p. 210.
8. *California Pastoral* (San Francisco, 1888), p. 758.
9. *The Missions and Missionaries of California* (San Francisco, 1912), II, xxxvii.
10. *California* (New Jersey, 1953), p. 335.
11. "Duhaut-Cilly's Account of California in the Years 1827–28," *California Historical Society Quarterly* VIII (June, 1929), 131.
12. Charles E. Chapman, *A History of California: The Spanish Period* (New York, 1923), p. 495.
13. See "A Symposium," *California Historical Society Quarterly* X (March, 1931), 79–83. Participants were Leslie E. Bliss, Henry Raup Wagner and Robert Ernest Cowan.
14. *Libros Californianos* (Los Angeles, 1931), p. 3.
15. *Viz.*, Leslie E. Bliss, Homer D. Crotty, Phil Townsend Hanna, J. Gregg Layne, Henry Raup Wagner and Robert J. Woods.
16. See *The Zamorano 80* (Los Angeles, 1945).
17. See *U.S. Iana (1650–1950)* (New York, 1963).
18. Charles Franklin Carter, *op. cit.*, 159.
19. Alexander Forbes, *California: A History of Upper and Lower California* (London, 1839), p. 200.
20. "The California Missions and their Visitors," XXIV (April, 1968), 319–336.
21. *The California Missions As Others Saw Them (1786–1842)* (Los Angeles, 1972). This book was selected by the Braille Institute of America for inclusion in its series for use by the blind.

1

Jean François de Galaup,
Comte de la Pérouse
(1741–1788)

*T*he *widely-diffused account of that "true theocracy"[1] enjoyed by the Christianized Indians of Provincial California, penned by Jean François de Galaup, Comte de La Pérouse, had its origin on the evening of September 14, 1786, when the two French ships,* La Boussole *and* L'Astrolabe, *entered Monterey Bay bearing the first foreign contingent to visit California after Spanish occupation. Commissioned by King Louis XVI to expand geographical knowledge by searching out such areas as the Northwest Passage, the Comte de la Pérouse was equally intent on appraising the commercial and political potentialities of the Pacific area.*

In 1797, the careful and extensive journals of Jean François de Galaup were gathered into four volumes and published at Paris as Voyage de la Pérouse Autour du Monde *under the editorship of M.L.A. Milet-Mureau. The popularity accorded the treatise can be gauged by the number of editions and abridgements, as well as translations into English, German, Swedish, Danish, Dutch, Italian, and Russian the work went through in the following quarter century.*

His personality is reflected in the particular vibrance the French seaman imparted to his account. Though he was in Monterey for a mere ten days, his recorded observations of that short span contain generally "accurate and comprehensive information concerning the climate, geography, resources, Indians, Mission system, and government of California."[2] In the style common to his contemporaries, he gave "voice to his sentiments instead of suppressing them."[3]

By his own admission, the Comte de la Perouse and his party were received at Mission San Carlos Borromeo "like lords of the parish making their first entry into their estates." The friars exhibited little reticence in discussing their activities and Galaup recorded that "the monks, by their answers to our questions, left us in ignorance of nothing concerning the regime of this kind of religious community…"

Though Galaup "had nothing to say against the character of the missionaries,"[4] his overall reactions to the Franciscan modus agendi were predominantly unfavorable. He did not believe that the system was suited to lift the natives from their primeval state. While testifying to the high purpose of the friars, Galaup "thought they erred in attempting to enforce a disciplined life upon a wild people, whose self-reliance, he felt, suffered from the mission system.[5]

The Comte de la Pérouse conceded that the Jesuits in Paraguay "were neither more pious nor more charitable" than their California counterparts. Nonetheless, he regarded the Society of Jesus as being considerably "more skillful" in its reduction plan. Seemingly scandalized at the sight of "men and women loaded with irons, others in the block," he hastened to admit that such punishments were "carried out with little severity." Whatever may have been the French observer's motives for comparing the Indians and their treatment to the slave system in the West Indies, "he stirred up a debate that lasted until long after the American occupation."[6]

Despite his critical attitude about certain features of mission life, Galaup "expressed his sincere admiration for the missionaries themselves,"[7] noting that they were "firmly convinced either by prejudice or by their own experience that reason is almost never developed in these people, which to them is sufficient motive for treating them as children."

Zephyrin Engelhardt probably overstated himself by identifying the "half-infidel Frenchman"[8] with that "bogus philosophy which culminated in the beheading or banishment of priests, monks, and helpless nuns"[9] from his motherland. And yet the "critical, though not unfriendly, analysis of the treatment accorded to the mission Indians,"[10] evident throughout Galaup's narrative, was surely influenced, at least to some degree, by the French philosophers, many of whose views he clearly endorsed.

Charles N. Rudkin felt that "La Perouse's ideas of the basic equality of all men and of the inequity of forced compliance with any form of ecclesiastical dogma, both derived from the Eighteenth Century philosophical revolution, plainly affected his account of the missions of California and furnished what basis there may be for Father Zephyrin Engelhardt's aspersions."[11]

Abstracting from the interpretative motives which Jean François de Galaup associated with the missionary enterprise, most disinterested readers are inclined to agree with the remarks of one critic of the missions who concluded, after reading the Comte de la Perouse's account of "absolute government," that "beneficent Christianity cannot precede civilization, nor succeed without it."[12]

References

1. The translation here utilized is that of Charles N. Rudkin, *The First French Expedition to California. Laperouse in 1786* (Los Angeles, 1959). The most recent edition is that edited by Malcomb Margolin and released by Heyday Books of Berkeley as *Monterey in 1786: The Journals of Jean Francois de La Perouse.*
2. Abraham P. Nasatir, *French Activities in California. An Archival Calendar-Guide* (Stanford, 1945), p.1.
3. Edward Weber Allen, *The Vanishing Frenchman* (Vermont, 1959), p. 68.
4. John S. Hittell, "California Under the Friars," *Californian* III (May, 1881), 432.
5. Andrew F. Rolle, *California* (New York, 1963), p. 97.
6. Robert J. Woods, *The Zamorano 80* (Los Angeles, 1945), p.38.
7. Robert Glass Cleland, *From Wilderness to Empire* (New York, 1954), Pp. 93–94.
8. *San Francisco or Mission Dolores* (Chicago, 1924), p. 109.
9. *The Missions and Missionaries of California* (San Francisco, 1912), II, 677.
10. Edward Weber Allen, "Jean Francois Galaup de Lapérouse," *California Historical Society Quarterly* XX (March, 1941), 48.
11. *Op. cit.*, p. 21.
12. J.D.B. Stillman, "Footprints of Early California Discoverers," *Overland Monthly* II (March, 1869), 258.

1786

The Fathers of the mission of Saint-Charles [San Carlos] invited us to dine with them and promised to show us in detail the administration of their missions, the Indian's way of living, their arts, their new customs and, in general, everything that might interest the curiosity of travellers. We accepted with alacrity offers which we should not have feared to solicit had we not been anticipated. It was arranged that we should go the next day but one. M. Fages[1] wished to accompany us and took upon himself to procure horses for us.

After having crossed a small plain covered with herds of cattle, on which were left only a few trees to shelter these animals from the rain or too great heat, we passed over some low ridges and heard the sound of bells announcing our arrival, of which the friars had been notified by a horseman sent ahead by the governor.

We were received like lords of the parish making their first entry into their estates. The president of the missions[2] wearing his cope, his aspergill in his hand, was waiting for us at the door of the church, which was lighted up as though for a great feast day. He led us to the foot of the great altar where he entoned the *Te Deum* as an act of thanksgiving for the happy outcome of our voyage.

Before entering the church we had crossed an open square in which the Indians of both sexes were ranged in line. Their faces showed no astonishment and left it doubtful whether we should even be a subject of their conversation during the rest of the day.

The church is very clean, although thatched with straw. It is dedicated to Saint-Charles and decorated with good enough pictures copied from Italian originals. There was a picture of Hell in which the painter seemed to have borrowed somewhat from the imagination of Calot, but as it is

11

absolutely necessary to appeal to the senses of these recent converts, I am convinced that such a representation has never been more useful in any country, and it would be impossible for the Protestant cult, which proscribes images and almost all the other ceremonial features of our Church, to make any progress whith these people. I doubt that the picture of Paradise which hangs facing that of Hell produces as good an effect on them. The quiet scene it represents and the sweet satisfaction of the blest who surround the throne of the Supreme Being are concepts too sublime from men like brutes, but there must be rewards alongside of the punishments and it was a bounden duty not to permit any change in the kinds of delights that the Catholic religion promises.

On leaving the church we passed the same rank of Indian men and women. They had not left their stations during the *Te Deum*, only the children had gone a little way off and stood in groups near the house of the missionaries, which is opposite the church, as are the several storehouses.

On the right is the Indian village, made up of about fifty huts which serve as lodging for the seven hundred and forty persons of both sexes, including children, who make up the mission of Saint-Charles or Monterey.

These huts are wretched as can be met with among any people. They are round, six feet in diameter by four high. Some staves as big around as an arm, fixed in the ground and leaning together in a vault above, make up the frame. Eight or ten bundles of straw badly arranged on these staves shield the inmates well or ill from the rain or wind, and more than half of the hut is left uncovered when the weather is fair. Their only precaution is for each to have near his house two or three trusses of straw in reserve.

This general architectural type of the two Californias has never been changed by the exhortations of the missionaries. The Indians say that they love the open air, that it is convenient to set fire to the house when one is eaten up by too many fleas, and build another, which takes less than two hours. The independent Indians who change their dwelling place frequently, as hunting peoples, have one more reason.

The color of these Indians which is that of negroes, the house of the friars, their storehouses which are built of bricks and plastered with mortar, the threshing floor where they trample out the grain, the cattle, the horses, everything, in fact, reminds us of a plantation in Santo Domingo or any other colony. Men and women are assembled at the sound of the bell. A friar conducts them to work, to church, or to other activities. It hurts us to say it but the resemblance [to the slave colony] is so great that we have seen men and women loaded with irons, others in the *bloc*, and, finally, the blows of the whip might have reached our ears, this punishment being also admitted, but carried out with little severity.

The monks, by their answers to our questions, left us in ignorance of nothing concerning the regime of this kind of religious community, for one can apply no other name to the regulations they have established. They are in charge of temporal as well as spiritual matters. The products of the soil are given over to their administration. There are seven hours of labor per day, two hours of prayer (four or five on Sundays and feast days, which are given over entirely to rest and religion). Corporal punishments are inflicted on Indians of both sexes who fail in their religious duties, and several sins which in Europe are left to divine justice are punished by irons or the *bloc*.[3] To complete the comparison with religious houses, from the moment a neophyte is baptized it is as though he had pronounced eternal vows. If he escapes to return to the home of his relatives in the independent villages he is summoned three times to return. If he refuses the missionaries appeal to the authority of the government which sends soldiers to tear him from the midst of his family and lead him back to the mission, where he is condemned to receive a certain number of blows of the lash.[4] These people have so little courage that they never oppose any resistance to the three or four soldiers who so evidently violate, with respect to the rights of man, and this custom, against which reason protests so strongly, is kept up because the theologians have decided that one cannot, in conscience, administer baptism to people so volatile unless government stands in some sort as god-father and voucher for their perseverance.

The predecessor or M. Fages, M. Phillippe de Neve dead four years since,[5] commander of the Internal Provinces of Mexico, a man full of humanitarian and a philosophical Christian [*Chrétien philosophe*],[6] had protested against this custom. He thought that the progress of the faith would be more rapid and the prayers of the Indians more agreeable to the Supreme Being if they were not forced. He would have desired a less monastic system, more civil liberty for the Indians, less despotism in the exercise of power by the *presidios* whose government might be confided to greedy and barbaric men. He thought further that it might be necessary to moderate their authority by setting up a magistrate who should have enough authority to guarantee them against harassment. This just man served his country from his childhood but he lacked the prejudices of his class and knew that military government is subject to many disadvantages when it is not moderated by any authority which can intervene. He must have felt, however, the difficulty of supporting this conflict of three authorities in a country so far from the general government of

Mexico since the missionaries who are pious, so respectable, are already in a state of open quarrel with the governor who, for his part, seemed to me to be a loyal soldier.

We wanted to witness the distributions which are made at each meal-time, and since one day is like another for this kind of friars, by sketching the history of a single day the reader is given to know that of the entire year.

Like the missionaries, the Indians rise with the sun and go to prayers and mass, which last for an hour. During this time in three great caul-drons in the middle of the plaza they cook the barley-meal, the grain of which has been roasted before it is ground. This sort of soup, which the Indians call *atole* and of which they are very fond, is not seasoned with butter or salt and for us would be a very flat-tasting dish.

Each hut sends to get the ration for all its inhabitants, in a bowl made of bark. There is no confusion nor disorder and when the cauldrons are empty the scrapings are distributed to the children who have best remembered the lessons of the catechism.

This meal takes three quarters of an hour, after which they all go to their labor. Some work the soil with the cattle, others cultivate the gar-den; in fact each is employed at the different needs of the settlement and always under the surveillance of one of the friars.

The women are charged with hardly more than the care of their homes and their children, and roasting and grinding the grain. This last task is very difficult and slow because they have no other means to accomplish it but to crush the grain on a stone with a roller. M. de Langle,[7] seeing this operation, presented his mill to the missionaries. It would be hard to ren-der them a greater service. Today four women will do the work of an (*sic*) hundred and time will be available to spin the wool of the sheep and weave some coarse cloth. But up to now the friars, more concerned with the interests of Heaven than with worldly advantages, have greatly neglected the introduction of the most ordinary crafts. They are so aus-tere themselves that they have not a single chamber heated by fire although the winter may sometimes be rigorous and the greatest anchorites have never led more edifying lives.

At noon the bells announce dinner. The Indians then leave their work and send for their rations in the same bowl as for breakfast, but this sec-ond stew is thicker than the first. Wheat and maize, pease and beans, are mixed with it. The Indians call it *poussole* [*posole*]. They resume work again from two o'clock until four or five. Then they attend evening prayers which last for an hour and are followed by another ration of *atole* like that for breakfast. These three distributions serve for the subsistence of the greater portion of the Indians and this very economical soup might be adopted in our years of scarcity, though it would be necessary to add some seasoning. The whole skill of this cookery consists of roasting the grain before it is reduced to meal. As the Indians have no earthen or metal dishes for this operation they do it in bark baskets over small fires of burning coals. They rotate this sort of dishes with such skill and rapidity that they succeed in making the grain swell and burst without burning the basket, though it is of very combustible material, and we can certify that the best roasted coffee does not approach in uniformity of roasting what the Indians can do with their grain. It is distributed every morning and the slightest cheating when it is given out is punished by the lash, but it is rarely that they expose themselves to this. These punishments are decreed by Indian magistrates called *caciques*. There are three in each mission, elected by the people from among those whom the missionaries have not disqualified. However, to give a true picture of this magistracy we will say that these *caciques*, like overseers of plantations, are but passive creatures, blind executors of the will of their superiors, and that their chief function is to act as beadles in the church and to maintain there an air of good order and contemplation. The women are never flogged in the public square but in a place shut up and far away, perhaps so that their cries may not excite too lively compassion, which might incite the men to revolt. The latter, on the contrary, are exposed to the view of all their fellow-citizens, that their punishment may serve as an example. They usually beg for mercy. Then the executioner lessens the force of the blows, but the number is always fixed irrevocably.

The rewards are small special allocations of grain out of which they make little cakes cooked over the coals, and on high feast days the ration is beef. Many eat it raw, especially the fat which to them is a dish as delicious as excellent butter or the best cheese. They skin any animal with the greatest of skill, and when it is fat, like ravens they make a croaking sound for pleasure, devouring with their eyes those parts of which they are fondest.

They are often permitted to hunt and fish on their own account, and on returning they usually give the missionaries some present of fish or game, but in so doing they regulate the amount to what is strictly necessary, increasing the amount, however, if they know that new guests are visiting their superiors. The women raise a few chickens around their huts, the eggs from which they give to their children. This poultry is the property of the Indians, as are also their clothing and the small furnishings for their homes and their hunting equipment. There has never been an incident of stealing among themselves although closing the house consists only in laying a simple truss of straw across the opening when all the inhabitants are absent.

These customs may appear patriarchal to some of our readers. They should take into consideration that in these establishments there is not a single household that contains objects to tempt the cupidity of the neighboring hut. Food being assured to the Indians there remains no other need for them but the desire to beget beings who must be as stupid as themselves.

The men in the missions have made greater sacrifices to Christianity than the women because polygamy had been permitted to them and it was even the custom to marry all the sisters of a family. The women, on the other hand, have gained the advantage of receiving exclusively the caresses of a single man. I must say, however, that in spite of the unanimous report of the missionaries of this supposed polygamy I cannot conceive how it could establish itself among a savage people for, the number of men being about equal to that of women, it must have resulted in forced continence for many unless conjugal fidelity was less rigorously enforced than it is at the missions, where the friars have constituted themselves guardians of the virtue of the women. An hour after supper they take care to shut up under lock and key all those whose husbands are absent as well as the young girls over nine years old, and during the daytime they confide them to the surveillance of matrons. So many precautions are still not enough and we have seen men in the *bloc* and women in irons for having outwitted the vigilance of these female Arguses[8] for whom two eyes are not enough.

The converted Indians have retained all of their former customs that their new religion does not forbid, the same huts, the same games, the same clothing. That of the richest consists of a mantle of otter skin which covers the back and falls below the groin. The laziest have only a simple bit of cloth that the mission supplies them to hide their nakedness, and a short mantle of rabbit skin covers their shoulders and reaches down to the belt; it is fastened by a cord under the chin. All the rest of the body is bare as is the head, although some have hats of straw, very well woven.

The dress of the women is a mantle of very badly tanned deer skin. Those of the missions are wont to make of it a little jacket with sleeves. This, with a little apron of reeds and a skirt of deer skin which covers their eyes and descends to mid-leg, is their only clothing. Young girls over nine years old wear only a simple belt and children of both sexes are entirely naked.

The hair of both men and women is cut about four inches from the roots. The Indians of the *rancheries* [*rancherías*] having no iron tools perform this operation with firebrands. They also make a practice of painting their bodies red, or black when they are in mourning. The missionaries have forbidden the first of these styles of painting but they have had to tolerate the other because these people are closely attached to their friends. They weep copiously when they are reminded of them although it may be a long time since they were lost. They even are offended if their names are inadvertently pronounced in their presence. The bonds of family are less strong than those of friendship. Children scarcely recognize their fathers. They leave his hut as soon as they are capable of supporting themselves, but they retain a longer attachment for the mother, who has brought them up with extreme gentleness and has whipped them only when they showed cowardice in their little combats with children of the same age.

The old men of the *rancheries*, who are no longer able to hunt, live at the cost of the whole village and in general are shown great consideration. The independent savages are very frequently at war, but fear of the Spaniards makes them respect the missions and is perhaps not the least of the causes of the growth of the Christian villages. Their arms are bows and arrows, tipped with flint, very artfully worked. The bows, of wood strengthened with beef tendons, are very superior to those of the natives of Port des Français [Lituya Bay].

We were assured that they ate neither their prisoners nor their enemies killed in war, but that when they have overcome and killed in battle chiefs or very brave men they eat some pieces, less as a sign of hate and vengeance than as homage which they render to their valor and in the belief that this food is proper to increase their own courage.[9] As in Canada they take the hair of the vanquished, and they tear out their eyes, which they have the art of preserving from decay and which they treasure carefully as symbols of victory. It is their custom to burn the dead and to deposit the ashes in cemeteries.

They have two games which occupy their leisure time. The first, to which they give the name *takersia*, consists of casting and rolling a little hoop, three inches in diameter, in a space ten fathoms square, cleared of vegetation and surrounded by a palisade. The two players have each a staff, as thick as an ordinary cane and five feet long. They try to throw this staff into the hoop while it is in motion. If they succeed they win two points, and if the hoop when it stops rolling simply rests on the staff they score one point. Three points constitute a game. This game furnishes violent exercise since either the hoop or the staff is always in motion.

The other game, called *toussi*, is quieter. It is played by four, two on a side. Each in hides a bit of wood in one of his hands while his partner makes a thousand gestures to divert the attention of the opponents. It is very curious for an observer to see them squatting face to face, maintaining the most profound silence, watching the facial expressions and the smallest circumstances that may help them to guess the hand that holds the piece of wood. They win or lose a point according as they have guessed well or ill, and the winner has the right to hide it in his turn. The game is for five points. The usual wager is some glass beads or, among the independent Indians, the favors of their wives.

The latter [the independent Indians] have no knowledge of a God or an Hereafter, except for some tribes to the south who had a confused idea of this before the coming of the missionaries. They located their Paradise in the midst of the ocean where the elect enjoyed a coolness which they seldom experienced on their burning sands, and they supposed Hell to be in the ravines of the mountains.

The missionaries, firmly convinced either by prejudice or by their own experience that reason is almost never developed in these people, which to them is sufficient motive for treating them as children, admit but very few communion.[10] These are the geniuses of the race who might have illuminated their century and their compatriots like Descartes and Newton, teaching them that four and four make eight, a computation beyond the capacity of a great many of them. The mission regime is not suited to lift them from this state of ignorance. There everything is concentrated on obtaining the rewards of the afterlife, and the most common arts, even surgery such as is practiced in our villages, are not exercised. Many children perish from hernias that the slightest skill could cure and our surgeons were so fortunate as to relieve a few, and to teach them to use bandages.

It must be admitted that if the Jesuits were neither more pious nor more charitable than these friars, they were at least more skillful. The immense structure that they set up in Paraguay must excite the keenest admiration, but one must always hold against their ambition and their prejudices that system of communism, so contrary to the progress of civilization, and too slavishly followed in the missions of California. This government is a true theocracy for the Indians. They believe that their superiors are in direct and continuous communication with God and that they make Him descend onto the altar every day. By reason of this belief the fathers live in the midst of the villages in the most complete safety. Their doors are not closed, even at night when they are asleep, although the history of their missions supplies the example of a slain friar.?11 It is know that this assassination was the sequel of a riot caused by an imprudent act, for homicide is a very rare crime, even among the independent Indians. It is not punished, however, except by general contempt. But if a man succumbs to the blows of many it is supposed that he has deserved his fate, since he had so many enemies.

Notes to the Text

1. Pedro Fages (1730–1794), a native of Catalonia, was Governor of California between September of 1782 and April of 1791.
2. Father Fermin Francisco de Lasuen (1736–1803) was then *Presidente* of the California missions.
3. Charles N. Rudkin has observed that "La Perouse's ideas of the basic equality of all men and of the iniquity of forced compliance with any form of ecclesiastical dogma, both derived from the Eighteenth Century philosophical revolution, plainly affected his account of the missions of California and furnish what basis there may be for Father Zephyrin Engelhardt's aspersions." See *La Perouse in California* (Los Angeles, 1959), p. 21.
4. One commentator has noted that "the traveler had the notion that the neophytes were chained and whipped for going off to see their pagan relatives or missing spiritual exercises. This is pure imagination. The neophytes were permitted to visit their people when they wished. Runaways, who merely departed and were not unjust or scandalous in their flight, caused the padres very little thought...The fugitives, who were brought back and flogged, had either abandoned wives and children, were refusing to bring their children for instruction, casting snares in the path of prospective neophytes, stealing cattle, or guilty of some other such crime." See James Culleton, *Indians and Pioneers of Old Monterey* (Fresno, 1950), p. 123.
5. Felipe de Neve (1727–1784) was styled by Hubert H. Bancroft as "one of California's ablest rulers."
6. This terminology identified the author, according to Engelhardt, with that "French bogus philosophy which culminated in the beheading or banishment of priests, monks and helpless nuns." See *The Missions and Missionaries of California* (San Francisco, 1912), II, 677.
7. Captain Paul-Antoine de Langle, a fellow traveller of La Perouse on their scientific expedition, was massacred in 1787 on Mauna, one of the Samoan Islands.
8. The reference here is to that many-eyed mythological being know as "the zealous watchman."
9. Here La Perouse relies on fable rather than fact.
10. If the natives were not encouraged to frequent the sacraments in the early years, it might well have been because of the difficulty they encountered in maintaining themselves in what theologians then considered the state of grace.
11. Alta California's proto-martyr, Father Luis Jayme (1740–1775), died during a revolt of the natives at San Diego. The Mallorcan friar came to the New World after successfully occupying the Chair of Theology at the Convento de Jesus at Palma.

2

George Vancouver
(1758–1798)

George Vancouver's three trips to California were made under orders "to explore the entire coast, to examine the extent of Spanish possessions, and to seize unclaimed territory."[1] In his reflections of the area, Vancouver "endeavored to be fair and just in describing what he saw, and even for what he thought faulty he made due allowances."[2] The seaman gave every indication of being "an intelligent and honest British sailor, a good representative of a good class of explorers and writers, plain of speech, and a reliable witness on matters which fell under his personal observation, and in which his national pride and prejudices were not involved."[3]

The captain's three volume account, published for G.G. and J. Robinson and J. Edwards at London in 1798, was initially released under the editorship of John Vancouver as A Voyage of Discovery to the North Pacific Ocean, and Round the World...performed in the Years 1790, 1791, 1792, 1793, and 1795, in the Discovery Sloop of War...[4]

The central theme of the California settlements by his time was that of spreading the Christian faith among the Indians. Vancouver recognized that motive, and his recorded observations show his interest and admiration for their spiritual accomplishments as well as their physical layouts.

Vancouver, like Laperouse, was "much impressed by the natural advantages of Alta California, but criticized the Spaniards for their failure to make due use of their surroundings, marvelling at the weakness of their establishments."[5] While noting that the natives at the four missions he visited were "well fed, better clothed than the Indians in the neighborhood," the English visitor "expected more improvement than he found" in California.[6]

Though he regarded the California natives as "certainly a race of the most miserable beings possessing the faculties of human reason," men "too stupid and indolent to benefit much from the efforts made in their behalf,"[7] Vancouver was moved by the manner in which "the uniform, mild disposition of this religious *order (the Franciscans) had never failed to attract the loyalties of the neophytes. Throughout his narrative, he "spoke of the conduct of the fathers as mild and kind-hearted and as never failing to attach to their interests the affections of the natives."⁸ He pointed out that the comforts the friars "might have provided in their own humble habitations, seemed to have been totally sacrificed to the accomplishment" of worthy places of prayer.*

George Vancouver was not a Catholic, nor was he familiar with the Spanish language. Yet his views of California and its missions are remarkably accurate. His account remains "superior to any of its kind, and constitutes the chiefest source of authority of that period."⁹

References

1. Andrew F. Rolle, *California*, A History (New York, 1963), p. 98.
2. Zephyrin Engelhardt, O.F.M.,. *The Missions and Missionaries of California* (San Francisco, 1912), II, 469.
3. Hubert Howe Bancroft, *History of California* (San Francisco, 1884), I, 526.
4. The excerpts here cited are from the annotated edition prepared by Marguerite Eyer Wilbur, *Vancouver of California, 1792–1794* (Los Angeles; 1954). This edition, forming Vols. IX, X and XXII of the *Early California Travel Series* was also published in a single volume.
5. Charles E. Chapman, *A History of California: The Spanish Period* (New York, 1923), p. 407.
6. John Walton Caughey, *California Heritage* (Los Angeles, 1964), p. 82.
7. Willard O. Waters, *Franciscan Missions of Upper California as seen by Foreign Visitors and Residents* (Los Angeles, 1954), n.p.
8. Theodore H. Hittell, *History of California* (San Francisco, 1898), II, 516.
9. Robert E. Cowan, *A Bibliography of the History of California and the Pacific West, 1510–1906* (San Francisco, 1914), p. 236.

1792–1793

Sunday the 18th, was appointed for my visiting the mission. Accompanied by Mr. Menzies[1] and some of the officers, and our friendly Señor Sal,[2] I rode thither to dinner. Its distance from the Presidio is about a league, in an easterly direction; our ride was rendered unpleasant by the soil being very loose and sandy, and by the road being much incommoded with low groveling bushes.

Its situation and external appearance in a great measure resembled that of the Presidio; and, like its neighborhood, the country was pleasingly diversified with hill and dale. The hills were at a greater distance from each other, and gave more extent to the plain, which is composed of a soil infinitely richer than that of the Presidio, being a mixture of sand and a black vegetable mould. The pastures bore a more luxuriant herbage, and fed a greater number of sheep and cattle. The barren sandy country through which we had passed, seemed to make a natural division between the lands of the mission and those of the Presidio, and extends from the shores of the port to the foot of a ridge of mountains, which border on the exterior coast, and appear to stretch in a line parallel to it. The verdure of the plain continued to a considerable height up the sides of these hills; the summits of which, though still composed of rugged rocks, produced a few trees.

The buildings of the mission formed two sides of a square only, and did not appear as if intended, at any future time, to form a perfect quadrangle like the Presidio. The architecture and materials, however, seemed nearly to correspond.

On our arrival, we were received by the reverend fathers with every demonstration of cordiality, friendship, and the most genuine hospitality. We were instantly conducted to their mansion, which was situated near, and communicated with the church. The houses formed a small oblong-square, the side of the church composed one end, near which were the apartments allotted to the fathers. These were constructed neatly after the manner of those at the Presidio, but appeared to be more finished, better contrived, were larger, and much more cleanly. Along the walls of this interior square, were also many other apartments adapted to various purposes.

Whilst dinner was preparing, our attention was engaged in seeing the several houses within the square. Some we found appropriated to the reception of grain, of which, they had not a very abundant stock; nor was the place of its growth within sight of the mission; though the richness of the contiguous soil seemed equal to all the purposes of husbandry. One large room was occupied by manufacturers of a coarse sort of blanket-ting, made from the wool produced in the neighborhood. The looms, though rudely wrought, were tolerably well contrived, and had been made by the Indians, under the immediate direction and superintendance of the fathers; who, by the same assiduity, had carried the manufacture thus far into effect. The produce resulting from their manufactory is wholly applied to the clothing of the converted Indians. I saw some of the cloth, which was by no means despicable; and, had it received the advantage of fulling, would have been a very decent sort of clothing. The preparation of the wool, as also the spinning and weaving of it, was, I understood, performed by unmarried women and female children, who were all resident with the square, and were in a state of conversion to the Roman Catholic persuasion. Besides manufacturing the wool, they are also instructed in a variety of necessary, useful and beneficial employ-ments until they marry, which is greatly encouraged; when they retire from the tuition of the fathers to the hut of their husband. By these means it is expected that their doctrines will be firmly established, and rapidly propagated; and the trouble they now have with their present untaught flock will be hereafter recompensed, by having fewer prejudices to combat in the rising generation. They likewise consider their plan as essentially necessary, in a political point of view, for insuring their own safety. The women and girls being the dearest objects of affection amongst these Indians, the Spaniards deem it expedient to retain con-stantly a certain number of females immediately within their power, as a pledge for the fidelity of the men, and as a check on any improper designs the natives might have for the missionaries, or the establishments in general.

By various encouragements and allurements to the children, or their parents, they can depend upon having as many to bring up in this way as they require: here they are well fed, better clothed than the Indians in the neighborhood, are kept clean, instructed, and have every necessary care taken of them; and in return for these advantages they must submit to certain regulations; amongst which they are not suffered to go out of the interior square in the day time without permission; are never to sleep out of it at night; and to prevent elopements, this square has no communication with the country but by one common door, which the fathers themselves take care of, and see that it is well secured every evening, and also the apartments of the women, who generally retire immediately after supper.

If I am correctly informed by the different Spanish gentlemen with whom I conversed on this subject, the uniform, mild, and kind-hearted disposition of this religious order has never failed to attach to their interest the affections of the natives, wherever they sat down amongst them; this is very happy circumstance, for their situation otherwise would be excessively precarious; as they are protected only by five soldiers who reside under the directions of a corporal, in the buildings of the mission at some distance on the other side of the church.

The establishment must certainly be considered as liable to some danger. Should these children of nature be ever induced to act an ungrateful and treacherous part, they might easily conceal sufficient weapons to effect any evil purpose. —There are only three fathers,[3] these live by themselves, and should any attempt be made upon them at night, the very means they have adopted for security might deprive them of any assistance from the guard until it might be too late; and individually, they could make but little resistance. Should a conspiracy for their destruction take place, the mission would soon fall, and there would be little doubt of the conspirators being joined by the Indians of the village, which is in the vicinity of the mission, and was said to contain six hundred persons, but on visiting it, I considered their number greatly over-rated. The major part of them, I understood, were converted to the Roman Catholic persuasion; but I was astonished to observe how few advantages had attended their conversion.

They seemed to have treated with the most perfect indifference the precepts, and laborious example, of their truly worthy and benevolent pastors; whose object has been to allure them from their life of indolence, and raise in them a spirit of emulous industry; which, by securing to them plenty of food and the common conveniences of life, would necessarily augment their comforts, and encourage them to seek and embrace the blessings of civilized society. Deaf to the important lessons, and insensible of the promised advantages, they still remained in the most abject state of uncivilization; and if we except the inhabitants of Tierra del Fuego,[4] and those of Van Dieman's land,[5] they are certainly a race of the most miserable beings, possessing the faculty of human reason, I ever saw. Their persons, generally speaking, were under the middle size, and very ill made; their faces ugly, presenting a dull, heavy, and stupid countenance, devoid of sensibility or the least expression. One of their greatest aversions is cleanliness, both in their persons and habitations; which, after the fashion of their forefathers, were still without the most trivial improvement. Their houses were of a conical form, about six or seven feet in diameter at their base (which is the ground) and are constructed by a number of stakes, chiefly of the willow tribe, which are driven erect into the earth in a circular manner, the upper ends of which being small and pliable are brought nearly to join at the top, in the centre of the circle; and these being securely fastened, give the upper part or roof somewhat of a flattish appearance. Thinner twigs of the like species are horizontally interwoven between the uprights, forming a piece of basket work about ten or twelve feet high; at the top a small aperture is left, which allows the smoke of the fire made in the centre of the hut to escape, and admits most of the light they receive: the entrance is by a small hole close to the ground, through which with difficulty one person at a time can gain admittance. The whole is covered over with a thick thatch of dried grass and rushes.

These miserable habitations, each of which was allotted for the residence of a whole family, were erected with some degree of uniformity, about three or four feet asunder in straight rows, leaving lanes or passages at right angles between them; but these were so abominably infested with every kind of filth and nastiness, as to be rendered not less offensive than degrading to the human species.

Close by stood the church, which for its magnitude, architecture, and internal decorations, did great credit to the constructors of it; and presented a striking contrast between the exertions of genius and such as bare necessity is capable of suggesting. The raising and decorating this edifice appeared to have greatly attracted the attention of the fathers; and the comforts they might have provided in their own humble habitations, seemed to have been totally sacrificed to the accomplishment of this favorite object. Even their garden, an object of such material importance, had not yet acquired any great degree of cultivations, through its soil was a rich black mould, and promised an ample return for any labour that might be bestowed upon it. The whole contained about four acres, was tolerably well fenced in and produced some fig, peach, apple, and other fruit-trees, but afforded a very scanty supply of useful vegetables; the principal part lying waste and over-run with weeds.

On our return to the convent, we found a most excellent and abundant repast provided of beef, mutton, fish, fowls, and such vegetables as their garden afforded. The attentive and hospitable behaviour of our new friends amply compensated for the homely manner in which the dinner was served; and would certainly have precluded my noticing the distressing inconvenience these valuable people labour under, in the want of almost all the common and most necessary utensils of life, had I not been taught to expect, that this colony was in a very different stage of improvement, and that its inhabitants were infinitely more comfortably circumstanced.

After dinner we were engaged in an entertaining conversation, in which, by the assistance of Mr. Dobson, our interpreter, we were each able to bear a part. Amongst other things, I understood that this mission was established in the year 1775, and the Presidio of San Francisco in 1778, and that they were the *northernmost settlements, of any description, formed by the court of Spain on the continental shore of North-West America, or the islands adjacent,* exclusive of Nootka, which I did not consider as coming under that description any more than the temporary establishment which, in the preceding spring had formed by Señor Quadra near Cape Flattery, at the entrance of the Straits of Juan De Fuca; and which has been already stated to be entirely evacuated. The excursions of the Spaniards seemed to be confined to the neighborhood of their immediate place of residence, and the direct line of country between one station and another; as they have no vessels for embarkation excepting the native canoe, and an old rotten wooden one, which was lying near our landing place. Had they proper boats on this spacious sheet of water, their journies would not only be much facilitated, but it would afford a very agreeable variety in their manner of life, and help to pass away many of the solitary and wearisome hours which they must unavoidably experience. I understood that the opposite side of the port had been visited by some soldiers on horseback, who obtained but little information; some converted Indians were found living amongst the natives of the northern and western parts of the port, who were esteemed by the Spaniards to be a docile, and in general a well-disposed people; though little communication took place between them and the inhabitants of this side. The missionaries found no difficulty in subjecting these people to their authority. It is mild and charitable, teaches them the cultivation of the soil, and introduces amongst them such of the useful arts as are most essential to the comforts of human nature and social life. It is much to be wished, that these benevolent exertions may succeed, though there is every appearance that their progress will be very slow; yet they will probably lay a foundation, on which the posterity of the present race may secure to themselves the enjoyment of civil society.

The next establishment of this nature, and the only one within our reach from our present station, was that of Santa Clara, lying to the southeastward, at the distance of about eighteen leagues, and considered as one day's journey. As there was no probability of our wood and water being completely on board in less than three or four days, I accepted the offer of Señor Sal and the reverend fathers, who undertook to provide us horses for an expedition to Santa Clara the following morning. At the decline of day we took our leave, and concluded a visit that had been highly interesting and entertaining to us, and had appeared to be equally grateful to our hospitable friends.

We arrived at the mission of Santa Clara, which according to my estimation is about forty geographical miles from San Francisco. Our journey, excepting that part of it through the morass, had been very pleasant and entertaining; and our reception at Santa Clara by the hospitable fathers of the mission, was such as excited in every breast the most lively sensations of gratitude and regard. Father Tomás de la Peña appeared to be the principal of the missionaries. The anxious solicitude of this gentleman, and that of his colleague Father José Sanchez, to anticipate all our wishes, unequivocally manifested the principles by which their conduct was regulated. Our evening passed very pleasantly, and after a most excellent breakfast next morning, the 21st, on tea and chocolate, we took a view of the establishment and the adjacent country.

The buildings and offices of this mission, like those of San Francisco, form a square, but not an entire enclosure. It is situated in an extensive fertile plain, the soil of which, as also that of the surrounding country, is black productive mould, superior to any I had before seen in America. The particular spot which had been selected by the reverend fathers for their establishment, did not appear so suitable to their purpose as many other parts of the plain within a little distance of their present buildings, which are erected in a low marshy situation for the sake of being near a run of fine water; notwithstanding that within a few hundred yards they might have built their houses on dry and comfortable eminences.

The stream of water passes close by the walls of the fathers' apartments, which are upon the same plan with those at San Francisco; built near, and communicating with the church, but appearing to be more extensive, and to possess in some degree more comforts, or rather less inconveniences, than those already described. The church was long and lofty, and as well built as the rude materials of which it is composed would allow, and when compared with the unimproved state of the country, infinitely more decorated than might have been reasonably expected.

Apartments within the square in which the priests resided, were appropriated to a number of young female Indians; and the like reasons were given as at San Francisco for their being so selected and educated. Their occupations were the same, though some of their woolen manufactures surpassed those we had before seen, and wanted only the operation of fulling, with which the fathers were unacquainted, to make them very decent blankets. The upper story of their interior oblong square, which might be about one hundred and seventy feet long, and one hundred feet broad, were made use of as granaries, as were some of the lower rooms; all of which were well stored with corn and pulse of different sorts; and besides these, in case of fire, there were two spacious warehouses for the reception of grain detached from each other, and the rest of the buildings, erected at a convenient distance from the mission. These had been recently finished, contained some stores, and were to be kept constantly full, as a reserve in the event of such a misfortune.

They cultivate wheat, maize, peas and beans; the latter are produced in great variety, and the whole in greater abundance than their necessities require. Of these several sorts they had many thousand bushels in store, of very excellent quality, which had been obtained with little labour, and without manure. By the help of a very mean, and ill contrived plough drawn by oxen, the earth is once slightly turned over, and smoothed down by a harrow; in the month of November or December, the wheat is sown in drills, or broadcast on the even surface, and scratched in with the harrow; this is the whole of their system of husbandry, which uniformly produces them in July or August an abundant harvest. The maize, peas, and beans, are produced with as little labour; these are sown in the spring months, and succeed extremely well, as do hemp and flax, or linseed. The wheat affords in general from twenty-five to thirty for one according to the seasons, twenty-five for one being the least return they have ever yet deposited in their granaries from the field; notwithstanding the enormous waste occasioned by their rude method of threshing, which is always performed in the open air by the treading of cattle. The product of the other grains and pulse bears a similar proportion to that of the wheat. I was much surprised to find that neither barley nor oats were cultivated; on enquiry I was given to understand, that as the superior kinds of grain could be plentifully obtained with the same labour that the inferior ones would require, they had some time ago declined the cultivation of them. The labours of the field are performed under the immediate inspection of the fathers, by the natives who are instructed in the Roman Catholic faith, and taught the art of husbandry. The annual produce is taken under the care of these worthy pastors, who distribute.it in such quantities to the several persons as completely answers all the useful and necessary purposes.

Besides a few acres of arable land, which we saw under cultivation near the mission, was a small spot of garden ground, producing several sorts of vegetables in great perfection and abundance. The extent of it, however, like the garden at San Francisco, appeared unequal to the consumption of the European residents; the priests, and their guard consisting of a corporal and six soldiers. Here were planted peaches, apricots, apples, pears, figs, and vines, all of which excepting the latter promised to succeed very well. The failure of the vines here, as well as at San Francisco, is ascribed to a want of knowledge in their culture; the soil and climate being well adapted to most sorts of fruit. Of this we had many evidences in the excellence of its natural unassisted productions. In this country the oak, as timber, appears to take the lead. A tree of this description near the establishment measured fifteen feet in girth, and was high in proportion, but was not considered by the the fathers as of an extraordinary size; and I am convinced, that on our journey we passed several oaks of greater magnitude. The timber of these trees is reputed to be equal in quality to any produced in Europe. The elm, ash, beech, birch, and some variety of pines, grew in the interior and more elevated parts of the country in the greatest luxuriance and abundance.

Our attention was next called to the village of the Indians near the mission. The habitations were not so regularly disposed, nor did it contain so many, as the village at San Francisco; yet the same horrid state of uncleanliness and laziness seemed to pervade the whole. A sentiment of compassion involuntarily obtruded on the mind in contemplating the natural or habitual apathy to all kind of exertion in this humble race. There was scarcely any sign in their general deportment of their being at all benefited, or of having added one single ray of comfort to their own wretched condition, by the precepts and laborious exertions of their religious instructors; whose lives are sacrificed to their welfare, and who seem entirely devoted to the benevolent office of rendering them a better and a happier people. They appeared totally insensible to the benefits with which they were provided, excepting in the article of food; this they now find ready at hand, without the labour of procuring it, or being first reduced by cold and hunger nearly to a state of famine, and then being obliged to expose themselves to great inconvenience in quest of a precarious, and often scanty means of subsistence. Not only grain, but the domestic animals have been introduced with success, amongst them; many of the natives have, by the unremitted labour of the fathers, been taught to manufacture very useful and comfortable garments from the wool of their sheep; for the introduction of this animal they ought to be highly grateful, since by the mildness of the climate, and the fertility of the soil, they are easily propagated and reared; and while they provided them with comfortable clothing, afford them also nourishing and delicate food. These advantages however seemed to have operated as yet to little purpose on the minds of these untaught children of nature, who appeared to be a compound of stupidity and innocence, their passions are calm; and regardless of reputation as men, or renown as a people, they are stimulated neither to the obtaining of consequence amongst themselves by any peaceful arts, nor superiority over their neighbours by warlike achievements, so common amongst the generality of the Indian tribes. All the operations and functions both of body and mind, appeared to be carried on with a mechanical, lifeless, careless indifference; and as the Spaniards assert they found them in the same state of inactivity and ignorance on their earliest visits, this disposition is probably inherited from their forefathers.

Further efforts are now making at this mission, to break through the gloomy cloud of insensibility in which at present these people are enveloped, by giving them new habitations; an indulgence that will most probably be followed by others, as their minds appear capable of receiving them. A certain number of the most intelligent, tractable, and industrious persons, were selected from the group, and were employed in a pleasant and well-adapted spot of land facing the mission, under the direction and instruction of the fathers, in building for themselves a range of small, but comparatively speaking comfortable and convenient habitations. The walls, though not so thick, are constructed in the same manner with those described in the square at San Francisco, and the houses are formed after the European fashion, each consisting of two commodious rooms below, with garrets over them. At the back of each house a space of ground is inclosed, sufficient for cultivating a large quantity of vegetables, for rearing poultry, and for other useful and domestic purposes. The buildings were in a state of forwardness, and when finished, each house was designed to accommodate one distinct family only; and it is greatly to be wished, for the credit of the creation, that this supine race of our fellow creatures may not long remain insensible to, and unconvinced of, the superior advantages they may derive, or the new comforts they may possess, by this alteration in their mode of living. It is by no means improbable, that by this circumstance alone they may be roused from their natural lethargic indifference, and be induced to keep themselves clean, and to exert themselves in obtaining other blessings consequent on civilized society. This once effected, the laborious talk of their worthy and charitable benefactors will wear the appearance of being accomplished; and should it be hereafter attended with a grateful sense of the obligations conferred, it is not possible to conceive how much these excellent men will feel rewarded, in having been the cause of meliorating the comfortless condition of these wretched humble creatures.

Our conversation admitted of no pause with these seemingly happy and benevolent priests; whilst we acquired much information we were highly entertained; and the day was far advanced by the time our curiosity was thus far gratified.

In compliment to our visit, the fathers ordered a feast for the Indians of the village. The principal part of the entertainment was beef, furnished from a certain number of black cattle, which were presented on the occasion to the villagers. These animals propagate very fast, and being suffered to live in large herds on the fertile plains of Santa Clara, in a sort of wild state, some skill and adroitness is required to take them. This office was at first intended to have been performed by the natives, but it was overruled by Señor Paries[6] an ensign in the Spanish army, who, with one of the priests of Señor Quadra's vessel,[7] had joined our party from a mission at some little distance called Santa Cruz. This gentlemen conceived the business of taking the cattle would be better performed by the soldiers, who are occasionally cavalry, and are undoubtedly very good horsemen. We mounted, and accompanied them to the field, to be spectators of their exploits. Each of the soldiers was provided with a strong line, made of horsehair, or of thongs of leather, or rather hide, with a long running noose; this is thrown with great dexterity whilst at full speed, and nearly with a certainty, over the horns of the animals, by two men, one on each side of the ox, at the same instant of time; and having a strong high-peaked pummel to their saddles, each takes a turn round it with the end of the line, and by that means the animal is kept completely at bay, and effectually prevented from doing either the men or horses any injury, which they would be very liable to, from the wildness and ferocity of the cattle. In his situation the beast is led to the place of slaughter, where a third person, with equal dexterity, whilst the animal is kicking and plunging between the horses, entangles its hind legs by a rope, and throws it down, on which its throat is immediately cut. Twenty-two bullocks, each weighing from four to six hundred weight, were killed on this occasion; eighteen were given to the inhabitants of the village, and the rest were appropriated to the use of the soldiers, and the mission, in addition to their regular weekly allowance of twenty-four oxen, which are killed for their service every Saturday: hence it is evident, as the whole of their stock has sprung from fifteen head of breeding cattle, which were distributed between this and two other missions, established about the year 1778; that these animals must be very prolific to allow of such an abundant supply. Their great increase in so short a time is to be ascribed to the rigid economy of the fathers, who would not allow any to be killed, until they had so multiplied as to render their expiration not easy to be effected. The same wise management has been observed with their sheep, and their horses have increased nearly at the same rate.

Although this village did not appear so populous as that as San Francisco, I was given to understand that there were nearly double the number of inhabitants belonging to it; and in consequence of the many unconverted natives in the neighbourhood of Santa Clara, several of the Christian Indians of good character were dispersed amongst their countrymen, for the purpose of inducing them to partake of the advantages held out to them, in which they had not been altogether unsuccessful. All who have offered themselves as converts have been admitted and adopted, notwithstanding the artifices of several, who have remained in and about the mission until they have acquired a stock of food and clothing, with which they have decamped. This improper conduct has, however, had no sort of effect on the benevolent minds of the fathers, who have not only uniformly supplied their wants on a second visit, but also those of many wandering tribes that would be at the trouble of asking their assistance.

Thus concluded our morning's entertainment, and we retired to dinner. In the convent a most excellent and abundant repast of the productions of the country was provided, which were in the greatest perfection. The day passed to the mutual satisfaction of all parties, and we found ourselves under some difficulty the next morning, Thursday 22d, to excuse ourselves from accepting the pressing solicitations of these good people, to prolong our stay at Santa Clara; this, however, necessity and not inclination obliged us to decline. We took our leave at an early hour, highly gratified by our reception and entertainment which had amply compensated for the fatigue or inconvenience attending so long a journey, performed in a way to which we were so little accustomed.

The mission of Santa Clara is situated at the extremity of the S.E. branch of port San Francisco, which terminates in a shallow rivulet extending some distance into the country, from whence, and the confines of the port in its vicinity, Santa Clara is well supplied with a variety of excellent fish.

Our reception at the mission (San Carlos Borromeo) could not fail to convince us of the joy and satisfaction we communicated to the worthy and reverend fathers, who in return made the most hospitable offers of every refreshment their homely abode afforded. On our arrival at the entrance of the Mission the bells were rung, and the Rev. Fermin Francisco de Lausen, father president of the missionaries of the order of St. Francis in New Albion, together the fathers of this mission,[8] came out to meet us, and conduct us to the principal residence of the father president. This personage was about seventy-two years of age,[9] whose gentle manners, united to a most venerable and placid countenance, indicated that tranquilized state of mind, that fitted him in an eminent degree for presiding over so benevolent an institution.

The usual ceremonies on introduction being over, our nine was pleasantly engaged in the society of the father president and his two companions, the priests regularly belonging to the mission of San Carlos, who attended us over their premises. These seemed to offer but little from those at San Francisco, or Santa Clara; excepting that the buildings were smaller, the plan, architecture, and materials exactly corresponding.

In their granaries were deposited a pretty large quantity of the different kinds of grain before noticed at the other establishments, to which was added some barley, but the whole was of an inferior quality, and the return from the soil by no means equal to that produced at Santa Clara. Here also was a small garden on the same confined scale, and cultivated in the same manner as observed at the other stations.

An Indian village is also in the neighbourhood; it appeared to us but small, yet the number of its inhabitants under the immediate direction of this mission was said to amount to eight hundred, governed by the same charitable principles as those we had before visited. Notwithstanding these people are taught and employed from time to time in many of the occupations most useful to civil society, they had not made themselves any more comfortable habitations than those of their forefathers; nor did they seem in any respect to have benefited by the instruction they had received. Some of them were at this time engaged under the direction of the fathers, in building a church with stone and mortar. The former material appeared to be of a very tender friable nature, scarcely more hard than indurated clay, but I was told, that on its being exposed to the air, it soon becomes hardened, and is an excellent stone for the purpose of building. It is of a light straw colour, and presents a rich and elegant appearance, in proportion to the labour that is bestowed upon it. It is found in abundance at no great depth from the surface of the earth; the quarries are easily worked, and it is I believe the only stone the Spaniards have hitherto made use of in building. At Santa Clara I was shown a ponderous black stone, that Father Tomas[10] said was intended to be so appropriated as soon as persons capable of working it could be procured. The lime they use is made from sea shells, principally from the ear-shell, which is of a large size and in great numbers on the shores; not having as yet found any calcareous earth that would answer this essential purpose. The heavy black stone is supposed to be applicable to grinding, and should it be found so to answer, it will be a matter of great importance to their comfort, since their only method of reducing their corn to flour is by two small stones placed in an inclined position on the ground; on the lower one the corn is laid, and ground by hand by rubbing the other stone nearly of the same surface over it The flour produced by this rude and laborious process makes very white and well tasted, though heavy bread, but this defect is said by the Spaniards to be greatly remedied when mixed with an equal proportion of flour properly ground.

After we had satisfied our curiosity in these particulars we rode round the neighbourhood of the mission. It was pleasantly situated, and the country, agreeably broken by hills and valleys, had a verdant appearance, and was adorned like that in the vicinity of Monterey, with many clumps and single trees, mostly of the pine tribe, holly-leaved oak, and willows; with a few trees of the poplar and maple, and some variety of shrubs, that rather incommoded our travelling, which was chiefly confined to one of the valleys, and within sight of the buildings. Through this valley a small brook of water about knee-deep, called by the Spaniards Rio Carmelo, takes its course, passes the buildings of the Mission, and immediately empties itself into the sea.

In this valley, near the sides of the Carmelo, a few acres of land exhibited a tolerably good plant of wheat; but as the soil here, as well as at Monterey, is of a light sandy nature, its productions are consequently inferior to the other two missions I had visited; yet I was given to understand, that the interior country here, like that at San Francisco, improves in point of fertility, as it retires from the ocean.

On our return to the convent, we found a most excellent repast served with great neatness, in a pleasant bower contructed for that purpose in the garden of the mission. After dinner we were entertained with the methods practised by the Indians in taking deer, and other animals, by imitating them. They equip themselves in a dress consisting of the head and hide of the creature they mean to take; with this, when properly put on and adjusted, they resort to the place where the game is expected, and there walk about on their hands and feet, counterfeiting all the actions of the animal they are in quest of; these they perform remarkably well, particularly in the watchfulness and the manner in which deer feed. By this means they can, nearly to a certainty, get within two or three yards of the deer, when they take an opportunity of its attention being directed to some other object, and discharge their arrows from their secreted bow, which is done in a very stooping attitude; and the first or second seldom fails to be fatal. The whole was so extremely well contrived and executed, that I am convinced a stranger would not easily have discovered the deception.

The mission (San Juan Capistrano) is very pleasantly situated in a grove of trees, whose luxuriant and diversified foliage, when contrasted with the adjacent shores, gave it a most romantic appearance; having the ocean in front, and being bounded on its other sides by rugged dreary mountains, where the vegetation was not sufficient to hide the naked rocks, of which the country in this point of view seemed to be principally composed.

The buildings of the mission were of brick and of stone, and in their vicinity the soil appeared to be of uncommon and striking fertility. It was founded in the year 1776, and is in latitude 33° 29', longitude 242° 35'. The landing on the beach in the cove seemed to be good; and had it not been for the very favorable gale with which we were now indulged, I should have been tempted to have passed a few hours at this very enchanting place.

Notes to the Text

1. Archibald Menzies (1754-1842) was himself the author of a description of Provincial California. *Cf.* Entry #3 in this volume.
2. Hermenegildo Sal (1746-1800) was in charge at San Francisco when Vancouver landed there. The British explorer gave Sal's name to a promontory south of San Luis Obispo Bay, north of Point Purisima in Santa Barbara County.
3. *Vg.* The three friars alluded to were Martin Landaeta, Antonio Danti and Diego Noboa.
4. Vancouver has in mind an archipelago area consisting of one large and several small islands separated from the mainland of South America by the Strait of Magellan.

5. The reference here is to a penal colony in Tasmania.
6. The author is possibly referring to Fernando Perez, *Alferez* of the San Francisco Company from 1792 to 1797.
7. Juan Francisco de la Bodega y Quadra (1744-1793), captain of the Spanish ship *Sonora*, was the discoverer of the Puerto de Bodega in 1775. *See.* Henry R. Wagner, "The Last Spanish Exploration of the Northwest Coast and the Attempt to Colonize Bodega Bay," *California Historical Society Quarterly* X (December, 1931), 313-345.
8. *Viz.* Pascual Martinez de Arenaza (c.1762-1799), Tomas de la Pena (1743-1806), Miguel Sanchez (1738-1803) and Jose Señan (1760-1825).
9. Father Lasuen was actually only fifty-six years old at the time. See. Finbar Kenneally, *Writings of Fermin Francisco de Lasuen* (Washington, 1965), I, 266n.
10. Father Tomas de la Pena (1743-1806) was already a veteran of two decades in missionary work in Alta California.

3

Archibald Menzies
(1754-1842)

Archibald Menzies, a Scottish surgeon and naturalist who accompanied George Vancouver to California in 1792-1793, came "to investigate the whole of the natural history of the countries visited..."[1] The Menzies narrative was unknown for over a century until its discovery in the British Museum. That part pertaining to California was translated by Alice Eastwood and published in 1924.[2] Menzies' account closely resembles that of Vancouver, though the latter dwells more extensively on details. For the most part, he gives a fair appraisal of the friars and their attempts to spread the Christian faith among the natives.

The Scottish physician spoke approvingly of the manner in which the Indians had assimilated the trades and mannerisms of civilized society, noting that "these are the happy effects of religious persuasions when conducted on the rational plans of industry & the supplying of necessary wants, & when inculcated by the mild influence of such exemplary Fathers." The contentment of the natives greatly impressed the visitor who expressed "no doubt but they will be induced to continue in pursuing that quiet industrious line of life which so easily gratifies all their wants & comforts their minds with the enjoyments of happiness here & hereafter."

Along with Vancouver, Menzies recognized and admired the motives of the missionaries. His descriptions of their establishments "show his interest and admiration for their spiritual accomplishments as well as their physical layouts."[3] He remarked, on one occasion, that his party could not "reflect without admiration on the patience, constancy & perseverance with which these worthy Fathers pursued their laudable object of Civilization, in a faithfull & humane discharge of their function, under the inconveniencies & sufferings to which they must be daily exposed in such distant & remote regions."

Menzies carefully recorded his recollections of Indian life at Missions Dolores,

Santa Clara, San Carlos and Santa Barbara, noting that "the painful constancy with which these abstemious Fathers maintain the religious observances of the Church of Rome in this distant region is a great proof of their indefatigable zeal & uncommon fortitude, for notwithstanding the inconveniencies & sufferings to which they are here daily exposed, yet they go patiently on encountering every difficulty with a manly perseverance & overcoming every obstacle by a noble principle of enthusiastic zeal & inward conviction of the importance of the object they pursue, in converting these poor Savages from that pagan state of darkness in which they have hitherto roamd at large in the Forests, to the enlightend paths of the Christian Religion & the practical knowledge of usefull Arts."

In Menzies' opinion, "a system of civilization conducted upon such humane & exemplary principles can never fail of attaining its end, even in a political view, by securing to the state in process of time a number of valuable & industrious subjects, reard up in the paths of virtue & morality under the mild auspices of these worthy Fathers, whose religious austerities must daily impress on their minds a lasting conviction of the exalted objects they pursue & whose little plans of industry so easy & natural, renders their manner of living less precarious & consequently more comfortable & happy than in their roving state. Thus influencd, these Proselytes act the part of gratefull & affectionate Children & gradually become usefull members of the Community, so that we cannot sufficiently applaud the persevering zeal of their humane conductors thro a process so tedious & difficult."

References

1. Charles Frederic Newcombe (Ed.), *Menzies' Journal of Vancouver's Voyage* (Victoria, B.C., 1923), p. x.
2. The excerpts here cited are reproduced from the Eastwood translation which appeared as "Menzies' California Journal," *California Historical Society Quarterly* II (January, 1924), 265-340.
3. Bern Anderson, *Surveyor of the Sea* (Seattle, 1960), p. 127.

1792-1793

O n our arrival at the Mission[1] the Venerable Fathers receivd us with open Arms & testified their satisfaction by every mark of civility attention & kindness. They provided an elegant & plentifull dinner for the whole party, which at their particular request was Cooked in the English Stile by our own Servants, & while it was getting ready, they took great pleasure in shewing us through every part of the Building of the Mission & its dependencies.

The Mission of San Francisco has been establishd about fifteen years & is situated near the sea side at the bottom of a pleasant fertile Valley where the surrounding Country lookd gay with rich verdure. It is at present under the direction & management of two Fathers of the Franciscian order of Friars,[2] & consists of a regular range of buildings inclosing a small Court of about twenty/yards square, faced round on the inside with Colonades, from which the entries to the different Granaries & Manufactories lead, but the only entrance to this Court is through a large Hall, where we din'd, & where the watchfull Fathers generally reside, so that nobody can enter or go out of this Building without their knowledge. The Church which is by far the largest Building takes up one side of the Square & every thing belonging to it is kept very clean & in good order; the entrance to it is from the end on the out side, but the Fathers have a private one for themselves from the inside of the Mission, with a Vestry where they keep & preserve their different Robes & Dress for Religious rites. Besides this compact building there are several separate houses for the Mechanics to work in & for Habitations for them & five Soldiers with their Families, which is conceivd necessary to guard the place from any sudden attack from the Natives. The whole of these buildings were of Mortar & Turfs & thatchd in the same manner as the

Houses at the Praesidio. There was also a small Garden fenced in containing about two Acres of Ground divided into quarters by cross walks & pretty well filld with a variety of Potherbs & Culinary Vegetables, together with a number of Fruit Trees, such as Apples Peaches Figs & Vines, but none of these were very productive or had yet bore any good Fruit; Whether this was owing to their not being of a good quality or their not agreeing with the Soil & Climate was uncertain.

But what particularly engagd our attention was a Village close to the Mission, which containd about five or six hundred Natives converted to Christianity by the indefatigable perseverance of these Humane Fathers. Their Habitations or Wigwams were aptly compard to a crowded cluster of Bee-hives each of which was of a hemispherical form about nine feet high & nearly the same in diameter & consisted of slender sticks or rods stuck in the ground & lashd together with thongs into the above form & afterwards closely thatchd all round with Bulrushes, excepting a small hole left on one side just sufficient to creep in at. The Fire is placd in the middle of the Wigwam & as no particular aperture is left at the top for the smoke to go out at, it was observd oozing out through the Thatch.

The Fathers industriously employ these Natives in cultivating the Land for their own subsistence & in spinning of Wool which they weave in Looms in the form of small Blankets for their own Clothing in a large Room within the Mission; We saw several of the Machines for this occupation. Others are reared up to Farming & to Mechanical Arts; so that they are now enabled to carry on every thing necessary for the subsistence & support of the Settlement within themselves, or at least with very little expense to the Mother Country. These are the happy effects of religious persuasions when conducted on the rational plans of industry & the supplying of necessary wants, & when inculcated by the mild influence of such exemplary Fathers.

These Proselytes appeard peaceable & docile in their behaviour & so contented with their situation, that we have no doubt but they will be induced to continue in pursuing that quiet industrious line of life which so easily gratifies all their wants & comforts their minds with the enjoyments of happiness here & hereafter. How different the comparison between them & the more Northern Tribes, who have been visited these eight years by commercial people, whose selfish Views have taught them duplicity, & whose avaricious objects have increasd their original ferocity, by the knowledge & exercise of those destructive Weapons with which they daily arm them, so that they seem to excel their civilized instructors in the refinement of their cruelties & the exercise of the most consummate frauds.

After spending the day agreeably with their Reverend Fathers we returnd in the evening highly satisfied with our cordial reception & impressed with a due sense of their hospitality & kind attention to every circumstance which they thought would please us. Nor could we reflect without admiration on the patience, constancy & perseverance with which these worthy Fathers pursued their laudable object of Civilization, in a faithfull & humane discharge of their function, under the inconveniencies & sufferings to which they must be daily exposd in such distant & remote regions.

The Missions are always a little removd from the Garrisons & are generally situated in commodious fertile spots, within fifteen or twenty leagues of one another, & round them the whole Agriculture of the Country is carried on under the care & management of the sagacious Fathers, who have their Ploughs Harrows & Teams with Oxen industriously employd, & who regulate the rural economy of the Farms in all their various branches & dependencies, as well as the more solemn duties of their avocations.

The painfull constancy with which these abstemious Fathers maintain the religious observances of the Church of Rome in this distant region is a great proof of their indefatigable zeal & uncommon fortitude, for notwithstanding the inconveniencies & sufferings to which they are here daily exposed, yet they go patiently on encountering every difficulty with a manly perseverance & overcoming every obstacle by a noble principle of enthusiastic zeal & inward conviction of the importance of the object they pursue, in converting these poor Savages from that pagan state of darkness in which they have hitherto roamd at large in the Forests, to the enlightend paths of the Christian Religion & the practical knowledge of usefull Arts.

Surely a system of civilization conducted upon such humane & exemplary principles can never fail of attaining its end, even in a political view, by securing to the state in process of time a number of valuable & industrious subjects, reard up in the paths of virtue & morality under the mild auspices of those worthy Fathers, whose religious austerities must daily impress on their minds a last conviction of the exalted objects they pursue & whose little plans of industry so easy & natural, renders their manner of living less precarious & consequently more comfortable & happy than in their roving state. Thus influencd, these Proselytes act the part of gratefull & affectionate Children & gradually become usefull members of the Community, so that we cannot sufficiently applaud the persevering zeal of their humane conductors thro a process so tedious & difficult.

Notes to the Text

1. *I.e. San Francisco or Mission Dolores, founded in 1776.*
2. The two friars alluded to were Antonio Danti and Martin Landaeta.

4

William Shaler
(1773-1833)

The "earliest published first hand description of California by an American"[1] and the initial one set to type in the United States, was written by William Shaler who fought his way out of San Diego Bay after the Lelia Byrd, "one of the first American ships to attempt trade with California,"[2] was cited for smuggling otter skins out of the country.

Though the Yankee sea captain was "an intelligent and able man, possessing considerable experience in literary, linguistic, and diplomatic matters,"[3] his account "is in error on some points," while in others "his remarks are open to question."[4] Throughout his recollections, Shaler is hostile and contemptuous towards the Spaniards whose policies he regarded as unprogressive and backward. "Terse and restricted in imaginative quality,"[5] those parts of the Connecticut-born trader's journal based on the earlier observations of Laperouse and Vancouver, give a fairly good description of the people, institutions and prospects of the province.

Shaler visited most of the missions, but apparently was poorly received at certain ones "for unlike his great predecessors he was a mere trader and as such he was looked upon with disfavor by the officials on the coast."[6] Perhaps it was this lack of enthusiasm on the part of his hosts that accounts for Shaler's generally unfavorable attitude towards the friars.

"A northwest fur trader of characteristic New England stuff,"[7] Shaler seems to have missed the whole purpose of the missionary enterprise. To him, those isolated outposts were little more than "valuable estates or plantations belonging to the king of Spain, and capable, in case of a conquest of this country, of furnishing abundant supplies of all kinds of provisions..."[8] Shaler regretted that "the notion of private property is not admitted among them." Each mission was, in his view, "an indivisible society, of which the fathers are the kings and pontiffs."

William Shaler's account was first published at Philadelphia as the Journal of a Voyage from China to the Northwestern Coast of America, in 1808.[9] It *was reprinted as an appendix in Robert Glass Cleland's* History of California: The American Period[10] *and again, in 1935, by Lindley Bynum at Claremont.*[11]

References

1. Willard 0. Waters, *Franciscan Missions of Upper California as seen by Foreign Visitors and Residents* (Los Angeles, 1954), Entry 3A.
2. J. Gregg Layne, "Annals of Los Angeles," *California Historical Society Quarterly* XIII (September, 1934), 204.
3. Hubert Howe Bancroft, *History of California* (San Francisco, 1885), II, 24.
4. John Walton Caughey, *California Heritage* (Los Angeles, 1964), p. 104.
5. Franklin Walker, *A Literary History of Southern California* (Berkeley, 1950), p.8.
6. Joseph B. Lockey, "Book Review," *Pacific Historical Review* V (September, 1936), 279.
7. Robert Glass Cleland, *A History of California: The American Period* (New York, 1927), p. 13.
8. The excerpts here cited are from the edition appended to Robert Glass Cleland, *A History of California: The American Period.*
9. *American Register* III, 137-175.
10. (New York, 1927), Pp. 470-482.
11. *Journal of a Voyage between China and the Northwestern Coast of America Made in 1804.*

1803-1805

The plan of civilization in the missions is to instruct the Indians in the Catholic religion, the Spanish language, the necessary arts, agriculture, etc.; but the notion of private property is not admitted among them; so that each mission forms an indivisible society, of which the fathers are the kings and pontiffs. The missionaries of the Franciscan order, in Upper California, have salaries of 400 dollars *per annum*; the Dominicans that are established below have but 350 dollars[1]. The missions of California may be considered as so many valuable estates or plantations belonging to the king of Spain, and capable, in case of a conquest of this country, of furnishing abundant supplies of all kinds of provisions, horses; etc.

I shall give the best account I am able of these missions, as far as I have information respecting them, together with the other establishments in the country, and its principal bays and harbours.

The missions of San Francisco, Santa Clara, and the Pueblo de San Josef, are within the jurisdiction of San Francisco. They are represented by Captain Vancouver as very fertile and flourishing, and are esteemed by the Spaniards to be among the richest establishments in the country.

Santa Cruz, near Point Ano Neuvo[2] and a pueblo of the same name in its neighborhood, form the northern frontier of the jurisdiction of Monterey: the first was founded in 1789, and the second in 1790.[3] Between that and Monterey stands La Soledad, and near the presidio, El Carmelo. Further down the coast are situated San Antonio, San Miguel, and San Luis; the latter is the last to the southward within this jurisdiction. Those missions are none of them far removed from the coast; they are reputed rich by the Spaniards in stock and grain; and the account given by Monsieur de la Perouse of the extraordinary fertility of El Carmelo, justifies that report.

The mission of San Luis is situated from six to twelve miles from the coast, in a fertile valley, watered by several streams; it has 1000 Indians attached to it, and its annual productions are 5000 *fanegas* of wheat, 1500 *fanegos* of corn, with barley, oats, and pulse in proportion; it has also vineyards, and a plenty of fruit. The stock belonging to this mission exceeds 1000 head of horned cattle, besides horses, sheep, hogs; goats, etc.; its buildings are said to be excellent; even the habitations of the Indians are stone and plaster. This mission has a commodious port, and a plenty of good timber.

The Purisima, situated near Point Conception; forms the northern frontier of the jurisdiction of Santa Barbara; it is watered by several streams, and is said to be little inferior to San Luis in fertility and abundance of stock.

Between this mission and Santa Barbara, was founded, in 1804, the mission of Santa Agnes (Ines) about three miles from the coast. It is well watered is in a fertile spot, and bids fair to be ranked among their richest establishments in a short time. Its productions the first year were 1500 fanegos of wheat, and 500 of corn; the wheat was the production of thirty fanegos sown, that is, fifty for one.

Santa Barbara is situated in the neighbourhood of the praesidio; it has 2400 Indians attached to it. I learnt no particulars respecting this mission, other than that it is very rich in stock and grain, vineyards and fruits.

San Buenaventura is situated about eighteen miles below the praesidio, half a mile distance from the sea, where there is good anchorage and safe landing; it stands on the left margin of a charming valley, and has an extensive plan to the southeast of it, which, when I was there, was covered with cattle, and the valley appeared to be cultivated as far as the eye could reach. This mission was founded in 1784;[4] it has 1200 Indians attached to it, and its stock of cattle is said to exceed 15,000 head, besides horses, mules, sheep, hogs, etc.; and its production in grain, wine, etc., are equally abundant.

San Fernando is situated between Buenaventura and the Pueblo de Los Angeles; whereabouts I am unable to say, or how far from the sea: the Spaniards report it to be a flourishing establishment.

The Pueblo de Los Angeles is about twenty-five or thirty miles in a northwest direction from the bay of San Pedro, and forms the southeastern boundary of the jurisdiction of Santa Barbara. This village is composed of about 100 families, many of whom are in easy circumstances; and some possess from 3000 to 5000 head of cattle. This part of the country is fertile, and produces large quantities of grain and pulse; they are also rapidly advancing in the culture of the vine, and the wine produced here is of a good quality.

San Gabriel is situated about twelve or fifteen miles north from the bay of San Pedro, and forms the northwest frontier of the jurisdiction of San Diego. I learnt few particulars respecting this mission. It has 1200 Indians attached to it, and is reported to be very rich in Californian wealth, that is, cattle, grain, and fruits; they informed me that last year sixty casks of wine were made at San Gabriel.

About thirty-five miles down the coast stands San Juan Capristano (Capistrano), close to the sea shore, where there is safe anchorage and good landing nine months in the year. The situation of this mission is very romantic and delightful; in a charming valley, thickly shaded with fine trees, through which runs a fine stream of water. I learnt few particulars respecting the mission of San Juan, but they say it is not inferior in wealth to any in California.

Not far from San Juan Capristano is another mission, called San Luis Rey, of the resources and situation of which I am utterly ignorant.

Near the praesidio of San Diego, is situated the mission of the same name. I know very little of this establishment, which is the last to the southward of the Franciscan order, except that it is esteemed inferior, in most respects, to all their others.

Notes to the Text

1. The missions of Peninsular California had been administered by the Order of Preachers or Dominicans since 1773. See Francis J. Weber, *The Missions and Missionaries of Baja California* (Los Angeles, 1968), Pp. 53 ff.
2. The reference here is to Bay Creek Island (San Mateo).
3. Mission Santa Cruz was actually founded in 1791 while the *pueblo*, Branciforte, was established six years later.
4. San Buenaventura Mission was begun on March 31, 1782.

5

Georg Heinrich,
Freiherr von Langsdorff
(1774-1852)

Georg Heinrich, Freiherr von Langsdorff, came to California as a surgeon for Nicolai Petrovich Rezanov on the first Russian expedition to circumnavigate the globe. He visited Missions San Francisco and San Jose, both of which he described in considerable detail, with praise for the prudence, kindness, paternal care and justice of the missionaries.

Known as a man who "held sacred the preeminence of scientific research over all other considerations,"[1] the German-born naturalist presented a realistic picture of the California missions in his narrative which generally corroborates the views earlier expressed by George Vancouver.

Though Langsdorff criticized the lack of technical progress and the wretched state of medical science, "his reports of the several Missions which he visited are minute, and, withal, more favorable to the training and discipline of the Indians by the padres than those given by most travellers."[2]

Langsdorff expressed admiration for the friars who voluntarily took upon themselves a "voluntary exile from their country, only to spread Christianity, and to civilize a wild and uncultivated race of men, to teach them husbandry and various useful arts, cherishing and instructing them as if they were their own children, providing them with dwellings, food, and clothing, with everything else necessary for their subsistence, and maintaining the utmost order and regularity of conduct."[3]

All things considered, the physician felt that "one cannot sufficiently admire the zeal and activity that carry them through labors so arduous, nor forbear to wish the most complete success to their undertaking."[4]

"Notwithstanding certain eccentricities of judgment, some amusing blunders arising from ignorance of the Spanish language, and a singularly unprepossessing face," Hubert Howe Bancroft regarded Langsdorff's narrative as "instructive and interesting..."[5]

Zephyrin Engelhardt, the Franciscan chronicler, praised the account as a "splendid report" and stated that "Bancroft, too, and the whole unfriendly tribe that followed him, could have learned the truth from this schismatic Russian, if documentary evidence had not been plentiful."[6]

The journal of the "brilliant reporter"[7] was published in two volumes by Frederich Wilmans at Frankfurt, in 1812, as Bemerkungen auf einer Reise um die Welt in den Jahren 1803 bis 1807. *A revised English translation of the chapters relating to California was privately printed by Thomas C. Russell at San Francisco, in 1927, as* Langsdorff's Narrative of the Rezanov Voyage to Nueva California in 1806.

References

1. Hector Chevigny; *Lost Empire, The Life and Adventures of Nikolai Petrovich Rezanov* (New York, 1944), p. 319.
2. HelenThroop Pratt, "Book Review," *California Historical Society Quarterly* VII (June, 1928), 197.
3. Thomas C. Russell (Trans.), *Langsdorff's Narrative of the Rezanov Voyage to Nueva California in 1806* (San Francisco, 1927), p. 52.
4. *Ibid.*
5. *History of California* (San Francisco, 1885), II, 67.
6. *San Francisco or Mission Dolores* (Chicago, 1924), p. 139.
7. Francis Florence McCarthy, *The History of Mission San Jose California, 1797-1835* (Fresno, 1958), p. 87.

1806

The name *"misión"* indicates an ecclesiastical establishment having for its object the propagation of the doctrines of the Roman Catholic church. In the *misiones* founded in the peninsula of Antigua California, as well as those in Nueva California, there are commonly two or three *padres*, who are protected in their holy work by the presidios, that is to say, the military government of the country. The padres in Nueva California are all frailes of the Franciscan order. Each of these frailes, before he comes from Spain to this part of the world for the purpose of christianizing the benighted natives, must enter into an engagement to remain here ten years, upon the expiration of which is optional with him whether he shall remain or not. On his voyage hither, as well as on his return if he should so decide he is maintained solely by the Spanish government,[1] and has nothing to think of but his Bible and prayer-book. None of these misioneros can acquire any property, so that it is impossible for one of them even to entertain the idea of enriching himself. Everything that the frailes can save or gain goes into the chest of the *misiones*. Hence, in case of their return to their native country, they are as poor as when they left it.

The number of *misioneros* brought every year from Europe to Vera Cruz is supposed to amount to three hundred. Each has an allowance of four hundred piastres annually, which is devoted to his own needs, and those of the community to which he belongs. Payment is not made in money, but in necessary or useful articles, — manufactured goods for clothing, household utensils, and the like. They are sent to them by the Franciscan College [of San Fernando], in Mexico, on which all the misiones in Nueva California are dependent, and are placed on board government vessels at San Blas, a port on the northwest coast of Mexico

50

(latitude 21° 30'N.). Among the principal goods are, linen and woolen cloth, wine, brandy, sugar, chocolate and cocoa, iron tools, wax tapers for church service, kitchen utensils, agricultural implements etc.

In the *provincia* of Nueva California, extending from San Francisco (latitude 32° 9'N.), there are at the present time nineteen hundred to a thosand *neófitos*. Protection for the misiones is afforded by, if I am not mistaken, six (four: San Francisco, Monterey, Santa Bárbara, and San Diego) *presidios*, but, all told, there are not more than from two hundred to three hundred cavalry.

The Misión Santa Clara de Asís, lying between San Francisco and Monterey, is, with regard to its fine situation, fertility of soil, population, and extent of buildings and grounds, considered the largest and richest misión. All the misiones have cattle in great numbers, and an abundance of other productions necessary to the support of man, and the padres, in general, conduct themselves with such prudence, kindness, paternal care, and justice, in their attitude towards the neófitos, that tranquility, happiness, obedience, and unanimity are the natural results of their methods. Corporal punishment commonly follows disobedience. The padres have recourse to the presidios only on very extraordinary occasions, as, for instance, when expeditions are sent out in pursuit of prospective converts, or when couriers carrying communications require protection, or as a precaution against sudden attacks.

The number of soldiers being so small, and their services so slight, it does not seem worth while to maintain an establishment for them. The Presidio de San Francisco has not more than forty, and it has three misiones under its protection. These are, San Fransicso (same name as the Presidio), Santa Clara, and San José, the last named being established but a few years ago (1797). There are seldom more than from three to five soldiers at any time at any misión, but this seemingly small number has hitherto been always found sufficient to keep the Indians under proper restraint. I was assured by a person worthy of credit that the Spanish *cortes* does not spend less than a million piastres annually for the support of the *misiones*, and their military establishments, in the two Californias, and that, too, without deriving any advantage from them, other than the spreading of Christianity in these provincias of Nueva España.

Each of the *frailes* has several horses for his own use, and when one starts out on an expedition for finding prospective *neófitos*, hs is always escorted by one or more soldiers, who precede him on the way. At such times the soldiers commonly throw over their breast and shoulders a deerskin mantle, which is intended as a protection against the arrows of the Indians, these being incapable of piercing leather. This mantle is worn on other occasions, also, as on dress parade, and when approaching a *presidio* or *misión*. By a royal command, it is not permissible for the *misioneros* to go any distance without military protection. As they carry only the bible and the cross as their personal protection, a military escort accompanies them at such times.

This information was imparted while we were enjoying our breakfast, after which we were taken around to see whatever was worthy of notice.

Behind the residence of the frailes there is a large courtyard, inclosed by houses. Here live the Indian women of the Misión, who are employed, under the immediate supervision of the *padres*, in useful occupations, such as cleaning and combing wool, spinning, weaving, etc. Their principal business is the manufacture of a woolen cloth and blankets for the Indians' own use. The wool of the sheep here is very fine and of superior quality, but the tools and looms are of a crude make. As the misioneros are the sole instructors of these people, who themselves know very little about such matters, scarcely even understanding the fulling, the cloth is far from the perfection that might be achieved.

All the girls and women are closely guarded in separate houses, as though under lock and key, and kept at work. They are but seldom permitted to go out in the day, and never at night. As soon, however, as a girl marries, she is free, and, with her husband, lives in one of the Indian villages belonging to the *Misión*. These villages are called *"las rancherías."* Through such arrangements or precautions the misioneros hope to bind the neófitos to the *misión*, and spread their faith with more ease and security. About a hundred paces form the buildings properly called the *Misión*, lies one of these Indian villages or barracks. It consists of eight long rows of houses, where each family lives separate and apart from the others. The Indian neófitos here are about twelve hundred in number.

The principal food of the Indians is a thick soup, composed of meat, vegetables, and pulse. Because of the scarcity of fish here, or the want of proper means of catching them, the *misioneros* obtained special dispensation from the pope allowing the eating of meat on fast-days.[2] The food is apportioned three times a day,—morning, noon, and evening,—in large ladlefuls. At mealtimes a big bell is rung, and each family sends a vessel to the kitchen, and is served as many measures as there are members. I was present once at the time the soup was served, and it appeared incomprehensible to me how any one could consume so much nourishing food three times a day. According to what we were told by our cicerone, from forty to fifty oxen are killed every week for the community. Besides this, meal, bread, Indian corn, pease, beans, and other kinds of pulse, are distributed in abundance, without any regular or stated allowance. After satisfying our curiosity at the ranchería, we inspected several other serviceable institutions for the promotion of production and economy in the establishment. There was a building for melting tallow, and another for making soap; there were workshops for locksmiths and blacksmiths, and for cabinet-makers and carpenters; there were houses for the storage of tallow, soap, butter, salt, wool, and ox-hides (these being articles of exportation), with storerooms for corn, pease, beans, and other kinds of pulse.

When one considers that in this way two or three *misionero padres* take upon themselves such a sort of voluntary exile from their country, only to spread Christianity, and to civilize a wild and uncultivated race of men, to teach them husbandry and various useful arts, cherishing and instructing them as if they were their own children, providing them with dwellings, food, and clothing, with everything else necessary for their subsistence, and maintaining the utmost order and regularity, of conduct —when all these particulars, I say, are considered, one cannot sufficiently admire the zeal and activity that carry them through labors so arduous, nor forbear to wish the most complete success to their undertaking.

Shortly before sunset we arrived at the *Misión*,[3] very much fatigued. It was now under the charge of two misioneros, Padre Luis [Gil yTaboada][4] and Padre Pedro De la Cueva.[5] The latter only was at the Misión. He received us with open arms, and sent at once horses to the shore to fetch our baggage and the sailor. We had left the sailor to take care of the bidarka, and he was now relieved by some Indians. Fray Luis was now at San Francisco on a short visit. On the morning of the 21st all the Indian *neófitos* were assembled to receive from Fray Pedro their allotted work for the day. He had promised, when I saw him at San Francisco, to entertain me with an Indian dance at his *Misión*, and he therefore now announced to them that they should have a holiday, and that they might dress themselves in their best and prepare for the dance. He distributed, for this purpose, a number of ornaments among the best dancers, who immediately withdrew with them to make the necessary preparations.

In the mean time Fray Pedro showed me about the buildings and grounds belonging to his Misión. They are of considerable extent, although it is only eight years since work was begun on them. Grain in the storehouses, as to quantity, greatly exceeded my expectations, there being over two thousand fanegas of wheat, and a proportionate quantity of maize, barley, peas, beans, etc. The kitchen-garden is exceptionally well laid out, and kept in very good order. The soil is everywhere productive, and the fruit-trees, although still small, are doing very well. A rivulet runs through the garden, with sufficient water to irrigate. Some vineyards have been planted within the past few years, with vines now yielding exceedingly well. The wine is sweet, and resembles Malaga.

The site of the establishment is exceedingly well chosen, and the common opinion is that the *Misión* will in a few years be one of the richest and best in Nueva California. The one and only disadvantage is, an entire lack of forests of tall timber. The native Indians have, now and then, thoughtlessly, simply to make a bonfire, set fire to the forests, and burned down large tracts, leaving few trees standing; hence timber for building purposes must be brought from a distance of several miles. But, in comparison with other misiones, this disadvantage is compensated by the presence, in the neighborhood, of chalk-hills and an excellent clay, whereby brick-kilns may be erected and the main structures built of brick.

The *Misión* is richer in grain than in cattle, and the number of cattle slaughtered weekly is hence much smaller than at Misión San Francisco, but the distribution of corn and pulse is much greater.

The interior arrangement and organization of this *Misión* is entirely the same as that of *Misión San Francisco*. The habitations of the Indians—las rancherías—are not yet finished, so that the neófitos live for the most part in families, in straw huts of a conical form.

Fray Pedro, who showed me about everywhere, invited me, when we had seen all that was worth seeing, to go and see the Indians getting ready for the dance. We went to a rivulet, by the side of which the dancers were gathered, very busy in smearing their bodies over with charcoal, red clay, and chalk. While one Indian was ornamenting his own breast, abdomen, and thighs, another was painting his back with various regular figures. Some were covering their nude bodies all over with down, which gave them rather the appearance of monkeys than of human beings. Their heads, ears, and necks were set off with a great variety of ornaments, but, except a covering tied around the waist, their entire bodies were nude. The women were at the same time, in their huts, performing the offices of the toilet, and were all, consistently with the customs of decorum, dressed. Their faces and necks, only, were painted, and they were adorned with a profusion of shells, feathers, corals, etc.

The Indians assembled in the courtyard toward noon. They are very different from the Indians of Misión San Francisco, as to size, appearance, and build. The men are well built, and almost all are above middling stature. Very few indeed are what may be called undersized. Their complexions are dark, but not negro-like, and if their physiognomy cannot absolutely be called pleasing, there is nothing about it that would provoke aversion. I thought that they strongly resembled the northern tribes. They have very coarse black hair, and some are possessed of extraordinary strength. In general, the women seem proportionately taller than the men, and many are over five feet high.

If there were not any, either among the men or women, that I could call handsome, I did not note in one the dull, heavy, and repugnant look of the neófitos of San Francisco. The Indians of this Misión are indeed generally considered the handsomest in Nueva California, and hence the Spanish soldiers, in the absence of Spanish women, often marry the Indian women of this Misión.

Notes to the Text

1. The author is in error. Provisions of the *Patronato Real* did not cover all the journeys of friars once they had arrived in the New World. Often these trips where financed by the privately endowed Pious Fund of the Californias.
2. Langsdorff confuses fasting and abstinence. In any event, it was true that the Indians were dispensed from the general law of the Church in the matter of Friday abstinence, though the reasons were other than "the scarcity of fish here."
3. *Viz*, San Jose, founded on June 11, 1797.
4. Father Luis Gil y Taboada (1773-1833) was a native of Santa Fe in the State of Guanajuato, Mexico. He was considered a fine administrator though plagued for most of his life with poor health.
5. Spanish-born Father Pedro de la Cueva (b.1773) left California shortly after Langsdorff's visit.

6

Otto von Kotzebue
(1787-1846)

The "Russian bear entered the picture in 1816"[1] in the person of Otto von Kotzebue whose ship, the Rurik, "fitted out by Count Nikolai Petrovich Romanzoff,"[2] dropped anchor in San Francisco Bay on October 2. For Kotzebue, an officer in the Russian Imperial Navy, it was the first of two visits to California which he made on successive voyages around the world.

The sea-captain "was enthusiastic about the country and had a keen eye to the future."[3] Beyond the area itself in its natural state and Spanish hospitality, however, Kotzebue "found nothing to praise."[4] Unhappily, "the Russian traveler saw things through very blue goggles, which fitted his nose ill, and kept him in habitual irritation."[5]

Kotzebue's description of the friars and their work does little credit to the missionary system. Although not denying "the mildness, the paternal anxiety of the missionaries," Kotzebue reported that they "had no quality but hospitality" and accused them of enslaving the natives "under the hypocritical pretense of conversion to Christianity."[6] While acknowledging that the natives led "a far better life in the missions than in their forests,"[7] he castigated the friars for not troubling themselves "to learn the language of the Indians" whom he categorized as "ugly, stupid, and savage."

Quite possibly, the Russian observer's exaggerations and prejudices of life at Missions Santa Clara, San Francisco and San Rafael is attributable, at least in part, to his reliance on the statements of José María Estudillo, a bitter foe of the padres. Hubert Howe Bancroft attributed Kotzebue's seemingly unjust criticism to his "imperfectly understood workings of the mission system."[8] That may well have been true for "what he reports regarding the California missions is based on hearsay from Mexican officials, having himself seen little of the missions."[9]

Judging from his account of the second expedition to California, in 1824,

Kotzebue had not mellowed in his appraisal. The whole answer for the Russian seaman's attitude is not immediately obvious. Perhaps, as Zephyrin Engelhardt concluded, Kotzebue was "typical of the poor individuals governed by prejudice, which will cause them to repeat their charges in spite of all the evidences to the contrary."[10]

The journal of Kotzebue's initial voyage was published simultaneously in German and English, in 1821. Nine years later, Kotzebue issued his observations of the second expedition which had circumnavigated the globe "to aid the Russian-American Company against smuggling by foreign traders."[11]

References

1. Gertrude K. Stoughton, *The Books of California* (Los Angeles, 1968), p. 17.
2. Alice Eastwood, "Early Botanical Explorers on the Pacific Coast and the Trees They Found There," *California Historical Society Quarterly* XVIII (December, 1939), 338.
3. E. O. Essig (Trans.), "The Russian Colonies in California," *California Historical Society Quarterly* XII (September, 1933), 208.
4. Hubert Howe Bancroft, *History of California* (San Francisco, 1885), II, 280.
5. William H. McDougal, "Vancouver's Visit to the Mission of Santa Clara," *Overland Monthly* XXI (January, 1893), 49.
6. Zephyrin Engelhardt, O.F.M., *The Missions and Missionaries of California* (San Francisco, 1913), III, 189.
7. The excerpts here cited are from *A Voyage of Discovery into the South Sea and Beerings Straits for the Purpose of Exploring a North-East Passage* (London,1821).
8. Hubert Howe Bancroft, *op. cit.*, II, 374.
9. Francis Borgia Steck, O.F.M, *A Tentative Guide to Historical Materials on the Spanish Borderlands* (Philadelphia, 1943), p. 100.
10. *San Francisco or Mission Dolores* (Chicago, 1924), p. 189.
11. Willard O. Waters, *Franciscan Missions of Upper California as seen by Foreign Visitors and Residents* (Los Angeles, 1954), Entry 9.

1816-1826

This afternoon, accompanied by all our gentlemen, I took a walk into the Presidio where we were received at the gate by the commandant, Don Louis d'Arguello,[1] and saluted with eight guns, and then conducted to his residence. I found the Presidio as described by Vancouver; the garrison consists of a company of cavalry, of which the commandant is chief and has only one officer of the artillery under his command.

The 4th, at eight o'clock in the morning, we all rowed to shore, and went into the Presidio to ride to the Mission, according to our promise, in company with the commandant. The horses were already saddled and we began our journey, accompanied by ten horsemen, all very fine and expert men, who manage their carbines and lances with the dexterity of our Cossacks. They owe their skill to constant practice, for it is well known, that the military in California serve only to protect the Mission against the incursions of the savages; besides, they assist the clergy to make converts among these tribes, and to keep those already converted in the new faith. The weather was extremely fine, and an hour's ride brought us to our journey's end, though about half of the road was sandy and mountainous. Only a few small shrubs here and there diversified the barren hills; and it was not till we arrived in the neighbourhood of the Mission, that we met with a pleasant country and recognized the luxuriant scenery of California. After passing through a street inhabited by Indians, which is the name given by the Spaniards here to the savage tribes, we stopped before a large building, adjoining the church, the residence of the missionaries and were received by five priests,[2] of whom three belonged to this Mission, and the two others had come from St. Clara to be present at the celebration of the festival; they conducted us to a large, dirty room, plainly furnished, where we were received with much respect. Precisely at ten we entered the church, which is spacious, built of stone,[3] and handsomely fitted up, where we already found several hundred half-naked Indians kneeling, who, though they understand neither Spanish nor Latin; are never permitted after their conversion to absent themselves from mass. As the missionaries do not trouble themselves to learn the language of the Indians, I cannot conceive in what manner they have been instructed in the Christian religion; and there is probably but little light in the heads and hearts of these poor creatures who can do nothing but imitate the external ceremonies which they observe by the eye. The rage for converting savage nations is now spreading over the whole South Sea, and causes much mischief, because the missionaries do not take pains to make men of them before they make them Christians, and thus, what should bring them happiness and tranquillity, becomes the source of bloody wars; as for example, in the Friendly Islands,[4] where the Christians and heathens reciprocally try to exterminate each other. I was surprised at observing that those who were not baptized were not suffered to rise from their knees during the whole ceremony; they were afterwards indemnified for this exertion by the church music, which seemed to afford them much pleasure, and which was probably the only part they comprehended during the whole service. The orchestra consisted of a violoncello, a violin, and two flutes; these instruments were played by little half-naked Indians, and were very often out of tune. From the church we went to dinner; where there was abundance of dishes and wine which is made by the missionaries themselves. After dinner they showed us the habitations of the Indians, consisting of long, low houses, built of bricks, and forming several streets. The uncleanliness in these barracks baffles description, and this is perhaps the cause of the great mortality; for of a 1000 Indians at St. Francisco, 300 die every year. The Indian girls, of whom 400 are in the mission, live separate from the men, likewise in such barracks both sexes are obliged to labour hard. The men cultivate the ground; the harvest is delivered to the missionaries, and stored in magazines; from which the Indians receive only so much as is necessary for their support. It serves also for the maintenance of the soldiers of the Presidio; but they are obliged to pay a very high price for the flour. The women spin wool, and weave a coarse stuff, which is used partly for their ordinary clothing, and partly exported to Mexico, and exchanged for other necessary goods. The costume of the Indians is faithfully represented in the drawings made by M. Choris.[5] This being a holiday, the Indians did no work, but divided into groups, amused themselves with various pastimes, one of which requires particular dexterity.

Two sit on the ground opposite each other, holding in their hands a number of thin sticks, and these being thrown up at the same time with great rapidity, they immediately guess whether the number is odd or even; at the side of each of the players, a person sits, who scores the gain and loss. As they always play for something, and yet possess nothing but their clothing, which they are not allowed to stake, they employ much pains and skill on little white shells, which serve instead of money.

The coast of California is inhabited by so many tribes, that there are frequently in the Mission, Indians of more than ten different races, each of which has its own language. As we were leaving the Mission, we were surprised by two groups of Indians, which were also composed of different nations. They came in military array; that is, quite naked, and painted with gay colours: the heads of the most were adorned with feathers, and other finery; some of them however had their long disordered hair covered with down, and their faces daubed in the most frightful manner. There is nothing remarkable in their war-dance, and I only regretted that I did not understand the words of their song. The physiognomy of these Indians is ugly, stupid, and savage, otherwise they are well formed, tolerably tall, and of a dark brown complexion: the women are short, and very ugly; they have much of the negro in their countenance, only that of a negro-head may be called handsome in comparison with theirs: they are principally distinguished from the negroes by their very long, smooth, and coal-black hair. The missionaries assured us that it was difficult to instruct them on account of their stupidity; but I believe that these gentlemen do not give themselves much trouble about it. They also told us, that the Indians came far from the interior of the country and voluntarily submitted to them, (which we likewise doubted,) that their instruction in religion immediately commenced, and that they were baptized sooner or later, according to their abilities. California is a great expense to the Spanish government which derives no other advantage from it, than that every year a couple of hundred heathens are converted to Christianity, who however die very soon in their new faith, as they cannot accustom themselves to the different mode of life. Twice in the year they receive permission to return to their native homes. This short time is the happiest period of their existence; and I myself have seen them going home in crowds, with loud rejoicings. The sick, who cannot undertake the journey, at least accompany their happy countrymen to the shore where they embark, and there sit for days together, mournfully gazing on the distant summits of the mountains which surround their homes; they often sit in this situation for several days, without taking any food, so much does the sight of their lost home affect these new Christians. Every time some of those who have the permission, run away; and they would probably all do it, were they not deterred by their fears of the soldiers, who catch them, and bring them back to the Mission as criminals; this fear is so great, that seven or eight dragoons are sufficient to overpower several hundred Indians.

Notes to the Text

1. Luis Antonio Arguello (1784-1830) had been Governor of California since 1822. *See* Raymond Kenneth Morrison, "Luis Antonio Arguello; First Mexican Governor of California," *Journal of the West* II (April, 1963), 193-204 and II (July, 1963), 347-361.
2. *Viz.* Fathers Ramon Abella (1764-1842), Vicente Pascual de Oliva (1780-1848), Buenaventura Fortuni (1774-1840), Magin Catala (1761-1830) and Jose Viader (b.1765). Between them, the last two friars spent seventy-four years at Mission Santa Clara.
3. Actually, it was an adobe church.
4. The reference here is to the Meridel Le Sueur.
5. The artistic accomplishments of Louis Choris, (1795-1828), a member of the von Kotzebue expedition, have been described as "the best and most elaborate of that period" by one chronicler. See Robert E. Cowan, *A Bibliography of the History of California and the Pacific West, 1510-1906* (San Francisco, 1914), p. 47.

7

Camille de Roquefeuil
(1781-1831)

The first of his three trips to California began on August 5, 1817, when Camille de Roquefeuil dropped anchor in San Francisco Bay. His ship, Le Bordelais, a three masted vessel of two hundred tons manned by a crew of thirty-four, was the initial ship flying the French flag to enter the port.

Roquefeuil, a lieutenant in the French Merchant Navy, was on "a strictly private and purely commercial venture."[1] The object of his expedition was "to demonstrate the possibility of trade with China in an effort to restore French foreign trade, practically at a standstill as the result of the Revolution and the Napoleonic Wars."[2]

The Chevalier in the Legion d'Honneur[3] visited Mission Dolores on several occasions and the narrative he left throws "much light on the situation at both the presidio and the Mission."[4] He sympathized with the aboriginal status of the natives, admitting that they were "the most carefree and the laziest men there are."[5] From personal experience he contended that they had "no more ability to reason than infants."

Although he probably was not a Catholic, Roquefeuil spoke favorably of the friars, noting that the church at Mission San Francisco "does credit to the piety and taste of the Fathers." The various shops and trades left much to be desired, in Roquefeuil's opinion, but they did "testify to the industry and the activity of these apostolic men."

The observations made by Roquefeuil were published at Paris, in 1823, as the Journal d'un voyage autour du monde, pendant les années 1816, 1817, 1818 et 1819. A condensed and rather inaccurate English translation was released at London in the same year by Sir Richard Phillips and Co. Alexander S. Taylor gathered those parts pertaining to the Pacific Slope for publication, on October 24, 1862, in the California Farmer. The first complete and adequate English translation was that of Charles N. Rudkin which appeared as Volume XXIII in the Early California Travel Series, Camille de Roquefeuil in San Francisco, 1817-1818.[6]

References

1. Abraham P. Nasatir, *French Activities in California. An Archival Calendar-Guide* (Stanford, 1945), p. 2.
2. Charles N. Rudkin (Trans.), *Camille de Roquefeuil in San Francisco, 1817-1818* (Los Angeles, 1954), p. vii.
3. The author is deeply indebted to Louis Vorms of the Consulat General de France a Los Angeles for the particulars about Camille de Roquefeuil's life. Further biographical data is available in René Cruchet, *Le tour du monde en 37 mois de Camille de ROQUE-FEUIL* (Bordeaux, 1952).
4. Zephyrin Engelhardt, O.F.M., *San Francisco or Mission Dolores* (Chicago, 1924), p. 160.
5. The excerpts here cited are from Charles N. Rudkin, *q.v.*
6. (Los Angeles, 1954) .

1817-1818

O n returning to Don Gabriel's house[1] I found there Father Ramon
Abella, Superior of the Mission (San Francisco), which I proposed
to visit. He congratulated me on my fortunate arrival, offered me the
resources of the missions and declared that he would be delighted to
receive me there.

The road which leads from the Presidio passes over some sand hills
which produce only coarse weeds, some broken, some stunted trees,
pines, oaks, holly, etc.; this region was still more desert-like than the
neighborhood of our anchorage. The mission cross raised on a staff
about fifty feet high, was visible from afar between the hills. The establishment is in a very irregular valley which extends southwesterly from
the heights in the north to a little arm of the sea at the south. The land
appeared to be much more fertile than that at the Presidio and the tem-
perature was sensibly warmer. When we arrived Father Ramon was
alone, his companion having gone to get in the harvest at Saint Matter
(San Mateo) with most of the Indians of the mission. The church is well
kept up and decorated with care; the holy vessels and the pictures are the
work of Mexican artists, and they are superior in richness and taste to
things of this sort that one generally sees in third class towns of France
and Germany. It may hold five or six hundred people; there is not a single seat. The whole does credit to the piety and taste of the Fathers. The
storehouses well stocked with wheat; peas; and other vegetable products,
the shops where they weave cloth which serves to clothe the Indians, and
the other workshops, although they leave much to be desired, testify to
the industry and the activity of of these apostolic men. I could only
glance in passing at the village and the cultivated land of the Indians.
The hours slipped by rapidly; it was nearly noon. The good Father want-

ed to have me stay for dinner but I had to refuse his invitation. We parted the best friends in the world, and the friar promised to send me every
day bread, vegetables, and other provisions of which we might have need.

Escorted by Don Manuel[2] I returned to the ship by a road which
goes directly from the mission to the bay of Hyerba Buena,[3] from
which it is not more distant than is the Presidio. We crossed some sand
hills, passably wooded, then went down into uncultivated intervales,
which, however, appeared to be fertile and which serve as pastures for
the cows and horses.

(On August 7. 1817)—I went to the mission to do business with Father
Ramon. The interview which I had with him confirmed what the officers
had told me of the carrying off of the peltries by Captain Wilchohrs,[4] an
American. I learned that the Indians, the most carefree and the laziest
men there are, had given up hunting which they had done only with their
ordinary indolence even in times of abundance which preceded the
incursion of the Kodiaks into the port of San Francisco. Because the
number of otters had been considerably diminished since the destruction
wrought by these foreigners, the Indians pretended there were no more,
and it was only with great difficulty that they could be hired to go on a
hunt, which had become more laborious and less productive. Father
Ramon promised me the few furs that remained in his hands and those
which he might be able to collect. This venerable friar appeared to be
about 55 years old and in robust health. He possessed a singular vivacity
which naturally had taken on a tinge of roughness in a man habituated to
commanding as master the most stupid savages in the world, among
whom he had lived for twenty years.

The frank open-mindedness of Father Ramon, combined with the reputation of his predecessors so favorably established by La Peyrouse and
Vancouver, made me lay aside a reserve which I never make use of unless
I am obliged to do so. I did not have to blame him for giving me false
hopes of the profit I might be able to get from the things I had brought
from Peru. The times had brought about great changes in the business
situation; most of these articles had depreciated greatly in price.

Returning on board I had the bread and vegetables which the Father
had sent us taken up by the boats, besides two fine sheep, some butter,
some dried tongues, etc. The soldiers of the Presidio also were beginning
to bring us poultry as well as baskets and other curiosities of the country.
We were also offered a very small otter skin, which we acquired. This
beginning of our trading was hardly brilliant.

(On August 9, 1817)—I went to the mission. Father Ramon showed me some workshops, the forge, the carpenter-shop, etc. This inspection led me to judge that industry, taken all around, is in its infancy in California. The garden is very well watered and produces an abundance of the principal vegetables, such as cabbage, onions, etc., as well as pears, apples, and some other fruits. It is about 100 *toises* (about 500 feet) square and is divided into three parts by two parallel walls. We went through the village (rancho): it forms a rectangle divided evenly into ten blocks by four parallel streets out across by one perpendicular. It has an hundred houses, or rather cabins, solidly enough constructed of bricks and roofed with tiles like all the buildings of the mission and the Presidio. The huts have only the four walls and the tiled roof, one door and sometimes a gable window. There is no furniture, and for their entire kitchen equipment a plaque for making griddle cakes (*tortillas*) and a kettle. The supply of dishes consists of stone wooden pots and buckets and some baskets so closely woven that they hold water. These last are the most remarkable product of the industry of the Californians. Some huts have a little oven and a bed made of wicker-work, covered with a cowhide. In one of those which we entered we found a sick woman lying on the straw and absolutely without help. Since the Fathers do not know how to use the few medicines that they have there is no infirmary, and these wretches, who have no more ability to reason than infants, are neither watched over nor cared for in their illnesses.[5] Every one of these habitations is a pool of filth and stench, partly because of the extreme negligence of the occupants, and partly because of the strips of dried meat with which they are draped.

At one end of the village we saw the little brook which we had crossed on arriving; at the other end is a little canal which it supplies and which furnishes water for the garden. This canal crosses an empty space which lies between the village and the shops. A plaza of sufficient extent lies between it and the buildings of the mission, which include the church, the lodging for the Fathers, the storehouses and the houses, little different from the huts of the Indians, intended for the detachment of guards. All these buildings form a solid line parallel to the village. The cemetery is next to the church, facing the garden.

Notes to the Text

1. Gabriel Moraga (1767-1823) was born at Sonora on the northern frontier of New Spain. Between 1783 and 1806 he held several positions, including that of magistrate of the Pueblo of San Jose and founder of the Villa de Branciforte. See Donald C. Cutter (Trans), *The Diary of Ensign Gabriel Moraga's Expedition of Discovery in the Sacramento Valley, 1808* (Los Angeles, 1957).
2. Manuel Gomez commanded the artillery at Monterey. He was subsequently promoted to lieutenant and remained in that position until 1822 when he and his wife, a daughter of Jose Maria Estudillo, left the province.
3. Since March 10, 1847, Yerba Buena has been known as San Francisco.
4. The author probably refers here to James Smith Wilcox, one of the many admirers of Concepcion Arguello, who "excused his illegal smuggling operations on the ground that they served to clothe the naked soldiers of the King of Spain, when for lack of raiment they could not attend mass, and when the most reverend fathers had neither vestments nor vessels fit for the church nor implements wherewith to till the soil." See Andrew F. Rolle, *California* (New York, 1963), p. 100.
5. Hubert Howe Bancroft remarked that the Indians "almost invariably preferred their own medicine-men; so that not infrequently the missionaries, with polite shrewdness...wisely abandoned their field to their more successful fellow practioners." See *California Pastoral* (San Francisco, 1888), p. 624.

8

José Bandini
(1771-1841)

José Bandini came to California in 1819, as Captain of the Reina de Los Angeles, *famed for being the first ship to fly the colors of independent Mexico. Though known as a militant Catholic,[1] Bandini felt "that the missions, with their monopoly of large-scale agriculture and the hide-and-tallow trade, claimed more land than they could use, thereby withholding property that might be better in the hands of private individuals."[2]*

Bandini's observations are not widely known in historical circles though it was from an extensive correspondence with this Spanish-born merchant that Alexander Forbes "derived much of the information published in his book."[3]

His nineteen page descrision, *probably the expansion of a letter written in September, 1828, to Eustace Barron, British vice-consul at Tepic, was used as the basis for a report drawn up by Juan Bandini for the* Comisario Principal de la Alta California *in 1830. The* descrision *was first published in its entirety in 1951, by Doris Marion Wright as* A Description of California in 1828 by José Bandini.

References

1. One of Bandini's sons became Archbishop of Lima.
2. Doris Marion Wright, *A Description of California in 1828 by José Bandini* (Berkeley, 1951), p. vi.
3. Hubert Howe Bancroft, *History of California* (San Francisco, 1886), IV, 151.

1819

In the territory there are twenty-one missions, which have been established at different times. In the year 1769 the first, San Diego, was founded. It is two leagues distant from the presidio of that name. The rest have been built consecutively, according to circumstances and necessity. The last was founded in 1822,[1] under the name of San Francisco Solano, and is the most northerly of all.

The buildings in some of the missions are more extensive than in others, but they are almost alike in form. The structures are of adobe, with sections of whatever size may be needed. In all of them there are comfortable living quarters for the ministers, warehouses for the storing of goods, granaries large enough for the grain, places for making soap, rooms for weaving, carpenter shops, forges, wine presses, cellars, large patios and corrals, separate apartments for the Indian youth of both sexes, and, finally, as many workrooms as the establishment may require. Adjoining these and connected with them are the churhces, which form a part of the mission building; all are of adequate size and are lavishly decorated.

The Indians live at a distance of more than two hundred *varas* from this structure in a village called a *rancheria*. In most of the missions these *rancherias* consist of some small adobe dwellings built in rows along the street, but in others the Indians have been allowed to keep their primitive customs, and their lodgings are nothing more than cone-shaped huts, at most probably four *varas* in diameter, with the vertex or point of the cone about two *varas* above the ground. They are made of rough poles covered with tule or grasses in such a way as to afford complete protection against all inclement weather. It seems to me that these *rancherias* are well suited to the innate slovenliness the Indians, since it is easy for them to replace their dwellings frequently, by burning some and putting up others immediately.

Near the mission on the opposite side there is a small barracks with enough rooms for the corporal and five soldiers, with their families. This reduced garrison is sufficient to check any attempted uprising of the Indians who have been taught, by means of some warning examples, to respect the small force. The picket has the additional duty of carrying the monthly correspondence or any special dispatches that it may occur to the government to send.

All the missions of Alta California are under the care of Franciscan missionaries, of whom there are at present twenty-seven, most of them of advanced age. Each administers one mission and in it has absolute authority. The labor of the fields, the harvest of grain, the slaughter of cattle, the work of the shops, and all of those things that may concern the mission are directed by the Padre; and he alone attends to the sales, purchases, and business agreements, without interference from anyone. Thus if a mission is fortunate enough to have a hard working and capable minister its neophytes will enjoy an abundance of the necessities of life; but poverty and misery in a mission give palpable evidence of the inactivity of him who directs it.

The missions have extended their holdings from one end of the territory to the other and have had a way of bounding one piece of property by the next, always opposing the private ownership of lands in between. They have unfeelingly appropriated the whole regions although for their planting and for the maintenance of their cattle they do not need all they possess. It is to be hoped that the new system of enlightenment and the need for encouraging the resident *gente de razon* will compel the government to take adequate measures to reconcile the interests of all.

Among all the missions there are recorded from twenty-one to twenty-two thousand Catholic Indians, but these are not equally distributed. Some establishments claim about three thousand souls, while others have scarcely four hundred. This difference accounts for the greater or lesser wealth of a mission. There are also a good many gentiles living in the farms or ranchos annexed to each mission; the number of these is undetermined.

The Indians are by nature slovenly and indolent, and their powers of understanding are greatly limited. In handicrafts they are imitators, never creators.[2] As their true character is one of vengeance and timidity, they are inclined toward treachery. They do not recognize kindness, and ingratitude is common among them. Their present education is not the most suitable one for bringing out their intellectual powers, but even if it were, I doubt that they would ever be capable of responding to good influences.

All of these Indians, because of their continual use of the *temescal*[3] as well as their great slovenliness and the inadequate ventilation of their dwellings, are weak and without vigor. The chills and rheumatism from which they suffer so much are the result of their customs. But that which destroys and retards their propagation more than anything else is the venereal disease with which most of them are so grievously afflicted. It should be noted that their constitutions are very susceptible to this contagion. Thus there is an enormous difference between deaths and births, doubtless exceeding 10 per cent a year. The missionaries try to make up this deficit from among the catechumens who live in the neighborhood.

In general, all the missions produce cattle, sheep, horses, wheat, maize, beans, peas, and other vegetables, and those situated to the south increase their output by means of vineyards and olive groves. Of all these articles the most profitable are the cattle, as they provide hides and tallow for a brisk trade with the vessels that reach these shores. This is the only means that either missions or private individuals have of supplying their needs, and thus they are obliged to do everything possible to stimulate this branch of commerce; most of them undoubtedly fix their whole attention upon it.

Hides have been collected here for the last six years. Before that, only those required by private individuals were turned to account, and the rest were wasted in the fields. But now foreign vessels export between thirty and forty thousand hides annually from the territory, and the *matanzas*[4] produce an almost equal number of *arrobas* of liquid tallow; and from the way in which this business is being carried on it is certain that within three or four more years the exportation of both products will be doubled. Hemp, flax, wine, olive oil, grains, and other agricultural products would be abundant if the export trade were stimulated, but as this is not done there is only such sowing and reaping as the territory itself requires.

Notes to the Text

1. Mission San Francisco Solano (Sonoma) was founded on July 4, 1823.
2. This statement is not universally true. At San Fernando, for example, the natives were known for their exceptional skill at basketweaving.
3. The *temescal* or "sweat house" was used as a cure-all for diseases.
4. *I.e.* Slaughter house.

9

Frederick William Beechey
(1796-1856)

Frederick William Beechey arrived in the harbor of San Francisco, on November 6, 1826, aboard his impressive ship, the Blossom, a twenty-six gun sloop of war. The London-born geographer "was a cold-eyed observer of the Missions and Indians and the friendly but reckless Spaniards."[1]

Generally regarded as "an excellent account of many aspects of the missions,"[2] the rear-admiral's memoirs correctly captured the underlying theme of the system by noting that "the object of the missions is to convert as many of the wild Indians as possible, and to train them within the walls of the establishment in the exercise of a good life, and of some trade, so that they may in time be able to provide for themselves and become useful members of civilized society."[3]

Beechey was "a rather stern critic"[4] and though "he was not blind to either the faults or excellences of the system or of the friars,"[5] his descriptions are generally fair. Even "that which sounds unfavorable, if interpreted by the circumstances of Mexican misrule and settlers' misrepresentations, will be found to speak well for the missionaries and their efforts."[6]

He affirmed that "the worthy and benevolent priests of the mission devote almost the whole of their time to the duties of the establishment, and have a fatherly regard for those placed under them who are obedient and diligent; and too much praise cannot be bestowed upon them, considering that they have relinquished many of the enjoyments of life, and have embraced a voluntary exile in a distant and barbarous country." Beechey further observed that the kindness of the padres was of such a nature that in some of the missions the converts were so attached to them that he had heard them declare "they would go with them if they were obliged to quit the country."

The impartiality[7] of the English seaman was not appreciably impaired by his Protestant background and he exhibited no hesitation in stating that the Indians converted to the Church "lead a far better life in the missions than in their

72

forests, where they are in a state of nudity, and are frequently obliged to depend solely upon wild acorns for their subsistence."

While the account of Frederick William Beechey's visit to California "added little to our knowledge of the country that could not have been gathered from the published accounts of his predecessors,"[8] the narrative "is important for the accurate and detailed description"[9] of the area's inhabitants.

Perhaps the supreme accolade paid to the Beechey account came from Hubert Howe Bancroft who felt that the "observations published in the voyager's narrative were perhaps more evenly accurate and satisfactory than those of any preceding navigator."[10]

The Narrative of a Voyage to the Pacific and Beering's Strait to Cooperate with the Polar Expeditions *was published in two volumes by Henry Colburn and Richard Bentley on the authority of the Commissioners of the Admiralty, at London, in 1831.*

References

1. Gertrude K. Stoughton, *The Books of California* (Los Angeles, 1968), p. 18.
2. W. Barclay Stephens, "Time and the Old California Missions," *California Historical Society Quarterly* XXXVII (December, 1958), 305.
3. The excerpts here cited are from *Narrative of a Voyage to the Pacific and Beering's Strait to Cooperate with the Polar Expedition* (London, 1831).
4. H.A. van Coenan Torchiana, *Story of the Mission Santa Cruz* (San Francisco,1933), p. 285.
5. Hubert Howe Bancroft, *History of California* (San Francisco, 1886), III, 123.
6. Zephyrin Engelhardt, O.F.M., *The Missions and Missionaries of California* (San Francisco, 1913), III, 264.
7. Willard 0. Waters, *Franciscan Missions of Upper California as seen by Foreign Visitors and Residents* (Los Angeles, 1954), Entry 11.
8. J.D.B. Stillman, "Footprints of Early California Discoverers," *Overland Monthly* II (March, 1869), 263.
9. Andrew F. Rolle, *California* (New York, 1963), p. 139.
10. Hubert Howe Bancroft, *op. cit.*, III, 122.

1826-1827

The missions have hitherto been of the highest importance to California, and the government cannot be too careful to promote their welfare, as the prosperity of the country in a great measure is dependent upon them, and must continue to be so until settlers from the mother country can be induced to resort thither. As they are of such consequence, I shall enter somewhat minutely into a description of them. In Upper California there are twenty-one of these establishments, of which nine are attached to the presidios of Monterey and Sán Francisco, and contain about 7000 converts. They are in order as follow from north to south:—

Sán Francisco Solano,	1822		1000
Sán Raphael	1817		250
Sán Francisco	1776		260
Sán Jose	1797		1800
Sánta Clara	1777		1500
Sánta Cruz	1797		300
Sán Juan	1797		1100
San Carlos	1770		200
La Soledad			300
		Total	6910

Sán Antonio	Buena Vistura
Sán Miguel	Sán Fernando
Sán Luis	Sán Gabriel
De la Purissima	Sán Juan Capistram
Sánta Ignes	Sán Luis Rey
Sánta Barbara	Sán Tomaso¹

I could not learn the number of Indians which are in each of the missions to the southward of Soledad, but they were stated collectively to amount to 20,000: on this head I must observe that the padres either would not say, or did not know exactly, how many there were, even in their own missions, much less the number contained in those to the southward: and the accounts were at all times so various that the above computation can be only an approximation. Almost all these establishments cultivate large portions of land, and rear cattle, the hides and tallow of which alone form a small trade, of which the importance may be judged from the fact of a merchant at Monterey having paid 36,000 dollars in one year to a mission which was not one of the largest, for its hide, tallow, and Indian labour. Though the system they pursue is not calculated to raise the colony to any great prosperity, yet the neglect of the missions would not long precede the ruin of the presidios, and of the whole of the district. Indeed, with the exception of two pueblos, containing about seven hundred persons, and a few farm houses widely scattered over the country, there are no other buildings to the northward of Monterey: thus, while the missions furnish the means of subsistence to the presidios, the body of men they contain keeps the wild Indians in check, and prevents their making incursions on the settlers.

Each mission has fifteen square miles of ground allotted to it. The buildings are variously laid out, and adapted in size to the number of Indians which they contain; some are enclosed by a high wall, as at Sán Carlos, while others consist merely of a few rows of huts, built with sunburnt mud-bricks; many are whitewashed and tiled, and have a neat and comfortable appearance. It is not, however, every hut that has a white face to exhibit, as that in a great measure depends upon the industry and good conduct of the family who possess it, who are in such a case supplied with lime for the purpose. It is only the married persons and the officers of the establishment who are allowed these huts, the bachelors and spinsters having large places of their own, where they are separately incarcerated every night.

To each mission is attached a well-built church, better decorated in the interior than the external appearance of some would lead a stranger to suppose: they are well supplied with costly dresses for processions and feast days, to strike with admiration the senses of the gazing Indians, and on the whole are very respectable establishments. In some of these are a few tolerable pictures, among many bad ones; and those who have been able to obtain them are always provided with representations of hell and paradise: the former exhibiting in the most disgusting manner all the torments the imagination can fancy, for the purpose of striking terror into the simple Indians, who look upon the performance with fear and trembling. Such representations may perhaps be useful in exhibiting to the dull senses of the Indians what could not be conveyed in any other way, and so far they are desirable in the mission; but to an European the one is disgusting, and the other ludicrous. Each establishment is under the management of two priests if possible, who in Upper California belong to the mendicant order of San Francisco. They have under them a major-domo, and several subordinate officers, generally Spaniards, whose principal business is to overlook the labour of the Indians.

The object of the missions is to convert as many of the wild Indians as possible, and to train them up within the walls of the establishment in the exercise of a good life, and of some trade, so that they may in time be able to provide for themselves and become useful members of civilized society. As to the various methods employed for the purpose of bringing proselytes to the mission, there are several reports, of which some were not very creditable to the institution: nevertheless, on the whole I am of opinion that the priests are innocent, from a conviction that they are ignorant of the means employed by those who are under them. Whatever may be the system, and whether the Indians be really dragged from their homes and families by armed parties, as some assert, or not, and forced to exchange their life of freedom and wandering for one of confinement and restraint in the missions, the change according to our ideas of happiness would seem advantageous to them, as they lead a far better life in the missions than in their forests, where they are in a state of nudity, and are frequently obliged to depend solely upon wild acorns for their subsistence.

Immediately the Indians are brought to the mission they are placed under the tuition of some of the most enlightened of their countrymen, who teach them to repeat in Spanish the Lord's Prayer and certain passages in the Romish litany; and also to cross themselves properly on entering the church. In a few days a willing Indian becomes a proficient in these Mysteries, and suffers himself to be baptized, and duly initiated into the church. If, however, as it not unfrequently happens, any of the captured Indians show a repugnance to conversion, it is the practice to imprison them for a few days, and then to allow them to breathe a little fresh air in a walk round the mission, to observe the happy mode of life of their converted countrymen; after while they are again shut up, and thus continue to be incarcerated until they declare their readiness to renounce the religion of their forefathers.

I do not suppose that this apparently unjustifiable conduct would be pursued for any length of time; and I had never an opportunity of ascertaining the fact, as the Indians are so averse to confinement that they very soon become impressed with the manifestly superior and more comfortable mode of life of those who are at liberty, and in a very few days declare their readiness to have the new religion explained to them. A person acquainted with the language of the parties, of which there are sometimes several dialects in the same mission, is then selected to train them, and having duly prepared them takes his pupils to the padre to be baptized, and to receive the sacrament. Having become Christians they are put to trades, or if they have good voices they are taught music, and form part of the choir of the church. Thus there are in almost every mission weavers, tanners, shoemakers, bricklayers, carpenters, blacksmiths, and other artificers. Others again are taught husbandry, to rear cattle and horses; and some to cook for the mission: while the females card, clean, and spin wool, weave, and sew; and those who are married attend to their domestic concerns.

In requital of these benefits, the services of the Indian, for life, belong to the mission, and if any neophyte should repent of his apostacy from the religion of his ancestors and desert, an armed force is sent in pursuit of him, and drags him back to punishment apportioned to the degree of aggravation attached to his crime. It does not often happen that a voluntary convert succeeds in his attempt to escape, as the wild Indians have a great contempt and dislike for those who have entered the missions, and they will frequently not only refuse to re-admit them to their tribe, but will sometimes even discover their retreat to their pursuers. This animosity between the wild and converted Indians is of great importance to the missions, as it checks desertion, and is at the same time a powerful defence against the wild tribes, who consider their territory invaded, and have other just causes of complaint. The Indians, besides, from political motives, are, I fear, frequently encouraged in a contemptuous feeling towards their unconverted countrymen, by hearing them constantly held up to them in the degrading light of *béstias!* and in hearing the Spaniards distinguished by the appellation of *génte de razón.*

77

The produce of the land, and of the labour of the Indians, is appropri-ated to the support of the mission, and the overplus to amass a fund which is entirely at the disposal of the padres. In some of the establish-ments this must be very large, although the padres will not admit it, and always plead poverty. The government has lately demanded a part of this profit, but the priests who, it is said, think the Indians are more entitled to it than the government, make small donations to them, and thus evade the tax by taking care there shall be no overplus. These donations in some of the missions are greater than in others, according as one estab-lishment is more prosperous than another; and on this, also, in a great measure, depends the comforts of the dwellings, and the neatness, the cleanliness, and the clothing of the people. In some of the missions much misery prevails, while in others there is a degree of cheerfulness and cleanliness which shows that many of the Indians require only care and proper management to make them as happy as their dull senses will admit of under a life of constraint.

The two missions of Sán Francisco and Sán Jose are examples of the contrast alluded to. The former in 1817 contained a thousand converts, who were housed in small huts around the mission; but at present only two hundred and sixty remain—some have been sent, it is true, to the new mission of Sán Francisco Solano, but sickness and death have dealt with an unsparing hand among the others. The huts of the absentees, at the time of our visit, had all fallen to decay, and presented heaps of filth and rubbish; while the remaining inmates of the mission were in as mis-erable a condition as it was possible to conceive, and were entirely regardless of their own comfort. Their hovels afforded scarcely any pro-tection against the weather, and were black with smoke: some of the Indians were sleeping on the greasy floor; others were grinding baked acorns to make into cakes, which constitute a large portion of their food. So little attention indeed had been paid even to health, that in one hut there was a quarter of beef suspended opposite a window, in a very offen-sive and unwholesome state, but its owners were too indolent to throw it out. Sán José, on the other hand, was all neatness, cleanliness, and com-fort; the Indians were amusing themselves between the hours of labour at their games; and the children, uniformly dressed in white bodices and scarlet petticoats, were playing at bat and ball. Part of this difference may arise from the habits of the people, who are of different tribes. Langsdorff observes, that the Indians of the mission of Sán José are the handsomest tribe in California, and in every way a finer race of men; and terms the neophytes of Sán Francisco pigmies compared with them. I cannot say that this remark occurred to me, and I think it probable that he may have been deceived by the apparently miserable condition of the people of Sán Francisco.

The children and adults of both sexes, in all the missions, are carefully locked up every night in separate apartments and the keys are delivered into the possession of the padre; and as, in the daytime, their occupations lead to distinct places, unless they form a matrimonial alliance, they enjoy very little of each other's society. It, however, sometimes happens that they endeavour to evade the vigilance of their keepers, and are locked up with the opposite sex; but severe corporal punishment, inflicted in the same manner as is practised in our schools, but with a whip instead of a rod, is sure to ensue if they are discovered. Though there may be occasional acts of tyranny, yet the general character of the padres is kind and benevolent, and in some of the missions, the converts are so much attached to them that I have heard them declare they would go with them, if they were obliged to quit the country. It is greatly to be regretted that, with the influence these men have over their pupils, and with the regard those pupils seem to have for their masters, the priests do not interest themselves a little more in the education of their converts, the first step to which would be in making themselves acquainted with the Indian language. Many of the Indians surpass their pastors in this respect, and can speak the Spanish language, while scarcely one of the padres can make themselves understood by the Indians. They have besides, in general, a lamentable contempt for the intellect of these simple people, and think them incapable of improvement beyond a certain point. Notwithstanding this the Indians are, in general, well clothed and fed; they have houses of their own, and if they are not comfortable, it is, in a great measure, their own fault; their meals are given to them three times a day, and consist of thick gruel made of wheat, Indian corn, and sometimes acorns, to which at noon is generally added meat. Clothing of a better kind than that worn by the Indians is given to the officers of the missions, both as a reward for their services, and to create an emulation in others.

If it should happen that there is a scarcity of provisions, either through failure in the crop, or damage of that which is in store, as they have always two or three years in reserve, the Indians are sent off to the woods to provide for themselves, where, accustomed to hunt and fish, and game being very abundant, they find enough to subsist upon, and return to the mission when they are required to reap the next year's harvest.

Having served ten years in the mission, an Indian may claim his liberty, provided any respectable settler will become surety for his future good conduct. A piece of ground is then allotted for his support, but he is never wholly free from the establishment, as part of his earnings must still be given to them. We heard of very few to whom this reward for servitude and good conduct had been granted; and it is not improbable that the padres are averse to it, as it deprives them of their best scholars. When these establishments were first founded, the Indians flocked to them in great numbers for the clothing with which the neophytes were supplied; but after they became acquainted with the nature of the institution, and felt themselves under restraint, many absconded. Even now, notwithstanding the difficulty of escaping, desertions are of frequent occurrence, owing probably, in some cases, to the fear of punishment—in others to the deserters having been originally inveigled into the mission by the converted Indians or the neophytes, as they are called by way of distinction to *Los Gentíles*, or the wild Indians—in other cases again to the fickleness of their own disposition.

Some of the converted Indians are occasionally stationed in places which are resorted to by the wild tribes for the purpose of offering them flattering accounts of the advantages of the mission, and of persuading them to abandon their barbarous life; while others obtain leave to go into the territory of the Gentiles to visit their friends, and are expected to bring back converts with them when they return. At a particular period of the year, also, when the Indians can be spared from the agricultural concerns of the establishment, many of them are permitted to take the launch of the mission, and make excursions to the Indian territory. All are anxious to go on such occasions, some to visit their friends, some to procure the manufactures of their barbarous countrymen, which, by the by, are often better than their own; and some with the secret determination never to return. On these occasions the padres desire them to induce as many of their unconverted brethren as possible to accompany them back to the mission, of course implying that this is to be done only by persuasions; but the boat being furnished with a cannon and musketry, and in every respect equipped for war, it too often happens that the neophytes, and the *génte de razón*, who superintend the direction of the boat, avail themselves of their superiority, with the desire of ingratiating themselves with their masters, and of receiving a reward. There are, besides, repeated acts of aggression which it is necessary to punish, all of which furnish proselytes. Women and children are generally the first objects of capture, as their husbands and parents sometimes voluntarily follow them into captivity. These misunderstandings and captivities keep up a perpetual enmity amongst the tribes, whose thirst for revenge is almost insatiable.

Morning and evening mass are daily performed in the missions, and high mass as it is appointed by the Romish Church, at which all the converted Indians are obliged to attend. The commemoration of the anniversary of the patroness saint took place during my visit at Sán José, and high mass was celebrated in the church. Before the prayers began, there was a procession of the young female Indians, with which I was highly pleased. They were neatly dressed in scarlet petticoats, and white bodices, and walked in a very orderly manner to the church, where they had places assigned to them apart from the males. After the bell had done tolling, several *alguazils* went round to the huts, to see if all the Indians were at church, and if they found any loitering within them, they exercised with tolerable freedom a long lash with a broad thong at the end of it; a discipline which appeared the more tyrannical, as the church was not sufficiently capacious for all the attendants, and several sat upon the steps without; but the Indian women who had been captured in the affair with the Cosemenes were placed in a situation where they could see the costly images, and vessels of burning incense, and everything was going forward.

The congregation was arranged on both sides of the building, separated by a wide aisle passing along the centre, in which were stationed several alguazils with whips, canes, and goads, to preserve silence and maintain order, and, what seemed more difficult than either, to keep the congregation in their kneeling posture. The goads were better adapted to this purpose than the whips, as they would reach a long way, and inflict a sharp puncture without making any noise. The end of the church was occupied by a guard of soldiers under arms with fixed bayonets; a precaution which I suppose experience had taught the necessity of observing. Above them there was a choir, consisting of several Indian musicians, who performed very well indeed on various instruments, and sang the *Te Deum* in a very passable manner. The congregation was very attentive, but the gratification they appeared to derive from the music furnished another proof of the strong hold this portion of the ceremonies of the Romish church takes upon uninformed minds.

The worthy and benevolent priests of the mission devote almost the whole of their time to the duties of the establishment, and have a fatherly regard for those placed under them who are obedient and diligent; and too much praise cannot be bestowed upon them, considering that they have relinquished many of the enjoyments of life, and have embraced a voluntary exile in a distant and barbarous country. The only amusement which my hospitable host of the mission of Sán José indulged in, during my visit to that place, was during meal times, when he amused himself by throwing pancakes to the *muchachos*, a number of little Indian domestics, who stood gaping round the table. For this purpose, he had every day two piles of pancakes made of Indian corn; and as soon as the *olla* was removed, he would fix his eyes upon one of the boys, who immediately opened his mouth, and the padre, rolling up a cake, would say something ludicrous in allusion to the boy's appetite, or to the size of his mouth, and pitch the cake at him, which the imp would catch between his teeth, and devour with incredible rapidity, in order that he might be ready the sooner for another, as well as to please the padre, whose amusement consisted in a great measure in witnessing the sudden disappearance of the cake. In this manner the piles of cakes were gradually distributed among the boys, amidst much laughter, and occasional squabbling.

Nothing could exceed the kindness and consideration of these excellent men to their guests and to travellers, and they were seldom more pleased than when any one paid their mission a visit: we always fared well there, and even on fast days were provided with fish dressed in various ways, and preserves made with the fruit of the country. We had, however, occasionally some difficulty in maintaining our good temper, in consequence of the unpleasant remarks which the difference of our religion brought from the padres, who were very bigoted men, and invariably introduced this subject. At other times they were very conversible, and some of them were ingenious and clever men; but they had been so long excluded from the civilized world, that their ideas and their politics, like the maps pinned against the walls, bore date of 1772, as near as I could read it for fly spots. Their geographical knowledge was equally backward, as my host at Sán José had heard of discoveries of Captain Cook;[2] and because Otaheite[3] was not placed upon his chart, he would scarcely credit its existence.

The Indians after their conversion are quiet and tractable, but extremely indolent, and given to intoxication, and other vices. Gambling in particular they indulge in to an unlimited extent: they pledge the very clothes on their backs, and not unfrequently have been known to play for each other's wives. They have several games of their own, besides some with cards which have been taught them by the Spaniards. Those which are most common, and are derived from the wild Indians, are *touseé*, called by the Spaniards *pares y nones*, odd or even; *escondido*, or hunt the slipper; and *takersia*.

The first though sometimes played as in England, generally consists in concealing a piece of wood in one hand, and holding out both for the guessing party to declare in which it is contained. The intense interest that is created by its performance has been amusingly described by Perouse. The second, *escondido*, needs no description; the last, *takersia*, requires some skill to play well, and consists in rolling a circular piece of wood with a hole in its centre along the ground, and throwing a spear through it as it rolls. If the spear pierces the hole, it counts ten towards the game; and if it arrests the wood in such a manner that it falls upon the spear, two is reckoned. It is a sport well calculated to improve the art of throwing the spear: but the game requires more practice to play it well than the Indians usually bestow upon it.

At some of the missions they pursue a custom said to be of great antiquity among the aborigines and which appears to afford them much enjoyment. A mud house, or rather a large oven, called *temeschal* by the Spaniards, is built in a circular form, with a small entrance, and an aperture in the top for the smoke to escape through. Several persons enter this place quite naked and make a fire near the door, which they continue to feed with wood as long as they can bear the heat. In a short time they are thrown into a most profuse perspiration, they wring their hair, and scrape their skin with a sharp piece of wood or an iron hoop, in the same manner as coach horses are sometimes treated when they come in heated; and then plunge into a river or pond of cold water, which they always take care shall be near the temeschal.

A similar practice to this is mentioned by Shelekoff[4] as being in use among the Konaghi, a tribe of Indians near Cook's River, who have a method of heating the oven with hot stones, by which they avoid the discomfort occasioned by the wood smoke; and, instead of scraping their skin with iron or bone, rub themselves with grass and twigs.

Formerly the missions had small villages attached to them, in which the Indians lived in a very filthy state; these have almost all disappeared since Vancouver's visit, and the converts are disposed of in huts as before described; and it is only when sickness prevails to a great extent that it is necessary to erect these habitations, in order to separate the sick from those who are in health. Sickness in general prevails to an incredible extent in all the missions, and on comparing the census of the years 1786 and 1813, the proportion of deaths appears to be increasing. At the former period there had been only 7,701 Indians baptised, out of which 2,388 had died; but in 1813 there had been 37,437 deaths to only 57,328 baptisms.

The establishments are badly supplied with medicines, and the reverend fathers, their only medical advisers, are inconceivably ignorant of the use of them. In one mission there was a seaman who pretended to some skill in pharmacy, but he knew little or nothing of it, and perhaps often did more harm than good. The Indians are also extremely careless and obstinate, and prefer their own simples to any other remedies, which is not unfrequently the occasion of their disease having a fatal termination.

The Indians in general submit quietly to the discipline of the missions, yet insurrections have occasionally broken out, particularly in the early stage of the settlement, when father Tamoral[5] and other priests suffered martyrdom. In 1823, also, a priest was murdered in a general insurrection in the vicinity of San Luis Rey;[6] and in 1827, the soldiers of the garrison were summoned to quell another riot in the same quarter.

The situations of the missions, particularly that of Sán José, are in general advantageously chosen. Each establishment has fifteen square miles of ground, of which part is cultivated, and the rest appropriated to the grazing and rearing of cattle; for in portioning out the ground, care has been taken to avoid that which is barren. The most productive farms are held by the missions of Sán José, Santa Clara, Sán Juan, and Sánta Cruz. That of Sán Francisco appears to be badly situated, in consequence of the cold fogs from the seas which approach the mission through several deep valleys, and turn all the vegetation brown that is exposed to them, as is the case of Shetland with the top of every tree that rises above the walls. Still, with care, more might be grown in this mission than it is at present made to produce. Sánta Cruz is rich in supplies, probably on account of the greater demand by merchant vessels, whalers in particular, who not unfrequently touch there the last thing on leaving the coast, and take on board what vegetables they require; the quantity of which is so considerable, that it not unfrequently happens that the missions are for a time completely drained. On this account it is advisable, on arriving at any of the ports, to take an early opportunity of ordering every thing that may be required.

A quantity of grain, such as wheat and Indian corn, is annually raised in all the missions, except Sán Francisco, which notwithstanding it has a farm at Burri Burri,[7] is sometimes obliged to have recourse to the other establishments. Barley and oats are said to be scarcely worth the cultivation, but beans, peas, and other leguminous vegetables are in abundance, and fruit is plentiful. The land requires no manure at present, and yields on an average twenty for one. Sán José reaps about 3,000 fanegas of wheat annually.

Hides and tallow constitute the principal riches of the missions, and the staple commodity of the commerce of the country: a profitable revenue might also be derived from grain, were the demand for it on the coast such as to encourage them to cultivate a larger quantity than is required by the Indians attached to the missions. Sán José. which possesses 15,000 head of cattle, cures about 2,000 hides annually, and as many bótas of tallow, which are either disposed of by contract to a mercantile establishment at Monterey, or to vessels in the harbour. The price of these hides may be judged by their finding a ready market on the Lima coast. Though there are a great many sheep in the country, as may be seen by the mission Sán José alone possessing 3,000 yet there is no export of wool, in consequence of the consumption of that article in the manufacture of cloth for the missions.

Husbandry is still in a very backward state, and it is fortunate that the soil is so fertile, and that there are abundance of labourers to perform the work, or I verily believe the people would be contented to live upon acorns. Their ploughs appear to have descended from the patriarchal ages, and it is only a pity that a little of the skill and industry then employed upon them, should not have devolved upon the present generation. It will scarcely be credited by agriculturists in other countries, that there were seventy ploughs and two hundred oxen at work upon a piece of light ground of ten acres; nor did the overseers appear to consider that number unnecessary, as the padre called our attention to this extraordinary advancement of the Indians in civilization, and pointed out the most able workmen as the ploughs passed us in succession. The greater part of these ploughs followed in the same furrow without making much impression, until they approached the padre, when the ploughman gave the necessary inclination of the hand, and the share got hold of the ground. It would have been good policy for the padre to have moved gradually along the field, by which he would have had it properly ploughed; but he seemed to be quite satisfied with the performance. Several of the missions, but particularly that of Santa Barbara, make a wine resembling claret, though not near so palatable, and they also distil an ardent spirit resembling arrack.

Notes to the Text

1. These charts are quite inaccurate. Perhaps the San Tomaso designated by the author is San Diego?
2. The details of Captain James Cook's expedition to Nootka in 1778 drew attention of France and other European nations to the possibilities of trade with the Pacific area. See James Cook and James King, *A Voyage to the Pacific* (London, 1784), 3 vols.
3. Vancouver probably here refers to Tahiti.

4. Paul Shelikov was the Russian Commandant at Fort Ross between 1829 and 1841.
5. The Jesuit, Father Nicolas Tamaral, died on October 3, 1734, at his mission post of San Jose del Cabo in Peninsular California.
6. The uprising actually took place at San Diego on November 4, 1775. During the insurrection, Father Luis Jayme was brutally clubbed to death by the mostly non-Christian natives.
7. The *rancho* at Buri-Buri was located in the northern part of present-day San Mateo County.

10

Harrison G. Rogers
(d. 1828)

Harrison G. Rogers was a chronicler with the fur brigade of Jedediah Smith, the first expedition to complete the overland trek to California from the east. He was with the exhausted party when it arrived at Mission San Gabriel, on Nomember 27, 1826.

The journal kept by Rogers "records with grateful appreciation the hospitable entertainment shown the Smith Party"[1] during their two-month sojourn at the fourth of California's missions.

A "sincere and devoted Protestant,"[2] Rogers "seemed to think that he knew all about Catholics by intuition,"[3] though his statements reveal only a shallow grasp of the Church's theological structure. He was a doctrinaire Calvinist, but expressed considerable admiration for the work of the missions. Rogers was fascinated by the "liberty of conscience"[4] allowed him and his party by their hosts. His respect for the missionaries, whom he calls "gentlemen of the first class, both in manners and habits," is obvious throughout the text of his observations.

Rogers' words of highest praise were "reserved for the jovial, friendly friars who were gracious and generous hosts,"[5] especially Fray Jose Bernardo Sanchez.

A fragment of the Rogers journal, rescued by Jedediah Smith from the Umpqua Indians of Oregon who killed Rogers in 1828, was later committed to the safety of the Missouri Historical Society. It was published by Harrison Clifford Dale in The Ashley-Smith Explorations and the Discovery of a Central Route to the Pacific, 1822-1829, in 1918. The volume was subsequently reissued, in 1941, by the Arthur H. Clark Company of Glendale.

References

1. Willard 0. Waters, *Franciscan Missions of Upper California as seen by Foreign Visitors and Residents* (Los Angeles, 1954), Entry 12.

2. George William Beattie, "San Bernardino Valley in the Spanish Period," *Historical Society of Southern California Annual* XII (1923), 23.
3. Zephyrin Engelhardt, O.F.M., *San Gabriel Mission* (San Gabriel, 1927), p. 153.
4. The excerpts here cited are from Harrison Clifford Dale, *The Ashley-Smith Explorations and Discovery of a Central Route to the Pacific, 1822-1829* (Glendale, 1941).
5. John Walton Caughey, *California* (New Jersey, 1953), p. 188.

1826-1827

November 28th. Mr. S. wrote me a note in the morning, stating that he was received as a gentleman and treated as such, and that he wished me to go back and look for a pistol that was lost and send the company on to the missionary establishment. I complyed with his request, went back, and found the pistol, and arrived late in the evening, was received very politely, and showed into a room and my arms taken from me. About 10 o'clock at night supper was served, and Mr. S. and myself sent for. I was introduced to the 2 priests[1] over a glass of good old whiskey and found them to be very joval friendly gentlemen, the supper consisted of a number of different dishes, served different from any table I ever was at. Plenty of good wine during supper, before the cloth was removed cigars was introduced. Mr. S.[2] has wrote to the governor,[3] and I expect we shall remain here some days.

29th.[4] Still at the mansion.[5] We was sent for about sunrise to drink a cup of tea, and eat some bread and cheese. They all appear friendly and treat us well, although they are Catholics by profession, they allow us the liberty of conscience, and treat us as they do their own countrymen, or brethren.

About 11 o'clock, dinner was ready, and the priest come after us to go and dine; we were invited into the office, and invited to take a glass of gin and water and eat some bread and cheese; directly after we were seated at dinner, and every thing went on in style, both the priests being pretty merry, the clerk and one other gentleman, who speaks some English. They all appear to be gentlemen of the first class, both in manners and habits. The mansion, or mission, consist of 4 rows of houses forming a complete square, where there is all kinds of macanicks at work; the church faces the east and the guard house the west; the N. and S. line comprises the work shops. They have large vineyards, apple and peach orchards, and

89

some orange and some fig trees. They manufacture blankets, and sundry other articles; they distill whiskey and grind their own grain, having a water mill, of a tolerable quality; they have upwards of 1,000 persons employed, men, women, and children, Inds. of different nations. The situation is very handsome, pretty streams of water running through from all quarters, some thousands of acres of rich and fertile land as level as a die in view, and a part under cultivation, surrounded on the N. with a high and lofty mou., handsomely timbered with pine, and cedar, and on the S. with low mou, covered with grass. Cattle—this mission has upwards of 30,000 head of cattle, and horses, sheep, hogs, etc. in proportion. I intend visiting the inner apartments to-morrow if life is spared. I am quite unwell to-day but have been engaged in writing letters for the men and drawing a map of my travels for the priests. Mr. Smith, as well as myself, have been engaged in the same business. They slaughter at this place from 2 to 3,000 head of cattle at a time; the mission lives on the profits. Saint Gabriel is in north latitude 34 degrees and 30 minutes. It still continues warm; the thermometer stands at 65 and 70 degrees.

30th. Still at Saint Gabriel; everything goes on well; only the men is on a scanty allowance, as yet. There was a wedding in this place today, and Mr. S. and myself invited; the bell was rang a little before sun rise, and the morning service performed; then the musick commenced serranading, the soldiers firing, etc., about 7 o'clock tea and bread served, and about 11, dinner and musick. The ceremony and dinner was held at the priests; they had an elegant dinner, consisting of a number of dishes boiled and roast meat and fowl, wine and brandy or ogadent, grapes brought as a dessert after dinner. Mr. S. and myself acted quite independent, not understanding their language, nor they ours; we endeavored to appoligise, being very dirty and not in a situation to shift our clothing, but no excuse would be taken, we must be present, as we have been served at their table ever since we arrived at this place; they treat (us) as gentlemen in every sense of the word, although our apparel is so indifferent, and we not being in circumstances at this time to help ourselves, being about 800 m. on a direct line from the place of our deposit.[6] Mr. S. spoke to the cammandant this evening respecting the rations of his men; they were immediately removed into another apartment, and furnished with cooking utensils and plenty of provisions, they say, for 3 or 4 days. Our 2 Ind. guides were imprisoned in the guard house the 2nd day after we arrived at the missionary establishment and remain confined as yet. Mr. S. has wrote to the commandant of the province, and we do not know the result as yet, or where we shall go from this place, but I expect to the N.W. I intended visiting the inner apartments to-day, but have been engaged in assisting Mr. S. in making a map for the priest and attending the ceremonies of the wedding.

December 1st, 1826. We still remain at the mansion of St. Gabriel; things going on as usual; all friendship and peace. Mr. S. set his black-smiths, James Reed[7] and Silas Gobel,[8] to work in the B.S. shop, to make a bear trap for the priest, agreeable to promise yesterday. Mr. S. and the interpreter went in the evening to the next mission,[9] which is 9 m. dis-tance from St. Gab. and called St. Pedro,[10] a Spanish gentleman from that mission having sent his servant with horses for them. There came an Itallian gentleman from Port Sandeago today by the name of John Battis Bonafast[11] who speaks good English, and acts as interpreter for all the American and English vessels that arrives in ports on the coast, quite a smart and intelligent man. The men all appear satisfied since there was new regulations made about eating. Mr. S. informed me this morning that he had to give Read a little floggin yesterday evening, on account of some of his impertinence; he appeared more complasant to-day than usual. Our fare at table much the same as at first, a plenty of everything good to eat and drink.

2nd. Much the same to-day as yesterday, both being what the Catholics call fast days;[12] in the morning after sunrise, or about that time, you have tea, bread and cheese, at dinner fish and fowl, beans peas, pota-toes and other kinds of sauce, grapes as a desert, wine, gin and water plenty at dinner. I could see a great deal of satisfaction here if I could talk there language, but, as it is, I feel great diffidence in being among them knot knowing the topic of there conversation, still every attention is paid to me by all that is present, especially the old priest. I must say he is a very fine man and a very much of a gentleman.[13] Mr. S. has not returned from the other mission as yet. This province is called the Province of New California; this mission ships to Europe annually from 20 to 25 thousand dollars worth of hides and tallow, and about 20 thousand dol-lars worth of soap. There vineyards are extensive; they make there own wine, and brandy; they have oranges and limes growing here. The Inds. appear to be much altered from the wild Indians in the mou that we have passed. They are kept in great fear; for the least offense they are correct-ed; they are compleat slaves in every sense of the word. Mr. S. and Laplant[14] returned late in the evening, and represents their treatment to be good at the other mission. Mr. S. tells me that Mr. Francisco[15] the Spanish gentleman that he went to visit, promises him as many horses and mules as he wants.

December 3rd., Sunday. About 6 o'clock the bell rang for mass, and they poured into church from all quarters, men, women and children; there was none of us invited therefore we all remained at our lodgings. The fare to-day at table much as usual; there was an additional cup of tea in the afternoon. The Inds. play bandy with sticks, it being the only game I have seen as yet among them. They play before the priests door. I am told they dance, both Spanyards and Inds., in the course of the evening.

12th. About sun rise, the bell rang and mass called; men women and children attended church; they discharged a number of small arms and some cannon while the morning service were performing. Their main church is upwards of 200 feet in length and about 140 in breadth made of stone and brick, a number of different apartments in it. They hold meeting in the large church every Sunday; the Spanyards first attend and then the Inds. They have a room in the inner apartment of the mission to hold church on their feast days. Their religion appears to be a form more than a reality. I am in hopes we shall be able to leave here in five or six days at most, as all hands appear to be anxious to move on to the north. Things in other respects much the same; the weather still continues to be good. In the evening there was kind of procession, amongst both Spanyards and Inds. I enquired the reason, I was told by a Mr. David Philips,[16] an Englishman, that this day, a year ago, the Virgin Mary appeared to an Ind. and told him that the 12th day of December should always be kept as a feast day and likewise a holliday among them and both Spaniards and Inds. believe it.[17]

13th. I walked through the work shops; I saw some Inds. blacksmithing, some carpentering, others making the wood work of ploughs, others employed in making spining wheels for the squaws to spin on. There is upwards 60 women employed in spinning yarn and others weaving. Things much the same, cloudy and some rain today. Our black smith(s) have been employed for several days making horse shoes and nails for our own use when we leave here.

14th. I was asked by the priest to let our black smiths make a large trap for him to set in his orange garden, to catch the Inds. in when they come up at night to rob his orchard. The weather clear and warm. Things in other respects much the same as they have been heretofore; friendship and peace prevail with us and the Spanyards. Our own men are contentious and quarrelsome amongst themselves and have been ever since we started the expedition. Last night at supper for the first time the priest questioned me as respected my religion. I very frankly informed him that I was brought up under the Calvinist doctrines and did not believe that it was in the power of man to forgive sins. God only had that power; and when I was under the necessity of confessing my sins, I confessed them unto God in prayer and supplication, not to man; I further informed him that it was my opinion, that men ought to possess as well as profess religion to constitute the christian; he said that when he was in his church and his robe on, he then believed he was equal unto God, and had the power to forgive any sing that man was guilty of, and openly confessed unto him, but when he was out of church and his common waring apparel on he was as other men, divested of all power of forgiving sins.

(December) 15th. I went out fowling with the commandant of the mission. I killed 7 brant and one duck, and the commandant killed 2 brants and a duck; the priest furnished me with shot. Two of our men went to work today; Arthur Black[18] and John Gaiter[19] "Now they are to get a horse a piece for 3 days work. Times much the same as they have been some time back; nothing new occurs.

16th. Late this morning a Mr. Henry (Edwards?) owner of a brig now lying in port, arrived at the mission; he appears to be a very much of a gentleman, and quite intelligent. His business here is to buy hides, tallow and soap, from the priest. Nothing new has taken place. Things much the same about the mission; the priest administered the sacrament to a sick Indian today, and he thinks he will die.

17th. The sick Indian that the priest administered the sacrament to yesterday, died last night, and was entered in there graveyard this evening; the proceedings in church similar to the last sabbath. Sunday appears to be the day that the most business is transacted at this mission; the priest plays cards both Sunday a(nd) weak a days, when he has company that can play pretty expert.

Monday, January 1st, 1827. This morning church was held before day; men, women and children attended as usual; after church, musick played by the Inds. as on sunday; wine and some other articles of clothing given out to the Inds. The priest keeps a memorandum of all articles issued to them. The fare at the table the same as other days, if any difference, not so good. Some rain last night and today; weather warm; showers alternate through the day like may showers in the states, and equally as pleasant; things in other respects much the same; no news from Mr. S. and I am at a loss how to act in his absence with the company, as he left no special instructions with me when he left here.

Tuesday 2nd. Still at the mission of San Gabriel; nothing new has taken place to-day; the men commenced work again this morning for the old padre; no news from Mr. S; friendship and peace still prevail. Mr.

Joseph Chapman,[20] Bostonian by birth, who is married in this country and brought over to the Catholic faith, came here about 10 o'clock a.m. to superintend the burning of a coal pitt for the priest. He is getting wealthy, being what-we tern a Yanky; he is jack of all trades, and naturally a very ingenious man; under those circumstances, he gets many favours from the priest, by superintending the building of mills, black smithings and many other branches of mechanidism.

W. 3rd. There was five or six Inds. brought to the mission and whiped, and one of them being stubbourn and did not like to submit to the lash was knocked down by the commandant, tied and severely whiped, then chained by the leg to another Ind who had been guilty of a similar offence. I rec'd a letter from Mr. S. this morning informing me that he had got his passports signed by the governor, by the intercession of the gentlemen officers, and that he would join me in a few days; he intended embarking on board Capt. Cunningham's[21] ship, and coming to St. Pedro, which is forty-five miles distant from San Gabriel.

6th, Saturday. This being what is called Epiphany or old Christmas day, it is kept to celebrate the manifestation of Christ to the gentiles, or particularly the Magi or wise men from the East. Church held early as usual, men, women, and children attend; after church the ceremonies as on sundays. Wine issued abundantly to both Spanyards and Inds., musick played by the Ind. band. After the issue of the mornings our men, in company with some Spanyards, went and fired a salute, and the old padre give them wine, bread, and meat as a treat. Some of the men got drunk and two of them, James Reed and Daniel Ferguson,[22] commenced fighting and some of the Spanyards interfered and struck one of our men by the name of Black,[23] which came very near terminating with bad consequence. So soon as I heard of the disturbance, I went among them, and passified our men by tolling what trouble they were bringing upon themselves in case they did not desist; and the most of them, being men of reason, adheared to my advice.

Our black smith, James Reeds come very abruptly into the priests dining room while at dinner, and asked for argadent; the priest ordered a plate of victuals to be handed to him; he eat a few mouthfuls, and set the plate on the table, and then took up the decanter of wine, and drank without invitations and come very near braking the glass when he set it down; the padre, seeing he was in a state of inebriety, refrained from saying anything.

Sunday 7th. Things carried on as on former sabaths, since I have been at the mission, church services morning and evening, issues to the Inds.

of wine and clothing; the priest in the evening threw oranges among the young squaws to see them scuffle for them, the activest and strongest would get the greatest share. Mr. Smith has not joined us yet.

Monday 8th. Last night there was a great fandago or dance among the Spanyards; they kept it up till nearly day light from the noise. The women here are very unchaste; all that I have seen and heard speak appear very vulgar in their conversation and manners. They think it an honnour to ask a white man to sleep with them; one came to my lodgings last night and asked me to make her a blanco Pickanina, which, being interpreted, is to get her a white child, and I must say for the first time, I was ashamed, and sew did not gratify her or comply with her requests seeing her so forward, I had no propensity to teach her. Things about the mission much the same. No news of Mr. S., and I am very impatient, waiting his arrival.

9th, Tuesday. Business going on about the mission as usual. About 8 or ten boys employed gathering oranges overseed by the commandant and the steward of the mission, old Antonio, a man of 65 years of age, who is intrusted with the keys of all the stores blonging to the mission; he generally is served at the priests table, and, from appearance, is very saving and trusty. I went out in company with Mr. McCoy this evening with our guns to amuse ourselves; I killed one brant and Mr. McCoy[24] killed nothing. Mr. S. still absent from the company.

Notes to the Text

1. *Viz.*, Jose Bernardo Sanchez (1778-1833) and Geronimo Boscana (1776-1831).
2. *Viz.*, Jedediah Smith (1799-1831), the first white man to reach California overland. He was an American trapper who came from Salt Lake City via the Colorado River and Mojave.
3. *Viz.*, Jose Maria Echeandia, (d. 1855) who harbored suspicions about Smith and his motives for coming to California.
4. *Viz.*, November 29, 1826.
5. The "mansion" was about four miles northeast of Mission San Gabriel.
6. The actual distance between Salt Lake City and Mission San Gabriel is closer to 600 miles.
7. James Read, one of the less desirable members of the Smith party, subsequently abandoned the expedition.
8. Silas Gobel, a "durable" follower of Smith, met his death at the hands of the Amuchabas in August of 1827.
9. The reference here is probably to the *Asistencia de Nuestra Señora de los Angeles.*
10. Obviously, the author is referring to Los Angeles. The distance from San Gabriel to San Pedro is thirty-four miles.

11. Juan Bautista Bonifacio (d. 1834) later became commander of the *Compania Extranjeria de Monterey*.
12. The preceding day, a Friday, would have been only a day of abstinence.
13. Smith expressed his admiration for Father Sanchez by naming the Sierra Nevada, in honor of the priest, "Mount Joseph."
14. Abraham Laplant was a veteran member of Smith's expedition of thirteen (fifteen-?) man who orginally set out for California.
15. Rogers probably refers here to Spanish-born Francisco Martinez; who was forced to leave California in 1827 because of his unwilling allegiance to Mexico.
16. According to Hubert Howe Bancroft, Philips was a cooper who came to California via Sonora. See *History of California* (San Francisco, 1886), IV, 776.
17. The author here alludes to the apparition of Our Lady of Guadalupe at Tepeyac to the fifty-five year old neophyte, Juan Diego, in December of 1531.
18. Arthur Black was one of the three fortunate escapees from the massacre in the Umpqua River country of Southern Oregon in 1828.
19. John Gaiter continued in Smith's employ until his death at the Umpqua in July of 1828.
20. Joseph Chapman (1785-1849) supervised the building of the first vessel of any importance on the California coast about 1831. Constructed at San Gabriel, the *Guadalupe* was launched at San Pedro.
21. Strangely, Captain William H. Cunningham's log for the ship Courier has nothing to say about his activities on shore in behalf of Jedediah Smith. See *Log of the Courier* (Los Angeles, 1958).
22. Daniel Ferguson (1798-1841) later deserted the Smith expedition and took up residence in Monterey.
23. This could refer to Arthur Black (See footnote #18) or, by derision, to Peter Ranne "a man of color," perhaps the first of his race to enter California.
24. Martin McCoy, was a long-time companion of Smith.

11

Auguste Bernard Duhaut-Cilly
(1790-1848)

Auguste Bernard Duhaut-Cilly, *"the first outlander to become intimately acquainted with, and describe, the then thriving Spanish California,"[1] arrived in 1826 aboard* Le Heros, *a 362 ton ship carrying thirty-two men on a trading voyage around the world.*

The French navigator's observations constitute "the most extensive contemporary account of California's missions and settlements"[2] for the period, visiting as he did more of those foundations than any other of the early visitors.

A person of deep religious convictions, Duhaut-Cilly was "an educated man, a close observer, and a good writer."[3] His observations about the missions, towards which he was "generally favorable,"[4] are, for the most part "accurate, well-written and interesting."[5]

Duhaut Cilly regarded the Franciscans as "men of distinguished merit and great discretion"[6] who were genuinely "hospitable to all" who approached the missions. While expressing a repugnance for the occasional slovenliness of the padres, the Frenchman's overall treatment of the friars "seems eminently fair and trustworthy,"[7] though frequently critical. He felt they were inordinately attached to their Iberian homeland, loving "the ground, the customs, everything, even the errors of their government."

The "vivid sketches"[8] of Auguste Bernard Duhaut-Cilly were initially published in two volumes at Paris, in 1834-1835, as Voyage autour da monde, principalement, a la Californie et aux Iles Sandwich. *The first complete translation, rendered into English by Charles F. Carter, was published in the* California Historical Society Quarterly, *in 1929, as "Duhaut-Cilly's Account of California in the Years 1827-1828."*

References

1. Phil Townsend Hanna in *The Zamorano 80* (Los Angeles, 1945), p. 24.
2. Wright Howes, *U.S. Iana* (New York, 1963), p.175.
3. Hubert Howe Bancroft, *History of California* (San Francisco, 1886), III, 130.
4. Willard O. Waters, *Franciscan Missions of Upper California as seen by Foreign Visitors and Residents* (Los Angeles, 1954), Entry 13.
5. Abraham P. Nasatir, *French Activities in California. An Archival Calendar-Guide* (Stanford, 1945), p. 4.
6. The excerpts here cited are from Charles Franklin Carter (Trans), "Duhaut-Cilly Account of California in the Years 1827-1828," *California Historical Society Quarterly* VIII (June, 1929), 130-166.
7. *Ibid.*, 132.
8. "The Flea in California History and Literature," *California Historical Society Quarterly* XV (December, 1936), 330.

1827-1828

I found Mission San Francisco very different from what it was when Vancouver visited it in 1794.

At that time it consisted of a chapel and a house forming two sides of a square. Not only has this square been completed since but a large church and a row of fairly large buildings, serving as store-houses and dependencies, have been added to it.

Beyond this solid wall of buildings, separated from it by a large court where flows a current of fine water, are the dwellings of the Indians attached to the mission. They are laid out in regular order, and cut by straight streets, made at equal distances. This establishment became, some years ago, one of the most important in California, as much from the wealth of its products as from the number of its Indians. In 1827 there remained of this wealth only the numerous houses necessitated by it, and of which the larger number were already falling into ruin.

When, in 1816, Roquefeuille visited this mission there were still seven hundred Indians; and when I arrived here there were not more than two hundred and sixty. This diminution of hands had proportionately reduced all the products, and this establishment has again become one of the poorest on the whole coast. That it should be made to come to this state of decay, it wanted merely the management of two successive missionaries without talent and energy. Fray Tomas[1] governed it after them, and under his administration it gave no promise of recovering; he was an excellent man, whose poor health made him indifferent to the handling of his business, and he willingly gave up the care of it to administrators, that he might enjoy the quietness he needed.

This worthy man gave me all the information that I asked of him concerning trade in Upper California. After a few days of calculation, I determined to profit by the advantageous prices the market offered.

But there was in this plan one quite serious inconvenience, which could be overcome only by taking a trip to Peru in the ship. The scarcity of ready money left no other means of exchange than cattle hides and tallow; and this latter article could be realized upon only at Lima, where I had known for a long time it sold well. As for the hides, it was easy to got rid of them by selling them again to the American captains who were in California in search of this commodity.

There was, even then, in the harbor a schooner belonging to that nation, engaged in this business; and we made an agreement with the supercargo of this ship, for all the hides we should gather, for which he agreed to pay us in *piastres* or in tallow.

This ship had sold her cargo on the west coast of Mexico, and had nothing aboard save money. But the *padres* wished to exchange their products only for the things they needed, so that the supercargo could only with difficulty obtain the hides he was seeking. The missionaries lived in constant fear that the government might extort from them contributions in silver, as that had occurred several times, and this was for them a powerful reason for preferring merchandise to coin.

I learned also from Fray Tomas that the favorable season for buying hides and tallow did not commence until the month of May, the time when the cattle are killed to extract from them the most profit; and that while waiting, we could bargain with all the missions.

This state of things suited us all the better, as we should have had no room on board at this time to load, and as we were obliged to return to Mazatlan after a short while, to carry out the engagement made with Don Ignacio Fletes, to deliver to him the merchandise we had sold him. It was, therefore, decided that, after having treated with the missions situated on the harbor of San Francisco, we should go down the coast, visiting all the other establishments, to the port of San Diego.

The immense port of San Francisco is divided into two branches, one of which goes toward the north, the other toward the east-southeast. Each of these two inner bays measures nearly fifteen leagues in lengths with a varying width of three to twelve miles; upon all this great extent, there are several islands, the largest of which is Los Angeles (Angel Island), north of the presidio.

Missions San Rafael and San Francisco Solano are on the borders of the northern branch; they are new and of slight importance.

On the shores of the eastern branch, beside Mission San Francisco with which the reader is already acquainted, are seen those of San Jose and of

Santa Clara, the finest and richest in this part of California. Near Santa Clara is found also the pueblo of San Jose, which is only a big village.

At every mission I visited I made a new friend. Hardly was I arrived at one than there grew up, between the missionary and myself, a trust, manifested at first by complaints against the government which had taken the place of the royal authority. This barrier overcome, I was made acquainted with all the harassments that this want of harmony necessarily produced. I was then told about the persons with whom I was to trade, to the minutest particular: it was in this way, above all, that I learned of the degree of solvency of each one: proofs which were of the utmost use to me and which I have never been sorry to have listened to: thus, during the whole course of my operations in California, I had only eight hundred *piastres* of bad credit.

Nearly all of these religious were men of distinguished merit and great discretion: the counsels they gave me came from no motive of hatred, and they had no other aim than to serve me, like a friend, like a brother; they knew well I would not make bad use of it, and that I received it from them only as business information. This was the result of the happiness they found in treating with a captain of their communion. Never would they have approached a like subject with an American or an Englishman. Their fine soul and their tolerance made them, truly, hospitable to all; but from simple duties of courtesy to complete indulgence of confidence, there was a world.

No situation is prettier than that of this mission. From the shore the ground rises so regularly by steps, that they might be said to be the symmetrical terraces of a fortification. I know not even if the grassy covering of an artificial work could ever equal the beauty of green sward clothing them like the carpet of green velvet spread out over the steps of a throne. The buildings are placed upon the third sward fronting the sea, and backed against a thick forest of large fir trees, which lend a new brilliance to the whiteness of their walls.

I went to Mission San Carlos, situated about five miles south from the presidio at Monterey. The road leading to it is winding, and it twists around among the hills carpeted by very verdant grass, and shaded by great fir trees and beautiful oaks. These trees are sometimes grouped so attractively they seem to have been planted by the hand of a skillful decorator: now they form avenues, rows or solid masses, now they are dense forests opening here and there, as if to allow the eye to wander over the plains of verdure, set in the midst of the woods in the most picturesque manner. In truth, the beautiful *lianas* of the tropics do not interlace here from one tree to another, like garlands; but the species are mingled, separated, reunited in so many ways; the soil is so clean, so fresh, so free from bushes, that nothing could add to the beauty of these hills. The forests of the torrid zone produce a more romantic effect; these have a more severe appearance.

Mission San Carlos is built upon a little bay, open to the southwest and offering neither shelter nor anchorage. It is poor and almost depopulated of Indians. Padre Ramon Abila[2] (the sudden bad weather having prevented him from re-embarking at Santa Cruz) had arrived by land. I found here also Padre Altimira,[3] a young missionary, and Padre Seria,[4] prefect and head of all the Franciscans of California, a man of distinguished merit and great virtue.

At this time he was in utter disgrace among the Mexicans, for having refused to take the oath to the constitution, and prevented his subordinates from consenting to it: he was also, in a manner, held as prisoner and kept in sight at San Carlos. The agents of the Mexican government considering him, therefore, as the main obstacle to the submission of all the other missionaries, would have liked to send him back to Mexico. Commandant Gonzalez[5] had already sought to sound my intentions, to learn if, on returning to Mazatlan, I would consent to take him; but I made that officer understand that, however disposed I was to do anything agreeable to his government, I would never make myself the instrument for any act of violence toward whomever it might be; and that I would not take the *padre prefecto* aboard unless he himself asked me to do so. This good missionary had feared that I might comply with the commandant's designs: and he showed me the liveliest gratitude when I disclosed to him my sentiments in this regard.

We went on foot to the mission, situated at the upper end of the plain a half-league from the presidio. The road leading to it ascends very slightly as it crosses a beautiful grassy meadow, where graze the horses used at the presidio and the cows supplying it with the daily milk. As we went on, the mission buildings presented a finer appearance. From the roadstead, we could have taken it for a mediaeval castle, with its lofty openings and belfry; approaching nearer, the building grows, and while losing none of its beauty, assumes little by little a religious aspect; the turret becomes a bell-tower; the bell, instead of announcing the arrival of a knight, rings for service or the angelus; the first illusion is destroyed, and the castle becomes a convent.

In front of the buildings, in the middle of a large square, is a playing fountain, whose workmanships quite imperfect as it was, surprised us the more, the less we expected to find in this country, so far from European refinement, that kind of luxury reserved with us for the dwellings of the wealthiest. After rising to a height of more than eight feet above the ground, the clear and sparkling water of this fountain fell again in broad sheets upon a descending series of stone basins forming altogether an octaganal pyramid; it filled a reservoir of the same shape to the brim, whence, issuing from the jaws of a bear, also in stone, it fell into a fine laver in stucco, around which some Indian women and Californian girls were busy washing. The latter looked at us from below through the beautiful tresses of their chestnut hair, and I presume the examination they made of two strangers was as perfect as it was swift.

In all countries the fair sex alone possess this gift of estimating an individual and particularly of seizing upon his oddities in a trice with a stealthy look. I saw one of these young girls smile almost imperceptibly; perhaps I myself was the cause of her mischievous mirth; but the rather grotesque appearance of my companion, his teeth calcined by the immoderate use of tobacco, and his simian head, on a slender body of four feet eight inches: all this should have quieted my self-love a little.

We went up a flight of several stops leading us to a long peristyle or cloister, supported by fifteen square pillars forming fourteen arches which, from a distance, give the mission that noble appearance which surprised us at the first sight of it. A feeble old padre was sitting there,[6] his age and condition making him so insensible to all taking pace about him, that scarcely did he see we were strangers when we bowed to him, and asked after his health. I saw easily that, to arouse his attention, it was necessary to take strong measurers: I leaned toward him, and spoke loudly enough to overcome his deafness: "I am a Frenchman; come from Paris, and I can give you quite recent news from Spain."

Never did a talisman produce a more magical effect than these few words, whose virtue I had already proved for drawing to myself the kindness and interest of these good fathers. The Spanish, in general, are extremely attached to their country: they love the ground, the customs, everything, even the errors of their government. I had no sooner pronounced these words than the old man, emerging from his lethargy, loaded me with compliments and such urgent questions, that I could not find an instant to reply to him. He recovered part of his past vigor, while speaking of his native land which he was to see no more.

The events, opening the way to the invasion of Spain by a French army, were known to him: he considered Fernando VII as a quasi-martyr, and the French as his liberators. Opinion and education often cause the same things to be looked at under very different aspects: while this poor religious rejoiced to learn that our troops were still in the peninsula, I could not prevent a painful remembrance from seizing upon my mind; and I recollected how impatiently we lately bore the presence of foreigners, and with what ill humor we counted the days still to pass before their departure, whatever might be the indebtedness certain persons believed we owed them. Very seldom, most seldom, is the aim of result of an invasion the welfare of the country occupied.

This old man was not the head of the mission; he filled no office, and was only supported here until God should bring his semi-existence to an end. It was entrusted to the direction of Fray Antonio Ripoll: the latter was engaged at the moment, and we took advantage of his absence to visit his garden which we found large, well planted and kept up. The paths, laid out methodically, were shaded by fine olive trees, and saw there at the same time the fruits of temperate climes and of the torrid zone. Banana trees spread their broad leaves between apple and pear trees; and with the ruby of the cherries were mingled the golden apples and the orange trees.

With more discretion and discernment Fray Antonio Ripoll,[7] a man of good countenance and distinguished mind, put to me some of the questions already asked of me by his aged companion; and when I had satisfied his curiosity, or rather his anxiety, he proposed to us an inspection of the mission buildings and the church.

The facade of this chapel is ornamented with six half-columns supporting a triangular front, bearing several statues of saints. The body of the church consists only of a nave with low arched roof, without side aisles. The construction of this edifice would have been nothing to excite surprise, had it been built by Europeans; but if one consider that it is the work of poor Indians, guided by an ecclesiastic; that it is erected in a country which, though it contains all the materials required, at least supplies them to the hand using them only in the rough state in which nature produces them; one cannot tire in admiration of the patience of this religious, the talent he has shown, and the care he must have taken for such a building.

With us, does one wish to undertake the erection of a building of this kind? Ten architects, with their plans and estimates, present themselves for it. One has merely to select the one most suitable; purchases are made from the furnishers; all the materials, ready to be put in place, are brought to the designated spot, without any one having to be concerned about a single thing other than to prove their quality and give them the finishing touch; lastly, the best workmen contend for the choice over their rivals.

Here, on the contrary, everything is in the rough, even to the men, and the first care of the builder has been to form his workmen. Out of the mere earth he has had to make bricks and tiles; to cut immense trees far away, and to bring them, by physical strength, over roads marked out expressly across ravines and precipices; to gather, at great expense, on the seashore, shells to make into lime; finally, everything, to the most trifling, connected with this edifice has cost preliminary labors, which must have increased the difficulty very much. One is, at the same time, astonished at the boldness of the plan and the perseverance in its execution: only a boundless zeal for the spread of religion can have made Padre Ripoll conqueror over so many obstacles. He has not, however, employed much more time for completing the building than would have been necessary in Spain: this church was begun in 1820, and finished in 1824.

The nave, the altar, and the vestry are decorated with paintings the best ones of which came from Mexico; the rest are from the hand of the Indians themselves. The pillars, frieze, framings and bases are marbled with a good deal of taste and decorated with arabesques passably executed. What heightens still more all this mass, and inclines one to be indulgent with regard to defects of architecture, is an excessive neatness, not found in our churches of the third, and even of the second order.

Fray Antonio's talent and solicitude have not been concentrated exclusively upon the building of his church: at the same time that he gave himself to this beautiful work, he was thinking also of feeding and clothing his Indians. We went to visit his woolen shops. There, in the buildings given up to this employment two hundred Indians of both sexes were busy at various kinds of labor: the women and children carded and spun the wool; the men planned and wove blankets, linsey-woolsey and, in particular, a coarse flannel resembling cloth before fulling. The establishing of various trades and machines had also been directed by the padre and executed by his Indians, out of whom he had made carperters, masons, blacksmiths, workmen, in fine, of all kinds essential for an establishment as large as this.

The project completely engrossing him at this time was a water-mill he was having built at the foot of a hill to the right of the mission. The water, brought for more than two leagues by a canal following the side of the mountains, was to fall from a height of about twenty feet upon the buckets of a wheel. The fall of this motive power was not vertical: it worked at an angle of about 35 degrees; the wheel also, instead of being vertical, was horizontal; it was a full circle, upon whose plane were arranged, like spokes, a sort of large, slightly concave spoons, which were to receive, one after another, the impulse and transmit the movement.

At first glance I was surprised that the padre, a man of judgment, should have preferred to have the fall inclined, when it wag so easy for him, in cutting a hill to a steeper slope, to make it much more powerful; for without being a hydrostatician, I readily perceived that his motive power lost the more of its force, the farther was it inclined from the vertical. But before expressing my opinion, reflection brought me back to the inventor's idea; and I believed I saw that whatever motive power he lost at first, he gained it from another side, in avoiding the friction from two sets of cog-wheels, since the turning grindstone would be fixed upon the axle of the wheel.

Another objection also can be made, in regard to the speed of rotation; for in this plan it is the same for both wheel and grindstone, while in our ordinary combination, the speed of the grindstone increases in the relation of the radius of the wheel to the radius of the axlehub. Besides, Fray Antonio's workmen being little skilled in mechanics, he avoided many imperfections by simplifying the machinery, and I had no doubt of the complete success of his undertaking. I brought to his attention, however, the fact that the quality of the stone he used for his grindstones, being made from the same stone, was not suitable; because being entirely composed of almost homogeneous parts, and of equal hardness, it would grow smooth too quickly. After dinner the president went to take his *siesta*, and we returned to the ship.

The 8th, Palm Sunday, I settled my accounts with the deputy's substitutes and paid him the import duties upon what I had sold at Santa Barbara. I then went to the mission to take leave of Fray Antonio, of the commandant general and of Don José Noriega.[8] I attended the ceremony for the day, which took place with extraordinary pomp. Branches of palm leaves, elegantly decorated with flowers and braids from the leaf itself, were distributed among all the *gente de razon*; the Indians had simple olive branches. The severity of Lent did not permit the padre to let us hear his music in the church. His Indians executed merely some chants with much taste and sweet melody; they made us hear Spanish and Latin words to the prettiest Italian airs.

After mass we returned to the padre's reception room, and the musicians gave a serenade to the commandant general. There were a large number of musicians, and all in uniform: although they executed tolerably some French and Italian *morceaux*, I noticed they had succeeded better in the chants. At the last I returned to the ship, and we set sail immediately.

106

Notes to the Text

1. *Viz.* Father Tomas Eleuterio Estenega (1790-1847), a native of Anzuola in the Province of Vizcaya, Spain, who came to California in 1820.
2. *Viz.* Father Ramon Abella (1764-1842) who labored in the California missions for forty-four years.
3. *Viz.* The "young" missionary, Fray Jose Altimira, was forty years of age when the author visited the mission.
4. Father Vicente de Sarria (1767-1835) served two terms as *Comisario-Prefecto*, 1812 to 1818 and 1824 to 1830.
5. Manuel Gonzalez, *comandante* of arms at Monterey from 1826 to 1828, was himself subsequently expelled from the province.
6. The "feeble old padre" was Father Antonio Jayme (1757-1829) a Mallorcan-born friar who had served in California since 1795.
7. Mallorcan Father Antonio Ripoll (b. 1785) retired to his native Spain the following year after serving a decade and a half in the missions.
8. Jose Antonio Julian De la Guerra y Noriega (1779-1858) was thus eulogized by Hubert Howe Bancroft: "No man in California ever came so near, by peaceful and legitimate means to absolute control of his district. He did not purchase popularity at the cost of independence, for many were his controversies, even with the friars, though he was their life-long friend and a devout churchman." See Joseph A. Thompson, O.F.M., *El Gran Capitan* (Los Angeles, 1961), p.167.

12

James Ohio Pattie
(1804-c. 1850)

James Ohio Pattie was an adventurer who came to the west, in 1828. After serving a term in prison for trapping without governmental authorization, he acquired permission from civil officials to visit the missions and to inoculate the natives against smallpox with a rare serum he supposedly brought from Kentucky.

There is an air of mystery about Pattie's shenanigans on the tour which, he claimed, took him to sixteen missions where he allegedly vaccinated 22,000 Indians. Apart from his own testimony, there is no evidence that he actually ever visited any of the old foundations. The peculiar combination of facts, legends and misinformation which Pattie crammed into his journal was dismissed by the Franciscan chronicler as one "wholesale" prevarication.[1]

The authoritative Henry Raup Wagner was more generous in his view, holding that "probably in the main the story can be accepted as true, due allowance being made for the lapse of time, making occurrences seem closer together than they really were."[2] Pattie was not highly regarded by Hubert Howe Bancroft who characterized him as "a self-conceited and quick-tempered boy, with a freedom of speech often amounting to insolence, and unlimited ability to make himself disagreeable."[3]

Throughout the text, Pattie exhibits an antagonistic attitude towards the overall missionary program, though he did feel kindly disposed to many of the individual padres whom he met on his journeys. In all fairness, it should be noted that a goodly portion of the narrative was substantially altered by the Reverend Timothy Flint who edited into the journal a considerable amount of sentiment and romance prior to its publication.

Pattie's literary laurels are as impressive as they are inconsistent. Robert Glass Cleland spoke highly of the accounts observing that "American literature has not yet produced a tale of adventure equal to his simple narrative."[4]

Andrew F. Rolle was less exuberant in his appraisal of this "first printed narrative of an overland journey to California"⁵ which he looked upon as "a mine of often unreliable but always fascinating information."⁶ Another authority claims that the itinerant vaccinator's narrative "remains the epic of the mountain men, perhaps more truly representing their attitudes, their experiences, and their adventures than any other book which has appeared on the subject."⁷

Unquestionably, Pattie's written observations have "an assured place in frontier literature" though they must be classified as "semi-fiction" rather than history.⁸

The journal was published by John H. Wood at Cincinnati, in 1831, as The Personal Narrative of James O. Pattie, of Kentucky, during an Expedition from St. Louis, through the vast regions between that place and the Pacific Ocean...

References

1. Zephyrin Engelhardt, O.F.M., *San Francisco or Mission Dolores* (Chicago, 1924), p. 408.
2. *The Plains and the Rockies. A Bibliography of Original Narratives of Travel and Adventure, 1800-1865* (Columbus, 1953), p. 74.
3. *History of California* (San Francisco, 1886), III, 171-172.
4. *A History of California: The American Period* (New York, 1927), p. 62.
5. J. Gregg Layne, *The Zamorano 80* (Los Angeles, 1945), p. 48.
6. *California* (New York, 1963), p. 172.
7. Franklin Walker, *A Literary History of Southern California* (Berkeley, 1950), p. 13.
8. William J. Ghent, *Dictionary of American Biography* (New York, 1934), XIV, 310.

1828-1829

On the 18th of January, 1828, I began to vaccinate; and by the 16th of February had vaccinated all the people belonging to the fort, and the Indian inhabitants of the mission of San Diego, three miles north of the former place.[1] It is situated in a valley between two mountains. A stream runs through the valley, from which ships obtain fresh water. An abundance of grain is raised at this mission. Fruit of all kinds, growing in a temperate climate, is also plentiful. The climate is delightfully equal. The husbandman here does not think of his fields being moistened by the falling rain. He digs ditches around them, in which water is conveyed from a stream, sufficient to cover the ground, whenever the moisture is required. Rains seldom fall in the summer or autumn. The rainy season commences in October; and continues until the last of December, and sometimes even through January; by which time the grass, clover and wild oats are knee high. When the rain does come, it falls in torrents. The gullies made in the sides of the mountains by the rains are of an enormous size.

But to return to my own affairs. Having completed my vaccinations in this quarter, and procured a sufficient quantity of the vaccine matter to answer my purpose, I declared myself in readiness to proceed further. I communicated the matter to one thousand Spaniards and Indians in San Diego.

February 28th the General[2] gave us each a legal form, granting us liberty on parole for one year, at the expiration of which period it was in his power to remand us to prison, if he did not incline to grant us our freedom. He likewise gave me a letter to the priests along the coast, containing the information that I was to vaccinate all the inhabitants upon the coast, and an order providing for me all necessary supplies of food and

110

horses for my journey these were to be furnished me by the people, among whom I found myself cast. They were, also, directed to treat me with respect, and indemnify me for my services, as far as they thought proper. The latter charge did not strike me agreeably; for I foresaw, that upon such conditions my services would not be worth one cent to me. However, the prospect of one whole year's liberty was so delightful, that I concluded to trust in Providence, and the generosity of the stranger, and think no more of the matter. With these feelings I set forth to the next mission, at which I had already been. It was called San Luis.

I reached it in the evening. I found an old priest,[3] who seemed glad to see me. I gave him the General's letter. After he had read it, he said, with regard to that part of it which spoke of payment, that I had better take certificates from the priests of each mission, as I advanced up the coast, stating that I had vaccinated their inhabitants; and that when I arrived at the upper mission, where one of the high dignitaries of the church resided, I should receive my recompense for the whole. Seeing nothing at all singular in this advice, I concluded to adopt it.

In the morning I entered on the performance of my duty. My subjects were Indians, the missions being entirely composed of them, with the exception of the priests, who are the rulers. The number of natives in this mission was three thousand, nine hundred and four.[4] I took the old priest's certificate, as had been recommended by him, when I had completed my task. This is said to be the largest, most flourishing, and every way the most important mission on the coast. For its consumption fifty beeves are killed weekly. The hides and tallow are sold to ships for goods, and other articles for the use of the Indians, who are better dressed in general, than the Spaniards. All the income of the mission is placed in the hands of the priests, who give out clothing and food, according as it is required. They are also self constituted guardians of the female part of the mission, shutting up under lock and key, one hour after supper, all those, whose husbands are absent, and all young women and girls above nine years of age. During the day, they are entrusted to the care of the matrons. Notwithstanding this, all the precautions taken by the vigilant fathers of the church are found insufficient.

I saw women in irons for misconduct, and men in the stocks. The former are expected to remain a widow six months after the death of a husband, after which period they may marry again. The priests appoint officers to superintend the natives, while they are at work, from among themselves. They are called *alcaldes*, and are very rigid in exacting the performance of the allotted tasks, applying the rod to those who fall short of the portion of labor assigned them. They are taught in the different trades; some of them being blacksmiths, others carpenters and shoe-makers. Those, trained to the knowledge of music, both vocal and instrumental, are intended for the service of the church. The women and girls sew, knit, and spin wool upon a large wheel, which is woven into blankets by the men. The *alcaldes*, after finishing the business of the day, give an account of it to the priest, and then kiss his hand, before they withdraw to their wigwams, to pass the night. This mission is composed of parts of five different tribes, who speak different languages.

The greater part of these Indians were brought from their native mountains against their own inclinations, and by compulsion; and then baptised; which act was as little voluntary on their part, as the former had been. After these preliminaries, they had been put to work, as converted Indians.

The next mission on my way was that, called St. John the Baptist.[5] The mountains here approach so near the ocean, as to leave only room enough for the location of the mission. The waves dash upon the shore immediately in front of it. The priest, who presides over this mission, was in the habit of indulging his love of wine and stronger liquors to such a degree, as to be often intoxicated.[6] The church had been shattered by an earthquake.[7] Between twenty and thirty of the Indians, men, women and children, had been suddenly destroyed by the falling of the church bells upon them. After communicating the vaccine matter to 600 natives, I left this place, where mountains rose behind to shelter it; and the sea stretched out its boundless expanse before it.

Continuing my route I reached my next point of destination. This establishment was called the Mission of St Gabriel. Here I vaccinated 960 individuals. The course from the mission of St. John the Baptist to this place led me from the sea-shore, a distance of from eighteen to twenty miles. Those who selected the position of this mission, followed the receding mountains. It extends from their foot, having in front a large tract of country showing small barren hills, and yet affording pasturage for herds of cattle so numerous, that their number is unknown even to the all surveying and systematic priests. In this species of riches St. Gabriel exceeds all the other establishments on the coast. The sides of the mountains here are covered with a growth of live oak and pine. The chain to which these mountains belong, extends along the whole length of the coast. The fort St. Peter stands on the sea coast, parallel to this mission.

My next advance was to a small town, inhabited by Spaniards, called the town of The Angels. The houses have flat roofs covered with bituminous pitch, brought from a place within four miles of the town,[8] where this article boils up from the earth. As the liquid rises, hollow bubbles like a shell of large size, are formed. When they burst, the noise is heard distinctly in the town. The material is obtained by breaking off portions, that have become hard, with an axe, or something of the kind. The large pieces thus separated, are laid on the roof, previously covered with earth, through which the pitch cannot penetrate, then it is rendered liquid again by the heat of the sun. In this place I vaccinated 2500 persons.[9]

From this place I went to the mission of St. Ferdinand, where I communicated the matter to 967 subjects. St. Ferdinand is thirty miles east of the coast, and a fine place in point of position.

The mission of St. Buenaventura succeeded. Not long previous to my arrival here, two priests had eloped from the establishment, taking with them what gold and silver they could lay their hands upon.[10] They chose an American vessel,[11] in which to make their escape. I practised my new calling upon 1000 persons in this mission.

The next point I reached was the fort of St. Barbara. I found several vessels lying here. I went on board some of them, and spent some pleasant evenings in company with the commanders. I enjoyed the contrast of such society with that of the priests and Indians, among whom I had lately been. This place has a garrison of fifty or sixty soldiers. The mission lies a half a mile N.W. of the fort. It is situated on the summit of a hill, and affords a fine view of the great deep. Many are the hours I passed during this long and lonely journey, through a country every way strange and foreign to me, in looking on the ceaseless motion of its waves. The great Leviathan too played therein.[12] I have often watched him, as he threw spouts of water into the air, and moved his huge body through the liquid surface. My subjects here amounted to 2600.[13] They were principally Indians.

The next mission on my route was that called St. Enos.[14] I vaccinated 900 of its inhabitants, and proceeded to St. Cruz, where I operated upon 650. My next advance was to St. Luis Obispo. Here I found 800 subjects. The mission of St. Michael followed in order. In it I vaccinated 1850 persons. My next theatre of operations was at St. John Bapistrano.[15] 900 was the number that received vaccination here. Thence, I went to La Solada, and vaccinated 1685, and then proceeded to St. Carlos, and communicated the matter to 800.

From the latter mission I passed on to the fort of Monte El Rey, where is a garrison of a hundred soldiers. I found here 500 persons to vaccinate. The name of this place in English signifies the King's mount or hill.

Forests spread around Monte El Ray for miles in all directions, composed of thick clusters of pines and live oaks. Numberless gray bears find their home, and range in these deep woods. They are frequently known to attack men. The Spaniards take great numbers of them by stratagem, killing an old horse in the neighborhood of their place of resort. They erect a scaffold near the dead animal, upon which they place themselves during the night, armed with a gun or lance. When the bear approaches to eat, they either shoot it, or pierce it with the lance from their elevated position. Notwithstanding all their precautions, however, they are sometimes caught by the wounded animal; and after a man has once wrestled with a bear, he will not be likely to desire to make a second trial of the same gymnastic exercise. Such, at any rate, is the opinion I have heard these express, who have had the good fortune to come off alive from a contest of this kind. I do not speak for myself in this matter as I never came so near as to take the close hug with one in my life; though to escape it, I once came near breaking my neck down a precipice.

From Monte El Rey I advanced to the mission of St. Anthony, which lies thirty miles E. from the coast. In it I found one thousand persons to inoculate. I had now reached the region of small pox, several cases of it having occurred in this mission. The ruling priest of this establishment[16] informed me that he did not consider it either necessary or advisable for me to proceed farther for the purpose of inoculating the inhabitants of the country, as the small pox had prevailed universally through its whole remaining extent. As I had heard, while in San Diego, great numbers had been carried off by it. I then told him that I wished to see the church officer who had been described to me by the first priest whom I had seen on my way up the coast. He furnished me a horse, and I set off for the port of San Francisco, vaccinating those whom I found on the way who had not had the small pox.

I reached the above mentioned place, on the twentieth of June, 1829. Finding the person of whom I was in search,[17] I presented him all the certificates of the priests of the missions in which I had vaccinated, and the letter of the General. I had inoculated in all twenty two-thousand persons. After he had finished the perusal of these papers, he asked me what I thought my services were worth? I replied, that I should leave that point entirely to his judgment and decision. He then remarked, that he must have some time to reflect upon the subject, and that I must spend a week or two with him. I consented willingly to this proposal, as I was desirous of crossing the bay at St. Francisco to the Russian settlement, called the Bodego.[18]

Notes to the Text

1. Mission San Diego is *neither* three miles *nor* north from the *presidio*. It is for statements such as this that "considerable doubt has been thrown upon Pattie's veracity." There is no evidence, outside his own narrative, that Pattie ever visited any of the missions. See William E. Smythe, *History of San Diego* (San Diego, 1907). p. 137. For a treatment of Pattie's charge that he could not obtain payment for his services without embracing the Catholic faith, See Zephyrin Engelhardt, O.F.M., *San Francisco or Mission Dolores* (Chicago, 1924), Pp. 407-410.
2. *Viz.*, José María Echeandia who published a decree in 1829 calling for the expulsion of all Spaniards.
3. Father José Joaquin Jimeno (1804-1856) was stationed at San Luis Rey at the time. He could hardly have been the "old priest" referred to by the author.
4. Pattie is wrong here. There were 2,860 natives then at San Luis Rey of whom approximately 500 resided at the Asistencia de San Antonio de Pala. *Cf.* Zephyrin Engelhardt, O.F.M., *San Luis Rey Mission* (San Francisco, 1921). p. 65.
5. Undoubtedly the author had his geography confused since his next stop would have been San Juan Capistrano.
6. Fray José Barona (1764-1831) was not addicted to alcohol, as the narrator would seem to indicate.
7. An earthquake had levelled the church at San Juan Capistrano on December 8, 1812.
8. Perhaps the author is referring to the La Brea tar-pits.
9. Hubert Howe Bancroft stated that the entire population of the town at the time of Pattie's visit amounted to only 770 (1160 if those outside the town's boundaries are included). See *History of California* (San Francisco, 1886), III, 632.
10. Pattie is referring to Fathers Jose Altimira of San Buenaventura and Antonio Ripoll of Santa Barbara who returned to Spain in January of 1828. A close investigation revealed that Altimira took a little box of cigars, his trunk and some rations. See Zephyrin Engelhardt, O.F.M., *San Buenaventura* (Santa Barbara, 1930), Pp. 62ff.
11. *Viz.*, The *Harbinger*.
12. The author here is referring to the mythical sea-monster often symbolic of evil in Old Testament literature.
13. Here again the numbers are out of proportion. In 1829 the population of the presidio *and* mission was less than 700 and the Indians numbered about 800.
14. Could this be Santa Ines?
15. A reference to San Juan Bautista?
16. The narrator may have in mind Fray Pedro Cabot (1777-1836) who spent thirty-two years in the California missions.
17. Jose Bernardo Sanchez (1778-1833) was *Presidente* in 1828-1829.
18. The Village of Bodega was located on the north shore of the Puerto de la Bodega (Sonoma). Between 1812 and 1841 the Russians were active in that area.

13

Jonathan S. Green
(1796-1878)

The Reverend Jonathan S. Green *"was a missionary sent from the Hawaiian Islands to explore the northwest coast and report on the feasibility of founding a mission to the Indians and a colony."[1] A representative of the American Board of Commissioners for Foreign Missions, "the first Protestant pastor to enter San Francisco Bay"[2] arrived, on September 30, 1829, aboard the* Volunteer.

Green visited Missions Dolores and San Carlos Borromeo where he was favorably impressed with the hospitality of the friars. The Congregationalist minister spoke of the two padres *at Carmel as "intelligent men, of good reputation."[3] He refused their invitation to attend religious services because of the antecedent bull fight which he found exceedingly distasteful.*

Obviously a fan of George Vancouver, Green relied heavily on the British seaman for background material. While admitting the loftiness of the "professed object" which lured the friars to the Pacific Slope, he expressed regret that so much was left undone in their attempts "to benefit the native inhabitants of California," most of whom he categorized as lewd, unclean, drunkards and notorious gamesters.

The Reverend Green betrayed an understandable religious bias by contending that results of missionary work among the natives might have been more effective "had the gospel been preached in its purity and simplicity to these men, had they been taught to read, and had the simple statements of the bible met their eyes." He went on to conjecture that "if the preaching of the gospel and the perusal of the bible" had changed "to a moral garden, the barren rocks, and to perennial spring the ever during winter, of Greenland, what could not the same means have effected on the pleasant hills, and the verdant, blooming vallies of New Albion?"

In any event, the report ultimately submitted by Jonathan Green advised against establishing, at that time, anything approaching the once-envisioned "New England Colony" in California.

Green's observations first appeared in the Missionary Herald *for November and December, 1830. They were reprinted, with only minor variations, at New York City, in 1915, for Charles Frederick Heartman as a* Journal of a Tour on the North West Coast of America in the Year 1829.

References

1. Willard O. Waters, *Franciscan Missions of Upper California as seen by Foreign Visitors and Residents* (Los Angeles, 1954), Entry 17.
2. Clifford M. Drury, "A Chronology of Protestant Beginnings in California," *California Historical Society Quarterly* XXVI (June, 1947), 164.
3. The excerpts here cited are from a *Journal of a Tour on the North West Coast of America in the Year 1829* (New York, 1915).

1829

The religion of California is the Roman Catholic. No other sect is tolerated. Many of the foreign residents have embraced the religion of the country, so far at least as they have found necessary to enable them to marry ladies of the country—it being impossible, with their present laws, for a Protestant to marry in California.

While at St. Francisco I visited the mission of that name, and when at Monterrey I visited that of St. Carlos. Both of these missions are situated about a league from the presidio of St. Francisco and Monterey. These missions are smaller than several others farther in the interior. That of Carlos, which is in a better condition at present, than the one of St. Francisco, is built much like a presidio. It is a square area, the sides of which are about 200 yards in length, inclosed by buildings used for work-shops, store-houses, the house of the "padre," and the church. At St. Francisco I was introduced to the only priest of the establishment, Padre Thomas des Tenega,[1] of the order of St. Francisco, a Spaniard, who has been here about twenty years. He is of a thin visage, and I should think of feeble health. The padre was very hospitable. He gave me a pressing invitation to visit the mission the next day, which was to be a great feast-day in honor of St. Francisco.[2] It being the Sabbath, I declined accepting the invitation, for though my curiosity might have been gratified by wit-nessing the ceremonies of the church, yet I could not conscientiously be present at an exhibition of "bull baiting," which was immediately to suc-ceed the church service. He appeared to be a man of considerable infor-mations and of a facetious temper. He showed me the interior of the church, pointed out the several saints which adorned the walls, and *smiled* when he showed me some paintings, which though they might petrify with terror the uninstructed Indians, were really ludicrous.

At the mission of St. Carlos I was introduced to padre Ramond,[3] and padre Saria,[4] who for many years had been stationed at that place. The latter is the prefect, or president of the spiritual affairs of all California. They are both aged, intelligent men, of good reputation. They seemed gratified that I had visited them, and made many inquiries respecting the mission at the Sandwich Islands. I gave them a short account of the operations of the American Board. Father Ramond took much pains to show me the church, the holy water, paintings, images, etc., assuring me, at the same time, that they only worshipped what these represented. I admitted that *he* might possibly employ them for this purpose, but I strongly suspected that the ignorant paid to them that homage which is due to God alone. He shook his head at such a suggestion, but as we could not converse, excepting through an interpreter, we dropped the subject. Each of these missions has about 300 Indians. There are twenty-one missions in upper California.

Those in the interior of the country are in a much more flourishing condition than those near the sea coast, the country being more favorable for cultivation, and temptations to sin in some respects being less numerous and strong. The average number of Indians belonging to this mission, is said to be one thousand. At each is one or more European padre, who has a few soldiers as a guard. These missions serve as inns, or resting places, for hunters and travellers, as there are no taverns in the country. Under the Spanish government, the influence of the padres was very great. Indeed the whole country was under their control. Their establishments of course have been, and continue to be, in a great measure, secular. They have accumulated large herds of cattle, horses and sheep, have traded with foreigners, and enriched their missions. Having this influence, and possessing these means, they have generally secured the good will of visitors, who speak of their hospitality in terms of commendation.

But to benefit the native inhabitants of California, was the professed object for which they came hither. And what has been the result of their labors with the Indians? On this subject I would speak with candor and kindness. The natives of this coast are, I admit, less intelligent than those who live farther north. Their countenances are dull and heavy, and they exhibit little evidence of possessing native strength of mind. In one respect, however, this has been favorable to their civilization and Christianization, as they have been pacific in proportion to their obtuseness of intellect. Such men the missionaries from the Roman Catholic church, more than fifty years since, gathered around them, and formed into societies under their immediate and constant superintendence, for the purpose of affording them instruction in the arts of civilized life, and in the doctrines and duties of Christianity. All this they attempted without giving them the Bible, or employing means to elevate them to the rank of thinking, intelligent beings. They fed them, taught them to cultivate the earth, to build themselves houses, and manufacture their own clothes. A few prayers in the Spanish language[5] they obliged them to commit to memory, and having baptized, they pronounced them good Christians. In 1792 Vancouver visited the missions of St. Francisco and St. Carlos. After describing the establishments and the method of controlling the Indians, he says:—"The missionaries found no difficulty in subjecting these people to their authority. It is mild and charitable, teaches them the cultivation of the soil, and introduces among them such of the useful arts as are most essential to the comforts of human nature and social life. It is much to be wished that these benevolent exertions may succeed, though there is every appearance that their progress will be very slow; yet they will probably lay a foundation, on which the posterity of the present race may secure to themselves the enjoyment of civil society."—Their efforts were at that time regarded in the light of an experiment. Little impression could be made on the minds of adult Indians, whose habits were confirmed; but here were their children, whose minds were unoccupied, and upon which they could have stamped their own image. In the light of an experiment, therefore, these efforts can be regarded no longer. And what is the result? After fifty years of toil, where are the smiling villages of industrious, intelligent mechanics? Where the happy neighborhoods of agriculturists? Where are found scenes of domestic bliss? Where are the indications of improved society? Where are seen those who have ceased to do evil, and learned to do well? None of these are to be found. It is admitted by all, with whom I have conversed on the coast, Catholic and Protestant, that these converted Indians, as they are called, are exceedingly degraded—much more so than their uncivilized neighbors. They are exceedingly uncleanly in their persons and habitations, are beastly drunkards, notorious gamesters, and are so many of them diseased in consequence of lewdness, that they are constantly dying off. They frequently run away from the missions, and lead on the untutored Indians to deeds of desperation. It is painful to see how little has been effected by men, many of whom doubtless have sincerely desired to benefit these Indians. But the history of these efforts among the pagans of California may not be lost, may not fail to be useful to the church. Had the gospel been preached in its purity and simplicity to these men, had they been taught to read, and had the simple statements of the bible met their eyes, what, by the blessing of God would have been effected? If the preaching of the gospel and the perusal of the bible, have changed to a moral garden, the barren rocks, and to perennial spring the ever during winter, of Greenland, what could not the same means have effected on the pleasant hills, and the verdant, blooming vallies of New Albion?

Notes to the Text

1. *Viz.*, Tomas Eleuterio Estenega (1790-1847), a many-talented friar who served at six missions during his quarter century in California.
2. It was probably September 17th, the Feast of the Stigmata of Saint Francis of Assisi.
3. *Viz.*, Father Ramon Abella (1764-1842) the Aragonese friar who arrived in the California in 1798.
4. *Viz.*, Father Vicente Francisco de Sarria (1767-1835), one of the ablest and most prominent of the Fernandinos.
5. Before receiving Baptism, the natives were obliged to know the *doctrina* which consisted of the Sign of the Cross, Our Father, Hail Mary, Creed; Acts of Faith, Hope and Charity; the Confiteor, Ten Commandments, Six Precepts, Seven Sacraments, the Necessary Points of Faith and the Four Last Things.

14

Alfred Robinson
(1807-1895)

Alfred Robinson "came to California in 1829 as a clerk on the trading vessel Brookline, married a native Californian, and became a resident for the remainder of his life."[1] "A bright, sensitive, and literate young man," the Massachusetts-born merchant personally witnessed "the stream of unfolding events which saw the pastoral province of Alta California transformed into the thirty-first state in the American union."[2]

Robinson's personal observations came about fortuitously. Originally, he intended only to publish Father Geronimo Boscana's Chinigchinich, a commentary on Indian life in and around Mission San Juan Capistrano. His envisioned "introduction" grew to such proportions as to completely over shadow the Boscana work.

The resultant "first English book on California to be written by a resident of the province"[3] was a natural outgrowth of Robinson's "intimate business and social relations with the best people of the Territory [which] afforded him excellent opportunities for the acquirement of accurate information."[4]

While his writings show "here and there the personal and political prejudices of the author,"[5] the account easily ranks among "the most valuable works in existence for the life and history of the period."[6] Robinson's narrative "gives a circumstantial account of all the missions as he found them, of the state of the country, and of the family life and amusements of the Californians."[7]

Robinson "wrote about the padres with a Yankee humor that is frequently delightful."[8] It should be noted, however, that he "became a Catholic because a Spanish lady [Ana Maria de la Guerra] would not have otherwise consented to marry him." Unquestionably, Baptism did not entirely cleanse him of "anti-Catholic rubbish."[9]

Life in California: During a Residence of Several Years in that Territory, comprising a Description of the Country and the Missionary

Establishments...to which is annexed A Historical Account of the Origin, Customs, and Traditions of the Indians of Alta-California *was initially published at New York in 1846, by Wiley & Putnam.*[10]
The following excerpt is an eyewitness account of the arrival at Santa Barbara of the Right Reverend Francisco Garcia Diego y Moreno, O.F.M., first Bishop of Both Californias, an event which signalled the end of the "provincial period," at least as far as ecclesiastical government is concerned.

References

1. Willard 0. Waters, *Franciscan Missions of Upper California as seen by Foreign Visitors and Residents* (Los Angeles, 1954), Entry 19.
2. Doyce B. Nunis, Jr., "Preface" to Alfred Robinson, *Life in California During a Residence of Several Years in that Territory* (New York, 1969), p. v-vi.
3. J. Gregg Layne in *The Zamorano 80* (Los Angeles, 1945), p. 54.
4. H. D. Barrows, "Alfred Robinson," *Historical Society of Southern California Annual* IV (1899), 234-235.
5. Hubert Howe Bancroft, *History of California* (San Francisco, 1866), V, 698.
6. Charles G. Chapman, *A History of California: The Spanish Period* (New York, 1923), p. 495.
7. Helen Throop Purdy, "Book Review," *California Historical Society Quarterly* IV (September, 1925), 299.
8. Franklin Walker, *A Literary History of Southern California* (Los Angeles, 1950), p. 34.
9. Zephyrin Engelhardt, O.F.M., *San Diego Mission* (San Francisco, 1920), p.187.
10. For biographical data, see Adele Ogden, "Alfred Robinson, New England Merchant in Mexican California," *California Historical Society Quarterly* XXIII (September, 1944), 193-218.

1829-1845

For a great length of time the Californians had been in anxious expectation of the coming of a bishop, who had been appointed for their diocese by his holiness, the Pope.[1] At length a courier arrived from St. Diego, on the 16th of December, 1841, announcing the fact of his having disembarked at that place. He came passenger on board of an English brig[2] from San Blas, accompanied by several priests,[3] two schoolmasters,[4] three school mistresses,[5] and four novitiates.[6] The news was received with the most enthusiastic expressions of joy by the inhabitants of Santa Barbara; guns were fired, and sky rockets let off in every direction. At the Mission the bells rang a merry peal, and the music of the band was heard at intervals, as its harmonious sounds floated through the air.

Several days subsequent to this demonstration of joy, we had an exhibition of the "Pastores,"[7] by the Indians of the Mission. They had been practising for some time, under the direction of Padre Antonio Jimeno,[8] and a great triumph was therefore anticipated over the performances of the *"gente de razon."* This exhibition took place on Sunday afternoons in the courtyard of Señor Noriega,[9] where four or five hundred persons were collected, to enjoy the amusement. Their performances were pronounced excellent, and I think they far surpassed those of the whites, which I had witnessed some years previous at St. Diego. At the conclusion of the "Pastores," a celebrated juggler came forward, and amused us a half hour longer, with some expert, and wonderful tricks of legerdemain.

The schooner *Leonidas* arrived, from St. Diego, with intelligence of the Bishop's intended embarkation at that place, in the barque *Guipuzcoana.* Her owner, Don José Antonio Aguirre,[10] had lately married there, the daughter of Señor Estudillo, and designed bringing his wife to Santa Barbara, where he had been preparing for some time previous, a suitable

124

residence. The venerable Bishop, and his retinue, had been invited to accompany the bridal party, and it was too good an opportunity for him to accomplish the remainder of his journey, to admit of a refusal. Great preparations were made, upon hearing this news, and all were anxious for the Bishop's arrival; for he was a functionary that but very few in California had ever beheld.

The vessel was in sight on the morning of the 11th of January, 1842, but lay becalmed and rolling to the ocean's swell. A boat put off from her side, and approached the landing-place. One of the attendants of his Excellency, who came in it, repaired to the Mission to communicate with the Father President.[11] All was bustle; men, women, and children hastening to the beach, banners flying, drums beatings and soldiers marching. The whole population of the place turned out, to pay homage to this first Bishop of California. At eleven o'clock the vessel anchored. He came on shore, and was welcomed by the kneeling multitude. All received his benediction—all kissed the pontifical ring. The troops, and civic authorities, then escorted him to the house of Don Jose Antonio,[12] where he dined. A carriage had been prepared for his Excellency, which was accompanied by several others, occupied by the President and his friends. The females had formed, with ornamented canes, beautiful arches, through which the procession passed; and as it marched along, the heavy artillery of the "Presidio" continued to thunder forth its noisy welcome. At the time he left the barque she was enveloped in smoke, and the distant report of her guns, was heard echoing among the hills in our rear.

The bride, with her mother and her sisters, remained on board till afternoon, when they, also, repaired to the festive scene.

At four o'clock, the Bishop was escorted to the Mission, and when a short distance from the town, the enthusiastic inhabitants took the horses from his carriage, and dragged it themselves. Halting at a small bower, on the road, he alighted, went into it, and put on his pontifical robes; then resuming his place in the carriage, he continued on, amidst the sound of music and the firing of guns, till he arrived at the church, where he addressed the multitude that followed him.

The Reverend Bishop Francisco Garcia Diego[13] is a Mexican, and a Friar of the Franciscan order. He had been a teacher of theology in Mexico, and afterwards, in 1833, was *"Comisario Prefecto"* of the Missions of Upper California. Having passed several years in the country, he knew well how to work upon the minds of the Californians, in order to win their esteem, and to make himself popular. Santa Barbara was selected to be the "Episcopal See;"[14] and plans were drawn up, for the erection of his Palace, a Cathedral, a Monastery, and a Theological School. The Inhabitants were called upon to unite in forwarding these plans, and the Bishop trusted for resources to the *"Fonda Piadosa de California,"* "Pious fund of California," in Mexico, for their accomplishment. Large piles of stones were heaped up, in several places, for laying the foundations of the above-named edifices; but, as the Mexican government have seen proper to appropriate this fund to less pious purposes, there they will undoubtedly remain, for some years, as monuments of the frailty of human speculations.

Notes to the Text

1. Fray Francisco Garcia Diego y Moreno, O.F.M., was appointed first Bishop of Both Californias by Pope Gregory XVI on April 27, 1840.
2. *Viz.,* the *Rosalind.*
3. *Viz.,* Friars Miguel Muro (1791-1848) and Francisco Sanchez (1813-1884), both members of the Apostolic College of Our Lady of Guadalupe at Zacatecas.
4. The "schoolmasters" were probably the above mentioned friars.
5. There were only two women in the party, Josefita Gonzales y Diego (d.1852), the bishop's niece and her elderly companion, known in the annals only as Doña Soledad.
6. The four *"novitiates"* were actually seminarians, *viz.,* Miguel Gomez (d.1856), Antonio Jimenez del Recio, Jose Maria Rosales and Doroteo Ambris (d.1883).
7. The *Pastorela* or Nativity Play was customarily performed on Christmas Eve, which, in this case, was about two weeks prior to the bishop's arrival at Santa Barbara.
8. Father Antonio Jimeno, a friar born in Mexico City, spent his thirty-one years in California at Missions Santa Cruz and Santa Barbara.
9. *I.e.* Jose Antonio Julian De la Guerra y Noriega (1779-1858), a prominent citizen of the channel town and a close friend of the padres.
10. Jose Antonio Aguirre was a kindly and helpful benefactor of the friars. He was married successively to two daughters of Jose Antonio Estudillo, Francesca and Rosario. The one here mentioned is Rosario.
11. *Viz.,* Father Narciso Duran (1776-1846) whose name "was more prominent than that of any friar over a long period…" See Angustias de la Guerra Ord, *Occurrences in Hispanic California* (Washington, 1956), p. 79.
12. *Viz.,* the wealthy merchant and ship-owner, Jose Antonio Aguirre. See Note #10 above.
13. For a biographical sketch of California's pioneer prelate, See Francis J. Weber, *Francisco Garcia Diego. California's Transition Bishop* (Los Angeles, 1972).
14. Actually the papal bulls designated San Diego as the episcopal seat. Only when that place proved inadequate did the bishop decide to relocate at Santa Barbara.

15

William Heath Davis
(1822-1909)

*T*he relatively late publication of William Heath Davis' memoirs afforded
the author an opportunity to include much data lacking in earlier chronicles. Davis first visited California when the missions were still relatively prosperous and populous. He subsequently witnessed the upheaval of provincial
times and the inauguration of a whole new breed of westerners, thus coming to
know first-hand many of the vexations rained on the mission system as it began
to crumble. There were few individuals of importance that Davis did not know
personally, a factor which makes his simple and straight-forward narrative "a
thoroughly readable account of life in Pastoral California."¹

"Many of the most glamorous incidents of Spanish Californian times"² can
be found in the "entertaining reminiscences of pioneer days"³ penned by Davis.
The Honolulu-born merchant, an affable, courteous and broadminded person,
was an active participant in the day and generation of which he has written so
well and convincingly. There was something of a prophetic ring to his observation that "when this State, imperial in its dimensions, shall have grown to an
empire itself, great will be the interest as to what were its beginnings, and as to
what manner of men they were who founded it."⁴

Davis "gives much concerning the padres and their simple but untiring
mission life..."⁵ Throughout his narrative he spoke admiringly of the friars,
the "original pioneers of California, beyond all others," as men who had "left
behind them, as mementos of their zeal and industry in the work in which they
were engaged, the Missions they built and conducted, besides other evidences,
less tangible, of their influence for the welfare of the people of California and
the whole world."

Davis considered the Franciscans to be decidedly "superior men in point of talent, education, morals and executive ability." To him they "seemed to be entirely
disinterested, their aim and ambition being to develop the country, and civilize

*and Christianize the Indians, for which purpose the Missions were established."
Davis noted that the friars had worked zealously and untiringly on behalf of the
neophytes and, from his point of view, "to them must be given the credit for
what advancement in civilization, intelligence, industry, good habits and good
morals pertained to the country at that day, when they laid the foundation of the
present advanced civilization and development of the country."*

*Financial embarrassment induced William Heath Davis to publish his recollec-
tions, in 1889, as* Sixty Years in California. A History of Events and Life in
California. *A considerably enlarged version, edited by Douglas S. Watson,
appeared in 1929, as* Seventy-Five Years in California. *In 1968, a third revised
and expanded edition, prepared by Harold A. Small, incorporated a number of
corrections from the author's own hand.*

References

1. Phil Townsend Hanna in *The Zamorano 80* (Los Angeles, 1945), p. 20.
2. Lawrence Clark Powell, *Libros Californianos* (Los Angeles, 1958), p. 50.
3. Caroline F. Hover *et al.*, *The Celebrated Collection of Americana Formed by the late Thomas Winthrop Streeter* (New York, 1968), Entry 3006.
4. The excerpts here cited are from the 1929 edition of *Seventy-Five Years in California*.
5. Robert Ernest Cowan, "Book Review," *California Historical Society Quarterly* VIII (June, 1929), 184.

1831-1833

The priests of California belonged to the Order of Franciscans. Their ordinary dress was a loose woolen garment, made whole and put on over the head, reaching nearly to the ground, of a plain drab or brownish hue, which was the color of the Order.[1] The dress was made with wide sleeves, a hood falling back on the shoulders, which could be drawn over the head when it was desired by the wearer, if the weather was cold or unpleasant; and at the waist was a girdle and tassels of the same material tied around the dress or habit, the tassels hanging down in front. Sometimes they were left untied. One requirement of the Order was that every priest should have shaven on the crown of the head a circular spot about three or four inches in diameter.[2] This I noticed among all of them. As the hair commenced growing it was again shaved, and this spot was always kept bare.

The priests at the various Missions were usually men of very pure character, particularly the Spanish priests. The first priests who established the Missions were directly from Spain.[3] They were superior men in point of talent, education, morals and executive ability, as the success of the Missions under their establishment and administration showed. They seemed to be entirely disinterested, their aim and ambition being to develop the country, and civilize and Christianize the Indians, for which purpose the Missions were established. They worked zealously and untiringly in this behalf, and to them must be given the credit for what advancement in civilization, intelligence, industry, good habits and good morals pertained to the country at that day, when they laid the foundation of the present advanced civilization and development of the country.

After the independence of Mexico, and its separation from Spain, the Missions of California passed under the control of Mexican priests, who

were also men of culture and attainments, generally of excellent character, but as a class they were inferior to their predecessors.[4] They were
always hospitable to strangers, all visitors were kindly received and entertained with the best they could offer, and the table was well supplied.
The wine which they made at the Missions was of a superior quality and
equal to any that I have drunk elsewhere.

In trading through the country and traveling from point to point it was
customary for travelers to stop at the Missions as frequently and as long as
they desired. This was expected as a matter of course by the priests, and had
the traveler neglected to avail himself of the privilege it would have been
regarded as an offense by the good Fathers. On approaching the Mission
the traveler would be met at the door or at the wide veranda by the Padre,
who would greet him warmly, embrace him and invite him in, and he was
furnished with the best the Mission afforded at the table, given one of the
best rooms to sleep in, attended by servants, and everything possible was
done to make him at home and comfortable during his stay. On leaving he
was furnished with a fresh horse, and a good *vaquero*[5] was appointed to
attend him to the next Mission, where he was received and entertained with
the same hospitality, and so on as far as the journey extended.

The last of the Mexican priests was Father Gonzalez, who presided in
'38 at the Mission of San José and who died some years ago at the
Mission of Santa Barbara at a very advanced age.[6] He was a noble man, a
true Christian, very much respected and beloved by all his people, and by
all who knew him. Whenever I went there he always welcomed me in the
most cordial manner, and the moment I saw him I felt drawn toward him
as by a lodestone. He would take me in and say, *"Sienta usted hijito"* (sit
down, my little son), and seating himself close by my side, he entertained
me in such delightful manner by his conversation, which flowed easily
and naturally in a continuous stream, that one hardly realized that he was
only an humble priest. His people greatly honored and loved him, and he
was known among them as "The Saint on Earth." There were some
exceptions among the priests as to general rectitude and excellence of
character, as there are everywhere; but as a class they were a fine body of
men of superior character, and accomplished a vast deal of good. The
priests were much respected by the people, who looked to them for
advice and guidance.

The supercargoes[7] of the vessels that were trading on the coast, of
course had occasion to visit all the settlements in the interior or along
the coast to conduct their business with the people, and to travel back
and forth up and down the country. In visiting down the coast they usual-

ly went on the vessels, which had a fair wind most of the time going south; but on coming up there was commonly a head wind, which made the voyage tedious, and the supercargoes then took to land and came up on horsebacks accompanied by a *vaquero*, stopping along from one Mission to another or at some rancho, where they were supplied with fresh horses whenever they required them, free of charge, by the Fathers of the rancheros. These horses were furnished as a matter of course with entire freedom and hospitality by the farmers and the Padres. When the traveler reached another stopping place he was provided with a fresh horse, and such a thing as continuing the journey on the horse he rode the day before was not to be thought of, so polite and courteous were these generous Californians.

The traveler had no further care or thought in regard to the horse he had been using, but left him where he happened to be, and the Padre or *ranchero* would undertake to send him back, or if this was not convenient it was no matter, as the owner would never ask any questions concerning his safety or return. It would have been considered impoliteness for the guest to express any concern about the horse or what was to become of him. Sometimes the traveler was furnished by the rancheros with part of a *caponera*, ten or twelve horses with a bell mare, and a *vaquero*, in order that he might continue his journey to the end without looking for other horses. He would travel along from day to day, changing his horse each day and sometimes oftener, and also that of his *vaquero*, and on reaching his journey's end the *vaquero* would return with the horses.

The Padres had stores at the Missions, to supply the wants of the Indians, as well as the Californians in the employ of the Missions. Their stock was necessarily large. They also supplied the rancheros with goods, taking in payment hides, tallow, fur and cattle. They also traded with the fur hunters, and gave in exchange for skins, goods and also gold and silver coin. The Fathers were first-class merchants. When they made purchases from vessels trading on the coast, they exhibited good judgment in their selections and were close buyers. The "Volunteer," in 1833, sold to the Missions bordering on the bay considerable quantities of goods, for cash. I remember that our supercargo, Sherman Peck,[8] spoke of the missionaries as shrewd purchasers, and strictly reliable men. It was a pleasure to deal with them. The Padres brought goods cheaper than the *rancheros*; their purchases being always larger, a reduction was made in prices, as a matter of policy, and to encourage good relations already existing.

One Mission would assist another with hides and tallow, or with fur, skins, or money, in payment for goods which it had purchased. The priest sometimes gave an order on another Mission, in favor of the supercargo, to furnish what was required. While my father was trading at the Refugio, the vessel had to wait several days, for payment for a portion of the goods sold to the Mission of Santa Barbara. Having paid over such gold and otter skins as it had on hand, this Mission sent out to the Mission of San Buenaventura at the east, and Santa Ynez on the west, for a further supply of skins, and coin, to pay for the balance of the goods. These numerous Missions were in reality one institution, with a common interest. The advancement of one was the general good and welfare of all. The goods purchased by one Mission were sometimes sent to others, partly for use, and in part for sale, as the range of distribution was thus widened. When one Mission had furnished another with money, or fur skins, or hides, or tallow, to assist it in paying for a large purchase, although there was no obligation to return the same, yet the Fathers were proud men, and it was their custom to return what they had borrowed, when they were able to do so from their new accumulations. While their interests were one, there was at the same time a friendly ambition on the part of each to conduct his Mission successfully, and not be outdone by any other Mission.

The Padres were the original pioneers of California, beyond all others. They have left behind them, as mementos of their zeal and industry in the work in which they were engaged, the Missions they built and conducted, besides other evidence, less tangible, of their influence for the welfare of the people of California and the whole world.

Notes to the Text

1. The missionaries in California originally wore gray habits and only after 1885, when the Golden State's friars were annexed to the American Province of the Sacred Heart, were members seen in brown. See Zephyrin Engelhardt, O.F.M., "Color of Fray Junipero Serra's Habit," *Franciscan Herald* V (September, 1916), 346-347.
2. The "tonsura," still worn in many predominantly Catholic countries, is the distinctive mark of the clerical state.
3. Alta California's earliest missionaries, mostly Spanish-born, were attached to Mexico City's Apostolic College of San Fernando.
4. After 1833, Mexican-born friars from the Apostolic College of *Nuestra Señora de Guadalupe* at Zacatecas took charge of the northernmost of the California missions.
5. A *vaquero* was the California-version of cowboy.
6. Father Gonzalez Rubio (1804-1875) came to California with Francisco Garcia Diego y Moreno in 1833. During the subsequent four decades he left an indelible mark upon everyone with whom he came in contact.

7. A *"supercargo"* was charged with the business affairs of a merchant ship.
8. Abel Stearns and Sherman Peck arrived at Monterey in July of 1829 on the *Dorotea*, a schooner purchased at San Blas by Jose De la Guerra y Noriega.

16

Hugo Reid
(1811-1852)

Hugo Reid was a naturalized Scottish-Mexican rancher who came to Mission San Gabriel in 1832. Shortly after his arrival at the fourth of the California Missions, Reid married Victoria Bartholomea, an Indian widow from the tribe of Comicrabit living at San Gabriel.

In in effort to vindicate the forebears of his bride, Reid "attracted much attention"[1] by writing a series of twenty-two letters which he published in the Los Angeles Star between February 21 and August 1, 1852. Though he "derived his information from traditions,"[2] many of Reid's thoughts were later canonized by Benjamin D. Wilson in the latter's report on Indian conditions in California.[3]

Reid was widely known as "one of the most interesting and picturesque characters" of the pueblo,[4] but to Zephyrin Engelhardt, the mission historian, the University trained Scotchman's observations and historical conclusions were decidedly "soured."[5] On the other hand, to John Nugent, editor of the San Francisco Herald, the letters "possessed a fund of information concerning the history of California" surpassing the observations of almost any other man in the state."[6]

Reid's enthusiasm for analyzing the evil times befalling the Indians in the post-mission era led him to conclusions that were "in emphatic disagreement"[7] with earlier accounts. His view that the natives "had been ruined by the Spaniards and the Franciscan mission system"[8] inclined Reid to the useful, but hardly valid post hoc, ergo propter hoc explanation of the admittedly sad state of Indian affairs in the mid-1850's.

Reid's "Letters on the Los Angeles County Indians" first appeared in the Los Angeles Star, in 1852, and nine years later in the California Farmer and Journal of Useful Arts. A condensed version, edited by Walter James Hoffman, appearing in the Bulletin of the Essex Institute XVI (January, 1885), was reproduced, in monograph form as Hugo Reid's Account of the Indians of

Los Angeles Co., Cal. *(Salem, 1885). An edition of 200 copies was released at Los Angeles in 1926, handset by Arthur M. Ellis, under the title* The Indians of Los Angeles County. *To her tastily-illustrated and authentically-annotated sketch of* A Scotch Paisano, *published at Berkeley in 1939, Susanne Bryant Dakin included the original letters as Appendix B. Robert F. Heizer edited the first complete and unabridged collection for the Southwest Museum in* The Indians of Los Angeles County. Hugo Reid's Letters of 1852 *(Los Angeles, 1968).*

References

1. William B. Rice, "Southern California's First Newspaper: The Founding of the *Los Angeles Star,*" *Historical Society of Southern California Quarterly* XXIII (March, 1941), 48.
2. Hubert Howe Bancroft, *History of California* (San Francisco, 1884), I, 180n.
3. See John Walton Caughey (Ed.), *The Indians of Southern California in 1852* (San Marino, 1952).
4. J. Gregg Layne, "Annals of Los Angeles," *California Historical Society Quarterly* XIII (September, 1934), 215.
5. *San Gabriel Mission* (San Gabriel, 1927), p. 354.
6. Quoted in Susanne B. Dakin, "Hugo Reid, Humanitarian," *Historical Society of Southern California Quarterly* XXXI (March-June, 1949), 59.
7. Franklin Walker, *A Literary History of Southern California* (Berkeley, 1950), p. 83.
8. Quoted from the 1926 edition of Hugo Reid's *The Indians of Los Angeles County.*

1832-1852

When the Priest came to found the Mission,[1] he brought a number of vagabonds, under the name of soldiers, to carry out the proposed plan. Some of these were masons, carpenters, etc. The priest having *converted* some few by giving them cloth and ribbons, and taught them to say *Amar a Dios*, they were baptized and cooperated in the work before them.

Baptism as performed, and the recital of a few words not understood, can hardly be said to be a conversion; nevertheless, it was productive of great advantage to the Missionaries, because once baptized they lost "caste" with their people, and had *nolens volens* to stop with the oppressor. This, of course, was put down by the Padre as a proof of the influence of religion on their minds, and the direct interposition of the Virgin Mary! Poor devils, they were the *Paraiha*[2] of the West! Not one word of Spanish did they understand—not one word of the Indian tongue did the Priest know.—They had no more idea that they were worshiping God, than an unborn child has of Astronomy. Numbers of old men and women have been gathered to the dust of their Fathers—and a few still remain—whose whole stock of Spanish was contained in the never-failing address of "Amar a Dios!" And whose religion, as Catholics, consisted in being able to cross themselves, under an impression it was something connected with hard work and still harder blows. Baptism was called by them *soyna*, "being Bathed", and strange to say, was looked upon, although such a simple ceremony, as being ignominious and degrading.

We are, of course, unable to say that the severe measures adopted emanated from the Priest; still there can be no doubt he either winked at the means employed by his agents, or else he was credulity personified! Baptism could not be administered by force to adults, it required a free act; so taking an Indian as guide, part of the soldiers or servants proceeded on expeditions after converts. On one occasion they went as far as the present Rancho del Chino, where they tied and whipped every man, woman and child in the Lodge at San Jose. On arriving home the men were instructed to throw their bows and arrows at the feet of the Priest, and make due submission.—The infants were then baptized, as were also all children under eight years of age; the former were left with their mothers, but the latter kept apart from all communication with their parents. The consequence was, first, the women consented to the right and received it, for the love they bore their offspring; and finally the males gave way for the purpose of enjoying once more, the society of wife and family. Marriage was then performed, and so this contaminated race, in their own sight and that of their kindred, became followers of Christ (?).

The Indians, from the beginning, never offered resistance or flew to arms, although they had ofttimes distinguished themselves in warfare with other tribes. At first, surprise and astonishment filled their minds; a strange lethargy and inaction predominated afterwards. All they did was to hide themselves as they best could from the oppressor.

From the first misnamed conversion until the arrival of Fray Jose Maria Salvadea,[3] they knew nothing about the various rites and ceremonies daily performed, and in which they took a part. No explication was, or could be offered, for the Indians only learned a few words of Spanish, and the Padres none of their language. The soldiers, it is true, picked up a smattering of the Indian tongue, but such words only, as to enable them to gratify with more ease their lust and evil propensities, and not to afford instruction.

But the Padre Jose Maria, who was a man of talent, and possessed of a powerful mind—which was as ambitious as it was powerful, and as cruel as it was ambitious—formed a new era in their existence. In a short time he mastered the language and reduced it to grammatical rules. He translated the prayers of the church, and preached every Sunday a sermon in their own tongue. His translation of the Lord's prayer, commencing with *Ayoinac* (our Father) is a grand specimen of his eloquence and ability.

He gave them, thereby, an insight of the Catholic religion, but did not in one iota alter their own. His predecessors had done nothing of the kind, and his successors, Padre Jose Bernardo Sanchez[4] and Padre Tomas Estenaga,[5] contented themselves in having their sermons translated sentence by sentence, to the Neophites, through an Indian interpreter, named Benito. On the death of Padre Tomas, the custom ceased.

FIRST MISSIONARY PROCEEDINGS

Having, at length, a sufficiency of Neophites to build with, ground was cleared and laid off; adobes were made and laid up; timber, cut in the neighboring mountains, was hauled; and at last a proper covering being required, tule or flags were put on, tied with nettle hemp made by the Indians, which formed a thatched roof suitable for present exigency. The Church had a steeple to it, which was afterwards taken down, having sustained damage during an earthquake. The present belfry was substituted instead.

In after years, not only were other buildings erected, but tile manufactured, and placed on all of the edifices, including four rows of new double houses, forming three streets for the married portion of the community. Living in houses, however did not suit their tastes; they were always vexed and annoyed with them, and debarred the satisfaction of burning them up according to usage, when their observances demanded it.

All this while, the former small stock of animals were carefully herded and were augmenting greatly.

Vine slips, fruit trees, and pulse, etc., were procured from Lower California. The first vineyard planted consisted of 3,000 Vines. It retains the name of *Vina Madre*, and from it sprang all the present generation of vineyards.[6]

A better class of people than the low vulgar soldiers, both men and women, were induced to emigrate from Sinaloa and Lower California. They were a great acquisition, as were likewise a few Indians from the latter place, who had been well instructed by the "Jesuits" in various arts.[7] The men among the newcomers served as *majordomos* and overseers in the different branches of industry carried on. And being likewise well acquainted with agriculture, and some of the required trades, their services were invaluable. The women were no less useful, for they taught the young female Indians to sew, and they became most expert at the business. Last and not least in the eyes of many besides the Priests, they instructed the older heads in the art of cooking, making of chocolate paste, preserves, and other edible knickknacks unknown for some time previous to our Missionary friends.

Water was brought to irrigate the crops, from numerous little streams, and more produce was raised than necessary for the sustenance of all. The Neophites were supplied with blankets and some few cotton goods, but not to any great amount.

Indians of course deserted. Who would not have deserted? Still, those who did had hard times of it. If they proceeded to other missions, they were picked up immediately, flogged and put in irons until an opportunity presented of returning them to undergo other flagellations. If they stowed themselves away in any of the *rancherias*, the soldiers were monthly in the habit of visiting them; and such was the punishment inflicted on those who attempted to conceal them, that it rarely was essayed. Being so proscribed, the only alternative left them was to take to the mountains, where they lived as they best could, making occasional inroads on the Mission property to maintain themselves. They were styled *hindas*, or runaways, and at times were rendered desperate through pursuit, and took the lives of any suspected of being traitors. They were always well informed of all passing at the Mission.—They sometimes, when things got too hot, went as far as the Tulares.

A considerable quantity of books to compose a library, were brought from the College of San Fernando, in Mexico, and a number of additional contributions were received during the time of Salvedea and Sanchez, from the same source, and also some by purchase from Lima. I cannot say much for the collection—it being nothing to compare with remnants of the Bibliothekes I have examined in Lower California, in the Missions established there, which are now, I am sorry to say, reduced to ashes.

The more valuable part of the works consisted of those treating on Theology and Law, with a scanty number of rather curious, quaint manuscripts; the balance being antiquated and erroneous productions on natural history, geography, etc., imparting little or no information. The best of the library has, long ere this, either been stolen or destroyed, and the refuse at the present time, consisting of some three or four hundred volumes is mere rubbish.

NEW ERA IN MISSION AFFAIRS

On the arrival of Padre Jose Maria Salvedea, cattle were plenty, as were likewise horses, mares, sheep and hogs. Cultivation was carried on to considerable extent, but it was to him that the after splendor of San Gabriel was due. He it was who planted the large Vineyards intersected with fine walks, shaded by fruit trees of every description, and rendered still more lovely by shrubs interspersed between—who laid out the orange garden, fruit and olive orchards—built the mill and dam—made fences of *tunas (cactus opuntia)* round the fields—made hedges of rose bushes—planted trees in the Mission square, with a flower garden and sun dial in the centre—brought water from long distances, etc., etc.

He likewise remodeled the general system of government, putting everything in order and to its proper use, and placing every person in his proper station. Everything under him was organized, and that organization kept up with the lash!

Thus people were divided into various classes and stations. There were *vaqueros*, soap makers, tanners, shoemakers, carpenters, black smiths, bakers, cooks, general servants, pages, fishermen, agriculturists, horticulturists, brick and tile makers, musicians, singers, tallow melters, *vignerons*, carters, cart-makers, shepherds, poultry keepers, pigeon tenders, weavers, spinners, saddle makers, store and key keepers, deer hunters, deer and sheep skin dressmakers, people of all work, and in fact every thing but coopers, who were foreign; all the balance, masons, plasterers, etc., were natives.

Large soap works were erected; tanning yards established; tallow works, bakery, cooper, blacksmith, carpenter, and other shops; large spinning rooms where might be seen 50 or 60 women turning their spindles merrily; and looms for weaving wool, flax and cotton. Then large store rooms were allotted to the various articles, which were kept separate. For instance, wheat, barley, peas, beans, lentils, chick-peas, butter, and cheese, soap, candles, wool, leather, flour, lime, salt, horsehair, wine and spirits, fruit, stores, etc., etc.

Sugar cane, flax and hemp, were added to the other articles cultivated but cotton wool was imported.

The *ranchos* belonging to the Mission were put on another footing, as were the sheep farms. A house was built at San Bernardino and other exterior operations carried out.—The principal ranchos belonging at that time to San Gabriel were San Pasqual, Santa Anita, Azusa, San Francisquito, Cucumonga, San Antonio, San Bernardino, San Gorgonio, Yucaipa, Jurapu, Guapa, Rincon, Chino, San Jose, Ybarras, Puente, Mission Viga, Serranos, Rosa Castillo, Coyotes, Saboneria, Las Bolsas, Alamitos and Cerritos.

A principal head *Mayordomo* commanded and superintended over all. Claudio Lopez[8] was the famed one during Padre Salvedea's administration, and although only executing the Priests' plans, in the minds of the people he is the real hero. Ask any one who made this, or who did that, and the answer on all sides is the same: *El difunto Claudio!* And great credit is due him for carrying out, without flogging, the numerous works set before him.

There were a great many other *mayordomos* under him, for all kinds of work, from tending of horses down to those superintending crops, and in charge of vineyards and gardens.

It is strange no medical man was kept on the establishment, as the number of people was great and the stock of medicines very large.—They were provided not by the pound, but by the *quintal!* Not in gallons, but in barrels full! Still all the dependence for medical aid (with the exception of midwives) was either on a casual foreigner employed or the premises. I know not why, but an Anglo-Saxon in those days was synonymous with an M.D. Many an *"Estrangero"* who never before possessed sufficient confidence in himself to administer even a dose of Epsom, after killing, God knows how many, has at length become a tolerable emperic. One thing in favor of the sick was, that after a lapse of years, the greater part of the drugs lost their virtue.

Indian *Alcaldes* were appointed annually by the Padre, and chosen from among the very laziest of the community; he being of the opinion that they took more pleasure in making the others work, than would industrious ones! From my own observation this is correct. They carried a wand to denote their authority, and what was more terrible, an immense scourge of raw hide, about ten feet in length, plaited to the thickness of an ordinary man's wrist!—They did a great deal of chastisement, both by and without orders. One of them always acted as overseer on work done in gangs, and accompanied carts when on service.

The unmarried women and young girls were kept as Nuns, under the supervision of an abbess, who slept with them in a large room.—Their occupations were various; sometimes they sewed or spun, at others they cleaned weeds out of the gardens with hoes, worked at the ditches or gathered in the crops. In fact, they were Jacks or jennies of no trade in particular.

The best looking youths were kept as pages to attend at table and those of most musical talent reserved for church service.

The number of hogs was great and were principally used for making soap. The Indians, with some few exceptions, refused to eat hogs, alleging the whole family to be transformed Spaniards! I find this belief current through every nation of Indians in Mexico. Why should they, without being aware of it, have each selected the hog more than any other animal to fix a stigma upon? It probably may be from its filthy habits; or, can something appertaining to the Jews be innate in them?

At San Francisquito, near the Mission, were kept the turkies, of which they had a large quantity. The dove-cote was along side of the soap works, and in an upper story, affording plenty of dung to cure leather and skins with.

The Padre had an idea that finery led Indians to run away, for which reason he never gave either men or women any other clothing (including shirts and petticoats) than coarse *frieze (Xerga)* made by themselves, which kept the poor wretches all the time diseased with the itch. If any handkerchiefs or cotton goods were discovered among them, the same was immediately committed to the flames.

He was an inveterate enemy to drunkenness, and did all in his power to prevent it, but to no purpose. He never flogged, however, while the influence of liquor lasted; but put them into the stocks, under care of a guard, until sober. Finding the lash alone was of no avail, he added warm water and salt to the dose, which was given until it ran out of the mouth again! It was of no use, the disease was as incurable as consumption.

Having found out the game practiced in regard to destroying the children born to the whites, he put down all miscarriages to the same cause. Therefore, when a woman had the misfortune to bring forth a still-born child, she was punished. The penalty inflicted was, saving the head, flogging for fifteen subsequent days, iron on the feet for three months, and having to appear every Sunday in church, on the steps leading up to the altar, with a hideous painted wooden child in her arms!

He had no predilection for wizards, and generally (as some one or another was always reporting evil of them), kept them chained together in couples and well flogged. There were, at that period, no small number of old men rejoicing in the fame of witchcraft, so he made sawyers of them all, keeping them like hounds in couples, and so they worked, two above and two below in the pit.

On a breach occurring between man and wife, they were fastened together by the leg, until they agreed to live again in harmony.

He was not only severe, but he was, in his chastisements, most cruel. So as not to make a revolting picture, I shall bury acts of barbarity known to me through good authority, by merely saying that he must assuredly have considered whipping as meat and drink to them, for they had it morning, noon and night.

Although so severe to the Indians, he was kind in the extreme to travelers and others.—There being so much beef, mutton, pork, and poultry, with fruits, vegetables and wines, that a splendid public table was spread daily, at which he presided. Horses to ride on were at their service and a good bed to sleep on at night. Whenever ready to start either up or down the coast, horses and a servant were at command to go as far as the next Mission.

Having brought the establishment and every thing connected with it, to the climax of perfection, he had still calculated on doing more. He purchased large quantities of iron, with the intention of railing in all of the vineyard and gardens. But, alas! even Catholic societies are not proof against the "capital sins" they so strongly condemn. Envy and jealousy stepped in and prevailed. He was ordered by his superior to the Mission of San Juan Capistrano. The loss of his favorite hobby capsized his reason, and after lingering for many years in a disturbed religious state of mind,[9] he at length expired, regretted by all who knew his worth and gigantic intellect.

BETTER TIMES

The Padre Jose Bernardo Sanchez had, for some time previous, been a colleague of Salvedeas but attended only to matters connected with the church. On the translation of Padre Jose Maria to San Juan, he became his successor. He was of a cheerful disposition, frank and generous in his nature, although at times he lost his temper with the strange, unruly set around him.

He was a great sportsman and capital shot, both with rifle and fowling piece. Although no one could complain of Salvedea, in regard to his kind treatment, still there was a certain restraint in his presence, arising from his austerity and pensiveness, which even custom did not erase from the mind. Padre Sanchez was different; his temper was governed according to circumstances. In Ecclesiastical affairs, his deportment was solemn; in trade he was formal; in the government of the Mission, active, lively and strict; in social intercourse he was friendly, full of anecdotes, fond of a joke, even to a practical one. Picnic parties were of weekly occurrence and generally held at the Mill, when, independent of a yearling heifer baked under ground, many other good things reigned on the table.

I cannot refrain from relating an anecdote connected with those parties of pleasure, as it shows the relish the old man had for anything ludicrous. A few of the actors are still alive, but the greater part have been gathered with the Padre, to the dust they sprang from.

Don J. M. M.,[10] an old Spaniard, who had large commercial relations with the Mission, having a negro cook, called Francisco, who was science itself in all relating to the kitchen, the Priest and M. made up a plan to carry out a joke at the expense of their guests. So having procured a fine fat little puppy, he was stuffed and roasted in a manner that would have tempted the most fastidious epicure to "cut and come again." This was brought on as a last course under the name of lamb, with an excellent salad to correspond.

All ate of it and praised it much, with the exception of the two concerned in the joke.—After concluding with a glass of wine, the old man enquired of his guests how they relished the Dog? No one would believe it, until the negro made his appearance with the head and paws on a plate. Then a mixed scene ensued, which brought tears into the old man's eyes, while he nearly killed himself with laughter. All, of course, were squeamish, but while the quiet portion retired to ease themselves, in discharging the detested food, the pugnacious remained to fight M. first, and do the other afterward. The Padre eventually procured harmony, but for many a day after, roast lamb and salad were viewed with suspicion by the former partakers of his cheer.

The same regulations which had been observed by his predecessor, were still in force under him, but more lenity was shown to the failings of the Neophites. Although the lash was ever ready, yet many other modes of chastising were adopted in its stead for minor offenses.

The general condition of the Indians was rendered better, and a more healthy state prevailed even in their morals. Many an Indian who had previously stolen and committed other acts of insubordination, from a vindictive spirit, now refrained from such deeds, through the love and good will held to their spiritual and temporal ruler.

The purchases made at one time seldom exceeded $30,000, consisting of domestics, bleached brown and printed; flannels, cloth, rebosas, silk goods, and, in fact, everything; besides supplies of sugar, panocha, rice, hosiery, etc. These goods were fitted up in two large stores for the accommodation, not only of the public, but for the necessities of servants and use of the Neophites. The females had their *freize (xerga)* converted into sweat-cloths, and more suitable garments provided them. This measure effected a great change, for now of a Sunday might be seen coming out of church, women dressed in petticoats of all patterns and colors, with their clean chemise protruding from the bosom, with a 'kerchief round the neck and rebosa round the shoulders; while the man had their pants, jacket, trousers, hat and fancy silk sash. Even the children sported in white or fancy shirt, with a handkerchief tied around the head.

This was, indeed, a transformation, and one for which they felt grateful. It elevated them to better thoughts and principles, and made them esteem themselves more than probably anything else would have done. Nor did the reformation stop here. The married people had not only sheets provided for their beds, but even curtains. It was the duty of the *Mayor-domo* to visit each room weekly and see that every article was kept clean and report accordingly. The Priest paid a monthly visit for the same end.

On coming out of Mass, the whole community was assembled and rations given to families for the ensuing week. Besides, each man received half a pint of spirits, and the women a pint of wine. *Panocha*, molasses and honey were distributed, and if required, clothing; as also two or three dollars each on occasions.—Although rations were given as stated, yet the Mission provided daily food for the laborers.

The Mission bell, on being rung, roused the *Alcades* from their slumbers, who in loud voice soon set all the world agog. Mass was heard, and again the bell rang to work. At eleven its notes proclaimed dinner, when in they flocked with their baskets to receive *posole* and a piece of beef. *Posole* consisted of boiled beans and corn or wheat. At twelve o'clock they were again warned to their labors, which concluded a little before sundown to afford them time to receive supper, which consisted of *atole* or mush. If a gang were at a distance, a copper kettle and attendant accompanied to provide food on the spot.

After twelve o'clock on Saturdays, soap was distributed, and all the world went a washing of clothes and persons, to make a decent appearance at church on Sunday. Saturday night was devoted to playing *peon*, and with few exceptions, none slept, for whites and Indians, men, women and children, were generally present.

After service, on Sunday, football and races were on the carpet until the afternoon, when a game called by the Scotch "shinty," and I believe by the English, "bandy," took place.—One set being composed of all men and one of all women. People flocked in from all parts to see the sport, and heavy bets were made. The Priest took a great interest in the game, and as the women seldom had less than half a dozen quarrels, in which hair flew by the handful, it pleased him very much. The game being concluded, all went to prayers, and so ended the Sabbath.

He died in 1833, regretted by all the community, and leaving every one who know him sad at his loss.

His course was a good one, yet probably the Padre Salvedea's was equally so. It was required in his time, no doubt, and the stop from the one to the other had a more beneficial tendency than had he from the first carried out measures such as those of Sanchez. He was succeeded by Padre Tomas Estenaga.

DECAY OF THE MISSION

The Mission, as received by the Padre Tomas was in a flourishing condition, but in 1834[11] (I think it was) the Mexican Congress passed a law secularizing all of the Missions, which each Indian was to receive his share of land, gardens and stock; but immediately on the top of it a change was effected in the general government, and instead of carrying out the law, they abolished it. They, however, secularized them and ordered Administrators to have charge instead of the clergy. These facts being known to the Padre Tomas, he (in all probability by order of his superior) commenced a work of destruction. The back buildings were unroofed and the timber converted into firewood. Cattle were killed on halves with people who took a lion's share. Utensils were disposed of, and goods and other articles distributed in profusion among the Neophites. The vineyards were ordered to be cut down, which, however, the Indians refused to do.

It did not require long to destroy what years took to establish. Destruction came as a thief in the night. The whites rejoiced at it. They required no encouragement, and seemed to think it would last forever. Even the mere spectators were gladdened at the sight, and many of them helped themselves to a sufficiency of calves to stock farms.

It is not the intention here to give a detail of all that occurred, as our line, as marked out from the first, relates merely to the Indians, and to other persons and things only so far as they are connected with them.

General Figueroa,[12] having been appointed political Chief and Commandant General of the territory, arrived, and his adjutant, Col. Nicholas Gutierrez,[13] received the Mission from the Padre Tomas, who remained as minister of the church with a stipend of $1500 per annum from the establishment, independent of his synod from the Pious Fund in Mexico.[14]

As a wrong impression of his character may be produced from the preceding remarks, in justice to his memory, be it stated that he was a truly good man, a sincere Christian and despiser of hypocrisy. He had a kind, unsophisticated heart, so that he believed every word told him. There has never been a purer Priest in California. Reduced in circumstances, annoyed on many occasions by the petulancy of Administrators, he fulfilled his duties according to his conscience, with benevolence and good-humor. The nuns who when the secular movement came into operation, had been set free, were again gathered together under his supervision and maintained at his expense, as were also a number of the old men and women. Everything he got was spent in charity upon those of the rancheria whom he considered as worthy of it and they remember him with gratitude and affection.

The Indians were made happy at this time in being permitted to enjoy once more the luxury of a tule dwelling, from which the greater part had been debarred for so long; they could now breathe freely again.

Administrator followed Administrator, until the Mission could support no more, when the system was broken up. I shall make no remarks here on their administration: it is to be presumed they complied either with their instructions or their own ideas.

The Indians during this period were continually running off. Scantily clothed and still more scantily supplied with food, it was not to be wondered at. Nearly all of the Gabrielions went north while those of San Diego, San Luis and San Juan overran this country, filling the Angeles and surrounding ranchos with more servants than were required. Labor in consequence was very cheap. The different Missions, however, had *Alcaldes* continually on the move, hunting them up and carrying them back, but to no purpose; it was labor in vain.

This was a period of demoralization. People from Sonora came flocking in to assist in the general destruction, lending a hand to kill off cattle on shares, which practice, when at last prohibited by government orders, they continued on their private account.

These Sonoreno overran this country. They invaded the *ranchería*, gambled with the men and taught them to steal; they taught the women to be worse than they were, and men and women both to drink. Now we do not mean or pretend to say that the Neophites were not previous to this addicted both to drinking and gaming, with an inclination to steal, while under the dominion of the church; but the Sonorenos most certainly brought them to a pitch of licentiousness before unparalleled in their history.

FINIS

Having given a sketch of the Angeles County Indians from the time they were the free, natal possessors of the soil, living contented in a state of nature, until these civilized times of squatting and legislative oppression, in which not only they but those bearing their blood in a fourth degree, are included, to the shame of this our country, and disgrace of the framers of such laws, I shall now conclude them, with a very short review of how far their ancient manners and customs remain in force among the handful left of a once happy people.

Their former lodges are not now in existence, and most of the Indians remaining in the county are from other parts—from Santa Ynez to San Diego. A few are to be found at San Fernando, San Gabriel and the Angeles. Those in service on ranchos are a mere handful. You will find at present more of them in the county of Monterey than in this, excluding the three places named above. Death has been busy among them for years past, and very few more are wanting to extinguish the lamp that God lighted! The Indians from the northwest coast killed great numbers years ago on the Islands. Those of San Clemente, the remains of which some eighteen years since were collected in caves on the Island, showed the whole of them to have been possessed of double teeth allround, both in the upper and under jaw.

I have previously mentioned that their language has deteriorated much since the conquest. Numerous causes affect all languages, and one of the many which did so to theirs, was the want of their former Councils held so frequently, in which their wise men spoke with eloquence suited to the occasion, using more dignity and expression, which naturally elevated the minds of all and gave a tinge of better utterance even in ordinary conversation.

They have at present, *two* religions—one of custom, and another of faith. Naturally fond of novelty, the Catholic one serves as a great treat—the forms and ceremonies an inexhaustible source of amusement. They don't quarrel with their neighbor's mode of worship, but consider their own the best. The life and death of our Saviour is only, in their opinion, a distorted version of their own life. Hell, as taught them, has no terrors. It is for whites, not Indians, or else their fathers would have known it. The Devil, however, has become a great personage in their sight; he is called *Zizu*, and makes his appearance on all occassions. Nevertheless, he is only a bugbear and connected with the Christian faith; he makes no part of their own. The resurrection they cannot understand, but a future state of spiritual existence is in accordance with their creed.

Their chiefs still exist. In San Gabriel remain only four, and those young. There are more, but of tribes formerly from the direction of San Bernardino. They have no jurisdiction more than to appoint times for the holding of Feasts and regulating affairs connected with the church. No standing Church remains nowadays; it is made yearly and consecrated when required, on any spot they choose to select.

Their food continues the same, with the addition made to the list of what the Spaniards introduced. Their clothing is of course distinct, and a cloak made of rabbit skins, has within this year or two become a novelty among themselves.

For a long time back, marriage has been performed in the Catholic Church; and only one instance of its fulfillment in their own *alone*, exists in the case of a young girl who contracted matrimony about three years ago. Marriage vows, I am sorry to say, are not very binding, although many examples of strict fidelity exist. Women undergo the same purification after childbirth as formerly, with the exception of such as were in the service of whites at their first parturition.

The seers have declined very much in their ability both of predicting events and doing harm; although instances of sickness occasionally occur of which they stand the blame. In performing cures, however, they still take the precedence of the other members of the faculty known as M.D.'s.

Ten years ago shell bead money was current in the Mission, not only between Indians, but between them and the whites. It is now extremely scarce, and hoarded from one year to another to use at their church ceremonies, and repurchased again for double its value.

Notes to the Text

1. *I.e.* San Gabriel, founded September 8, 1771.
2. The author here apparently had in mind a *pariah*, a member of the low caste of Southern India and Burma and one rejected and despised by society.
3. Fray Jose Maria Zalvidea (1780-1846) served at San Gabriel between 1806 and 1827.
4. Jose Bernardo Sanchez (1778-1833) was a native of Robledillo, Ciudad Rodrigo, Spain. In addition to San Gabriel, the friar also served at Missions San Diego and Purisima Concepcion during his twenty-eight years in California.
5. Thomas Eleuterio Estenega (1790-1847) was stationed at San Gabriel between 1837 and 1845.
6. While the vineyards at San Gabriel were widely known for their fine grapes, it is thought that the first successful planting was made at San Juan Capistrano in 1779.
7. The Jesuits had not labored in Peninsular California since 1768.
8. Claudio Lopez y de Mora was manager of Mission San Gabriel for over forty years. He had come to California with Francisco Palou in 1773. His family was connected with the distinguished Lancasters (Alencaster) of Spain and Mexico. See Francisca Lopez de Belderrain, "The Awakening of Paredon Blanco Under a California Sun," *Historical Society of Southern California Annual* XIV (1928), 65-79.
9. One sympathetic author concedes that "there were some idiosyncrasies which increased with age, which carried him at least to the borders of a broken mind." See Angustias de la Guerra Ord, *Occurrences in Hispanic California* (Washington, 1956), p. 84.
10. Juan Ignacio Mancisidor was an old friend of Father Sanchez who was living in retirement at the mission.
11. The confiscation decrees, promulgated on November 3, 1834, declared San Gabriel a curacy of the first class.
12. Jose Figueroa (1792-1835), an Aztecan mestigo, was a veteran of the Sonora frontier. He was Governor of California between 1833 and 1835.
13. Spanish-born Nicolas Gutierrez came to California in 1833 with Governor Jose Figueroa. He was acting governor after Figueroa's death until May of 1836.
14. It should be noted that the friars at San Gabriel declined the stipend provided by the government.

17

John Coulter
(unk.)

The narrative of John Coulter has been "greatly discredited and adjudged as unreliable,"[1] so much so that one authority is even "doubtful if he ever saw California."[2] Hubert Howe Bancroft described the Coulter account as one "of absurdly impossible personal adventures, with allusions to magnificent ruins and relics of antiquity."[3]

Whatever may have been the author's real or imagined frame of reference, the treatise of the Irish physician is, for the most part, favorable to the missionaries who, he maintained, were "without exception, a pleasant set of men." Coulter seems to have confused the Franciscans with their Jesuit predecessors in Peninsular California. His descriptions of the natives and their way of life is as colorful as it may have been apochryphal.

Coulter's observations of California were related in the seventh chapter of his Adventures on the Western Coast of South America, and the Interior of California, *published at London, in 1847.*

References

1. Robert E. Cowan, *A Bibliography of the History of California and the Pacific West, 1510-1906* (San Francisco, 1914), p. 57.
2. Willard O. Waters, *Franciscan Missions of Upper California as seen by Foreign Visitors and Residents* (Los Angeles, 1954), Entry 22.
3. *History of California* (San Francisco, 1886), III 411.

1835

I was soon quite well, and enjoyed the agreeable conversation of the Padre[1] extremely; he proposed a visit round the different missions that are situated about this bay, as he had not seen any of his brethren for some time; I was pleased with his intentions, and after a few preliminary preparations, we started off and visited the missions, making a few days' stay at each, enjoying the lively, humane, and agreeable conversation of the Padres, who were without an exception, a pleasant set of men. There were five missions established round this great bay of St. Francisco; they were named as follows; the mission of Dolores, St. Clara, St. José, St. Francis Solana, and St. Rafail.

They were all built in the same manner, an immense walled-in enclosure, entered by gates; a range of houses, or rather rooms, were erected all along the walls, with a door and windows in each, the roof extending about eight feet clear of the houses, supported by posts, and forming a *piazza*, or corridor, the entire length of the range; the flooring of both apartments, and corridor, were formed of square red tile, generally washed every day, and had a very clean appearance: at most of the missions, the roofing of the houses, church, sheds for cattle, &c. were all tile.

At an angle of this great square, generally, the chapel is erected: they have all loud toned bells, the tolling of which is heard afar off; and, in one instance, from its vicinity to calm water and mountainous ground, each knock on the bell was echoed several times, conveying an unusual sound to the ear of the listener. There are few of these missions that have not good accommodation for from one thousand to fifteen hundred families to dwell in, besides the cattle sheds.

You may form an idea of the extent of these stations, when I state, that from my own observation, and the information I received from the

151

Padres, that amongst the five missions I have mentioned, there are, at least, five thousand Indians living in, and attached to, the establishments, and between two and three hundred whites; both the missions and white residents own thousands of horses, mules, and sheep, domesticated; they will sell you a bullock for four or five dollars, as many sheep as you require for something less than one dollar a head, and if you have no cash, they will take goods in exchange.

I may say, most of their fancy goods, grains, &c. come from the Sandwich Islands, and they give in trade for them, the fur skins of various animals, timber sawed up into planks and boards, hides, tallows cheese, &c. In conversation with the different Padres, I was highly entertained by their detailing to me anecdotes respecting the first formation of these Jesuit[2] missions, and conversion of the Indians to the Roman Catholic religion. When their predecessors[3] first came, and erected these establishments, they were not on the extensive scale they are at present.

A small inclosure, a small chapel, and a few houses, sufficed to accommodate the few that accompanied them.

The Indians were in a wild and perfectly un-Christianised state, and the various tribes that inhabit and hunt through the country not infrequently formed temporary alliances for the purpose of making a descent upon the mission and plundering it of every article it contained. Thus, frequently the establishments were laid waste. Still the Jesuits[4] persevered, obtained a fresh supply of necessaries, cultivated patches of land about them, lived on its produce, the fish out of the bay and river, the game from the forest, and ultimately succeeded in the establishing of their missions.

One of the padres here, who had put in a long service at his mission, told me that the last act of hostility towards them was against his establishment. The "Wallack" and the "Shoshons," or Snake Indians, formed an alliance and advanced on the mission with overwhelming force and in a very formidable manner. When they came near the gate or entrance, they yelled and warhooped fearfully; but, instead of making a useless defence and getting his followers all scalped, he flung open the gates and walked out boldly to meet them unarmed and alone.[5]

This act staggered the wildest of the wild men that he now confronted. Several of the chiefs and a number of warriors passed him, leaving the chief body of the men outside. They searched the entire establishment minutely over for guns or ammunition, and, finding nothing but a few well-worn spades, shovels, and other implements of agriculture, they kicked those about, and, with feelings of the most profound contempt, they left the mission.

A head chief of the "Wallacks" had a few words of Spanish, and addressed the padre, who was waiting their pleasure outside, with "What use live here? no gun, no deer, plenty of buffalo, plenty elk, plenty every thing. No gun, no shoot. Pshaw! dig, dig the ground, no good. Big fool you, big fool all. Go to sleep." And, after giving a withering look of contempt at his reverence, he joined his own peoples and the entire party set off as they came, yelling and shouting, without taking any thing with them.

The missions were never troubled by the wild Indians afterwards, but they were often plundered and left nearly in ruins by various gangs of fellows getting up temporary revolutions on a small scale, merely for the purpose of more effectually plundering the missions and, I may add, the houses of the Spanish, Mexican, American, and European residents of the country. These gangs of robbers (I can term them nothing else) are formed of runaway seamen from whalers, runaway sailors and marines from men-of-war, and a number of Indians, whose scamping propensities make them outcasts from their tribes.

To return to the hospitable Padres: they informed me, that after the Indians ceased to annoy them, they continued their agricultural pursuits for some time, yet no Indians came in; a general council was held between them, and it was resolved to entrap some of the wild Indians, bring them to the mission by force, if necessary, treat them kindly for a little while, and let them go again. To succeed in this project, it was necessary to procure thirty or forty friendly Indians from the more southern missions, that had been longer established; these Indians were soon at the new missions, and stragglers from the various surrounding tribes brought in, fastened by the feet and hands.

At first, they had an idea they were going to be killed, or tortured for former doings; but when they saw no signs of hostility at the mission, the cords that tied their hands and feet cast off, themselves free, and an abundant meal spread out before them, they seemed more at their ease; after a few days of good living, the Padres would give them a present of a small quantity of gunpowder, to kill game with, or perhaps a small axe, kettle, or some minor article; then the gates would be opened, and the Indians would walk out, accompanied by one of the fathers, shaking them by the hand; and with looks of kindness, and signs conveying to them the impression, that they were welcome back at any time to the mission. The Indians, in marching off, generally gave the most provokingly ludicrous looks, laughing outright, as much as to say, "This is the best joke ever we knew."

This, as it were, kidnapping system, was continued for some time, and with the desired effect, for when the present of powder was out, they came in for more, lounged about the mission for a few days, and went away again; at last their friends came with them, some bringing their squaws and children, and experiencing such continued kindness, and snug quarters, they finally settled at the mission, and hundreds soon followed the example. The accommodation at the various establishments became too limited; then it was that the Indians first commenced manual labour, to extend the area of the mission square, by building extensive walls, and many houses, inside, for the accommodation of their friends who were anxious to join them: thus these missions became enlarged to the extent they now are.

The Padres now have perfect control over the Indians of the missions, they insist on their performance of their allotted work, during a certain number of hours each day, either in agricultural pursuits, or tending the immense droves of cattle that are grazing around the mission. Previous to the hour of prayers, particularly on Sunday mornings, the Padre will take a look into the chapel, and if they are not all there before the tolling of the bell ceases, he will mount a mule, ride round the square, whip in hand, and drive the lazy fellows on before him: it seemed to create prime fun amongst the rest, when any one would catch a blow of the Padre's whip across the legs. After the working hours are over, these mission squares present a very animated scene,— violins and guitars playing in a lively manner, to the waltzers and fandango dancers, on one sides whilst groups of Indians, with their own dull sounding drums, and guttural songs, are merely at work dancing in their own wild, yet picturesque, way, at another side of the square, the centre being occupied by groups of Indians engaged earnestly at their various games.

Sunday, after prayers, is the day appointed for the great merry making; the Indians then enjoy, outside the mission, horse-racing, bull, dog, bear, badger, and cock fighting; one must see a scene of this kind to form an idea of it; the yells and whoops of the Indians as the business of the day proceeds; the groans and roars of the tortured bulls, bears, and dogs, that are fighting; the singing of the women, the dancing of the men, on boarded platforms erected for the purpose; the beating of the drums,—all combine to make such an infernal noise, that one who is present for the first time will gladly put a finger in each ear, and run away from it.

There is only one part of this wild exhibition to be admired, and that is, the personal appearance of the Indians: on particular occasions of this kind, they invariably put on the costume they wore whilst in their original wild state; all their ornaments are carefully arranged, their paint laid on in

154

their most perfect manner, and when excited by their various games, as they move rapidly to and fro, their general aspect is magnificent.

Notes to the Text

1. The author is referring to Father Lorenzo Quijas, the Ecuador-born friar who worked in the California missions for eleven years before his departure in 1844.
2. There were no Jesuit-founded missions in Alta California.
3. By "predecessors," Coulter apparently means the Fernandino friars who were replaced by missionaries from Zacatecas at the northern missions after 1833.
4. *Cf.* Note #2 above.
5. Perhaps this is a reference to the Indian uprising of 1824, the most violent revolt in the history of the missions.

18

Alexander Forbes
(1778-1863)

The English vice-consul at Tepic, Alexander Forbes, wrote "the first book to relate exclusively to California."[1] The "vivid and charming" narrative,[2] containing a wealth of historical material, was primarily a propagandistic endeavor "to bring about British colonization"[3] written to focus attention on the Californias and "the feasibility of their acquisition by the British crown."[4]

Though there is reason to doubt if the English merchant ever personally visited the area, "he was brought constantly in contact with intelligent men who were familiar with the country."[5]

Forbes was among that group of typically cold Englishmen "imbued with the intolerance of Protestantism" who were "inclined to ridicule and cast insinuations on the activities of the Fathers."[6] He regarded the natives attached to the missions as "slaves under another name."[7] "Severe critic of the system that he was,"[8] Forbes was deeply impressed by "the unbounded affection and devotion invariably shown towards them by their Indian subjects."

The English diplomat had no reason to doubt "the sincerity and honesty of the religious missionaries."[9] Although he "cannot be accused of partiality" for the friars,[10] Forbes remarked that he had never heard that the missionaries of California "ever betrayed their trust, or exercised inhumanity; and the testimony of travellers who have visited this country is uniformly to the same effect."

In fact, Forbes paid the friars and their system the ultimate compliment by saying that "...assuredly there are few events in history more remarkable on the whole, or more interesting, than the transformation, on the great scale, wrought by the Jesuits and Franciscans in Paraguay and California."

Alexander Forbes' observations were first published at London, in 1839, as California: A History of Upper and Lower California. The 368 page tome was reprinted at San Francisco, in 1919, by Thomas C. Russell with an introduction by Herbert Ingram Priestley.

References

1. Robert Ernest Cowan, *A Bibliography of the History of California and the Pacific West, 1510-1906* (San Francisco, 1914), p. 88.
2. Franklin Walker, *A Literary History of Southern California* (Berkeley, 1950), p. 37.
3. John Walton Caughey, *California* (New Jersey, 1953), p. 223.
4. Theodore H. Hittell, *History of California* (San Francisco, 1898), II, 293.
5. Hubert Howe Bancroft, *History of California* (San Francisco, 1886), IV, 151.
6. Marguerite Eyer Wilbur (Trans.), *Duflot de Mofras' Travels on the Pacific Coast* (Santa Ana, 1937), I, 141.
7. The excerpts here cited are from *California: A History of Upper and Lower California* (London, 1839).
8. Daniel D. McGarry, "Educational Methods of the Franciscans in Spanish California," *The Americas* VI (January, 1950), 348.
9. Joachim Adam, "A Defense of the Missionary Establishments of Alta California," *Historical Society of Southern California Annual* III (1896), 36.
10. Zephyrin Engelhardt, O.F.M., *The Missions and Missionaries of California* (San Francisco, 1912),III, 557.

1835

THE MISSIONS—These establishments are all formed on the same plan and consequently greatly resemble each other. They vary, however, according to their extent, standing, and population, and also according to the individual character of the directing fathers for the time being. Each mission is governed by one or more missionaries, all friars of the order San Francisco. One of these is styled *Prefect*, and not President as was formerly the case.[1] Through him is (or was) carried on all the public correspondence with the government of Mexico; but he has no power superior to the others, and each may be said to be absolute in his own mission. Each mission has allotted to it, in the first instance, a tract of land of about fifteen miles square, which is generally fertile and well suited for husbandry. This land is set apart for the general uses of the mission, part being cultivated, and part left in its natural condition and occupied as grazing ground. The buildings of the mission are, like the Presidio, all on the same general plan, but are varied according to the locality and number of the inhabitants. Most of the missionary villages or residences are surrounded by a high wall enclosing the whole; others have no such protection but consist of open rows of streets of little huts built of bricks: some of these are tiled and whitewashed and look neat and comfortable; others are dirty and in disrepair and in every way uncomfortable. In the mission of Santa Clara, which in several respects excels the others, the houses of the Indians form five rows or streets, which compared with the old straw huts must be considered really comfortable: and this is the greatest improvement that has taken place in the domestic civilization of these people at the missions. The buildings are generally built in the form of a square or part of a square, the church usually forming a portion of the elevation. The apartments of the fathers, which are often spacious, the granaries and work-shops compose the remainder. The Indian population generally live in huts at about two hundred yards distant from the prinicipal edifices; these huts are sometimes made of *adobes*, but the Indians are often left to raise them on their own plan; *viz.* of rough poles erected into a conical figure, of about four yards in circumference at the base, covered with dry grass and a small aperture for the entrance. When the huts decay, they set them on fire, and erect new ones; which is only the work of a day. In these huts the married part of the community live, the unmarried of both sexes being kept, each sex separate, in large barn-like apartments, where they work under strict supervision. The store houses and workshops, at some of the larger missions, are of great extent and variety. There may be seen a place for melting tallows, one for making soaps, workshops for smiths, carpenters, &c., storehouses for the articles manufactured, and the produce of the farms; viz. stores for tallow, soap, butter, salt, wool, hides, wheat, peas, beans, &c. &c. &c. Four or five soldiers have their residence a few yards further off, and are meant to watch the Indians, and to keep order; but they are generally lazy, idle fellows: and often give the missionary more trouble than all his Indians; and instead of rendering assistance increase his troubles. But in all Spanish countries, nothing can possibly be done without soldiers, and the idea of having any public establishment without a guard of soldiers would appear quite ridiculous.

The church is, of course, the main object of attraction at all the missions, and is often gaudily decorated. In some of the missions where there is good building-stone in the vicinity, the external appearance of the sacred building is not unseemly; in other missions the exterior is very rude. In all of them the interior is richer than the outside promises. In several there are pictures, and the subject of these is generally representations of heaven or hell, glaringly coloured purposely to strike the rude senses of the Indians. Pérouse says that the picture of hell in the church of San Carlos has, in this way, done incalculable service in promoting conversion; and well remarks that the protestant mode of worship, which forbids images and pompous ceremonies, could not make any progress among these people. He is of opinion that the picture of paradise in the same church, has exerted comparatively little effect on account of its tameness: but Langsdorff tells of wonders in this way wrought by a figure of the virgin represented as springing from the coronal of leaves of the *Agave Americana*, or great American aloe, instead of the ordinary stem! The priests also take care to be provided with rich dresses for the same purpose of inspiring awe.

The object of the whole of the Californian or missionary system being the conversion of the Indians and the training of them up, in some sort, to a civilized life, the constant care of the fathers is and ever has been directed towards these ends. The children born in the missions are, of course, devoted to the missionary discipline from their infancy; but the zeal of the fathers is constantly looking out for converts from among the wild tribes on the borders of their territories. Formerly when the missionaries were strangers in the land, and the natives were numerous, and spread around their settlements, there was no lack of materials on which to exercise their converting zeal. But for a good many years the case has been different; the natives have become fewer in number and have been gradually receding from the missionary territory: the very progress of conversion has necessarily occasioned this.

New means of obtaining converts have been therefore had recourse to; and there can be no doubt that some of these means go far beyond the bounds of legitimate persuasion. It would be injustice to tax the Fathers with openly sanctioning much less directing the more severe of these means; yet they cannot be altogether ignorant of them, and must be regarded as encouraging them indirectly. And, indeed, it must be admitted that with their particular views of the efficacy of baptism and ceremonial profession of christianity in saving souls, the conversion of the Indians even by force, can hardly be otherwise regarded by them than as the greatest of benefits conferred on these people and therefore justifying some severity in effecting it. No one who has seen or known any thing of the singular humanity and benevolence of these good Fathers will for a moment believe that they could sanction the actual cruelties and bloodshed occasionally wrought in their name by the military and more zealous converts. Certain it is, however, that every encouragement is held out to all, who shall bring in *Gentiles* for conversion. Converts that can be depended on are stationed in the vicinity of the haunts occupied by their wild brethren, whose business it is to represent their own condition in the most favourable light possible, with the view of inducing them to join the missionary fold. Others are permitted to pay visits to their kindred of more distant tribes, with the same views, and are almost expected to bring back converts with them. "At a particular period of the year also" we are told by Captain Beechey, "when the Indians can be spared from the agricultural concerns of the establishment, many of them are permitted to take the launch of the mission and make excursions to the Indian territory. On these occasions the padres desire them to induce as many of their unconverted brethren as possible to accompany them back to the mission, of course implying that this is to be done only by persuasion; but the boat being furnished with a cannon and musketry, and in every respect equipped for war, it too often happens that the neophytes and the *gente de razón*, who superintend the direction of the boat, avail themselves of their superiority, with the desire of ingratiating themselves with their masters and of receiving a reward. There are, besides, repeated acts of aggression which it is necessary to punish, all of which furnish proselytes. Women and children are generally the first objects of capture, as their husbands and parents sometimes voluntarily follow them into captivity."

One of these proselytising expeditions into the Indian territory occurred during the period of Captain Beechey's visit in 1826, which ended in a battle with the loss, in the first instance, of thirty-four of the converted, and eventually in the gain (by a second expedition sent to avenge the losses of the first) of forty women and children of the invaded tribes. These were immediately enrolled in the list of the mission, and were nearly as immediately converted into Christians. The process by which this was effected is so graphically described by Captain Beechey that it would be doing him injustice to use any words but his own

"I happened (he says) to visit the mission about this time and saw these unfortunate beings under tuition, They were clothed in blankets, and arranged in a row before a blind Indian, who understood their dialect, and was assisted by an alcalde to keep order. Their tutor began by desiring them to kneel, informing them that he was going to teach them the names of the persons composing the Trinity, and that they were to repeat in Spanish what he dictated. The neophytes being thus arranged, the speaker began: *"Santissima Trinidada, Dios, Jesu Christo, Espiritu Santo"*—pausing between each name, to listen if the simple Indians, who had never spoken a Spanish word before, pronounced it correctly or anything near the mark. After they had repeated these names satisfactorily, their blind tutor, after a pause added, *"Santos"*— and recapitulated the names of a great many saints which finished the morning's tuition."

After a few days, no doubt,[2] these promising pupils were christened, and admitted to all the benefits and privileges of Christians and *gente de razón*. Indeed I believe that the act of making the cross and kneeling at proper times and other suchlike mechanical rites, constitute no small part of the religion of these poor people. The rapidity of the conversion is, however, frequently stimulated by practices much in accordance with the primary kidnapping of the subjects. "If, as not unfrequently happens, any of the captured Indians show a repugnance to conversion, it is the practise to imprison them for a few days, and then to allow them to breathe a little fresh air in a walk around the mission, to observe the happy mode of life of their converted countrymen; after which they are again shut up, and thus continue incarcerated until they declare their readiness to renounce the religion of their forefathers." As might be believed, the ceremonial exercises of the Roman Catholic religion, occupy a considerable share of the time of these people. Mass is performed twice daily, besides highdays and holidays, when the ceremonies are much grander and of longer duration; and at all the performances every Indian is obliged to attend under the penalty of a whipping; and the same method of enforcing proper discipline as in kneeling at proper times, keeping silence, &c., is not excluded from the church service itself. In the aisles and passages of the church, zealous beadles of the converted race are stationed, armed with sundry weapons of potent influence in effecting silence and attention, and which are not sparingly used on the refractory or inattentive. These consist of sticks and whips, long goads, &c., and they are not idle in the hands of the officials that sway them.

The following is the course of proceedings in the missions, on ordinary occasions; and as there is little or no variety in their monotonous life, the picture may be received as a general one. It was thus witnessed by Pérouse, and it is equally extant at the present time. The Indians as well as the missionaries rise with the sun and go to mass, which lasts about an hour. While this is in progress the breakfast is prepared, the favorite *Atole* or pottage, which consists of barley flour, the grain being roasted previously to grinding. It is cooked in large kettles, and is seasoned with neither salt nor butter. Every cottage or hut sends for the allowance for all its inmates, which is carried home in one of their bark baskets. Any overplus that remains, is distributed among the children as a reward for good behaviour, particularly for good lessons in the catechism. After breakfast, which lasts about three quarters of an hour, they proceed to their labours, either out of doors or within. At noon the dinner is announced by a bell, and the Indians quitting their work go and receive their rations as at breakfast time. The mess now served is somewhat of the same kind as the former, only varied by the addition of maize, peas and beans: it is named *pozzoli*. After dinner they return to their work, from two to four or five; afterwards they attend evening mass[3] which lasts nearly an hour, and the day is finished by another supply of *atole*, as at breakfast. In the intervals of the meals and prayers, the Indians are of course variously employed according to their trade or occupation, that is to say, either in agricultural labours, according to the season, or in the store-rooms, magazines, and laboratories of the mission. The women are much occupied in spinning, and other little household labours, the men in combing wool, weaving, melting tallow, &c., or as carpenters, shoemakers, bricklayers, blacksmiths, &c. One of the principal occupations of the missions is the manufacturing a coarse sort of cloth from the wool of their own sheep, for the purpose of clothing the Indians. The grinding of the corn is left almost entirely to the women, and is still performed by a hand mill. All the girls and widows are kept in separate houses during the day while at work, being only permitted to go out occasionally, like boys at school. The unmarried of both sexes, as well adults and children, are carefully locked up at night in separate houses, the keys being left in the keeping of the Fathers; and when any breach of this rule is detected, the culprits of both sexes are severely punished by whipping, the men in public, the women privately.

It is obvious from all this, that these poor people are in fact slaves under another name; and it is no wonder that Pérouse found the resemblance painfully striking between their condition and that of the negro slaves of the West Indies. Sometimes, although rarely, they attempt to break their bonds and escape into their original haunts. But this is of rare occurrence, as, independently of the difficulty of escaping, they are so simple as to believe that they have hardly the power to do so, after being baptised, regarding the ceremony of baptism as a sort of spell which could not be broken. Occasionally, however, they overcome all imaginary and real obstacles and effect their escape. In such cases, the runaway is immediately pursued, and as it is always known to which tribe he belongs, and as, owing to the enmity subsisting among the tribes, he will not be received by another, he is almost always found and surrendered to the pursuers by his pusillanimous countrymen. When brought back to the mission he is always first flogged and then has an iron clog attached to one of his legs, which has the effect of preventing his running away and marking him out *in terrorem* to others.

Notwithstanding this dark picture of the general mode of life of the converted Indians, it must not be imagined that it is one of much real hardship, or that it is generally thought so by the parties themselves. On the contrary, it accords too well with the native indolence of their character and total defect of all independent spirit. It is true, that the system tends most powerfully to keep up and to aggravate the natural defects in their character, and to frustrate all prospect of true civilization and all rational improvement; still it cannot be said that they are discontented; if they lead the life of grovelling animals, they have at least their negative happiness. If they are cribbed like the stalled ox, they are fed like him, and they have hardly more care or fear for the future than he has.

The bliss is theirs
Of that entire dependence that prepares
Entire submission, lot what may befall…
No forecast, no anxieties have they:
The Jesuit governs and instructs and guides;
Food, raiment, shelter, safety he provides:
Their part it is to honor and obey,
Like children under wise paternal sway.

Their labour is very light, and they have much leisure time to waste in their beloved inaction, or in the rude pastimes of their aboriginal state. These last consist chiefly of dances and certain games, and gambling of various kinds. Of two games they are especially fond, and spend much of their time, like boys as they are, in their performance. They are thus described by La Perouse."The first, to which they give the name of *taker-sia*, consists in throwing and rolling a small hoop, of three inches in diameter, in a space of ten square fathoms, cleared of grass. Each of the two players holds a stick into the hoop whilst it is in motion; if in this they succeed they gain two points, and if the hoop, when it stops, simply rests upon their stick, they gain one by it: the game is in three points. This game is a violent exercise, because the hoop or the stick is always in motion.

The other game named *Toussé* is more easy. They play it with four, two on each side; each in his turn hides a piece of wood in his hands, whilst his partner makes a thousand gestures to take off the attention of the adversaries. It is curious enough to a bystander to see them squatting down opposite to each other, keeping the most profound silence, watching the features and most minute circumstances which may assist them in discovering the hand which conceals the piece of wood; they gain or lose a point, according to their guessing right or wrong, and those who gain, have a right to hide in their turn. The game is five points and the common stake is beads."

These and other games of chance, some of them learnt from the Spaniards, as those at cards, are indulged in to a criminal excess; and frequently they lose in this way, all they can call their own, the clothes off their backs, the favours of their wives, and even their wives themselves. This picture is not softened by the addition of intoxications a vice not infrequent in the missions.

From the total subjection in which the Indians grow up and live, never being taught or indeed allowed to act and hardly to think for themselves, it could scarcely be expected that they should attain any real knowledge of life or independence of conduct, even if they had been originally of a better stock; as it is, they are, in regard to the capacity and power of acting as members of a civilized community, on a lower scale than even the domesticated negroes of the West Indian colonies: they are reduced to the state of mere automatons, totally subjected to the direction and guidance of others. It has accordingly been invariably found that, when any of them have been set at liberty or placed in a position to act for themselves, by leaving the missions or otherwise, they were utterly incapable of maintaining themselves; nay even so stupid as to be incapable of exercising the office of a beggars even when their very existence seemed at stake. This seems hardly credible, yet it is a fact.

The extreme state of debasement in which they are held, not only has deprived them of their mental powers, but it has diminished their physical strength; they are not only stupid and pusillanimous but puny and feeble. It is well known that savages are prone to be filthy in their habitations; but in their natural state their living so much in the open air, their exertions in hunting and diversions, counteract this cause of disease; but at the missions, the Indians being still allowed to live in all their native filthiness, and their lives being now comparatively sedentary, with little corporeal and less mental exercise, they inevitably grow up debilitated in body as well as in mind. And how could it be otherwise?

All thoughts and occupations to commute,
To change their air, their water, and their food,
And those old habits suddenly uproot,
Conform'd to which the vital powers pursued
Their functions,—such mutation is too rude
For man's fine frame unshaken to sustain.

Great numbers fall a prey to fevers, dysenteries, and other acute diseases. Langsdorff tells us that the missionaries informed him that upon the least illness they become wholly cast down and lose all courage and care for recovery, refusing to attend to the diet or any thing else recommended for them. Chronic diseases of various kinds are also prevalent and add to the mortality. Syphilis prevails to a frightful extent, being indeed almost universal not only among the Indians but the Creoles and Spaniards:[4] it produces frightful ravages among the former, as they refuse all treatment of it even when this is accessible to them, which is not always the case. These circumstances, with the natural tendency which all the Indian race have to diminish in numbers in a state of civilization, much more in a state of bondage, make the loss of life very great in the missions: and now that fresh recruits can be procured with difficulty, and under recent events probably not at all, and consequently the stock maintained only by the procreation of those already domesticated, it is probable that the whole race will gradually diminish and in a few generations more will become entirely extinct.

In concluding this sketch of the present state of the domesticated Indians of Californias which unquestionably betrays a lamentable want of judgment and sound philosophy on the part of the men who have been the original founders and are still the strenuous supporters of the system under which these melancholy results have arisen, it would be extreme injustice not to place in the strongest contrast with their want of judgment, the excellent motives and most benevolent and christian-like intentions by which they have been always influenced. Considering the perfectly absolute and totally irresponsible power possessed by the missionaries over the Indians, their conduct must be allowed to have been invariably marked by a degree of benevolence and humanity and moderation, probably unexampled in any other situation. To each missionary is allotted the entire and exclusive management of his mission. He is the absolute lord and master of all his Indians, and of the soil; he directs without the least interference from others, all the operations and economy of the establishment, agricultural, mechanical, maunfacturing, and commercial; and disposes, according to his will and pleasure, of the produce thereof. He allots his lands, orders his seed time and harvest, distributes his cattle; encourages, chastises, and commands all the human beings under his charge; and all this without being accountable to any power on earth; for by a convenient fiction, this property belongs to the Indians, and the Indians are slaves. There are, I fear, few examples to be found, where men enjoying such unlimited confidence and power, have not abused them. And yet I have never heard that the missionaries of California have not acted with the most perfect fidelity, or that they ever betrayed their trust, or exercised inhumanity; and the testimony of all travellers who have visited this country is uniformly to the same effect. On the contrary, there are recorded instances of the most extraordinary zeal, industry, and philanthropy in the conduct of those men. Since the country has been more opened, strangers have found at their missions, the most generous and disinterested hospitality, protection, and kindness; and this without one solitary instance to the contrary that I have ever heard of.

I cannot avoid this opportunity of gratifying my feelings, by noticing in a more especial manner one of those worthy men as affording a recent example of what I have said of their order.

Father Antonio Peyri[5] took possession of the mission of San Luis Rey, in the year 1798. He first built a small thatched cottage, and asked for a few cattle and Indians from the mission. After a constant residence of thirty-four years at this place, he left it stocked with nearly sixty thousand head of domesticated animals of all sorts, and yielding an annual produce of about thirteen thousand bushels of grain, while the population amounted to nearly three thousand Indians! He left also a complete set of buildings; including a church, with inclosures, &c. Yet after these thirty-four years of incessant labors in which he expended the most valuable part of his life, the worthy Peyri left his mission with only what he judged to be sufficient means to enable him to join his convent in the city of Mexico, where he threw himself upon the charity of his order. The toll of managing such an establishment would be sufficient motive for a man of Father Peyri's age to retire; but the new order of things which has introduced new men and new measures,—when the political power has been entrusted to heads not over-wise, and to hands not over-pure, when the theoretical doctrines of liberty and equality have been preached while oppression and rapine have been practised,—has doubtless accelerated his resignation. Whatever his motives may have been, his voluntary retirement in poverty, to spend his remaining days in pious exercises, must be applauded by the religious; and his noble disinterestedness by all. At his mission, strangers of all countries and modes of faith, as well as his fellow subjects, found always a hearty welcome, and the utmost hospitality. Many of my countrymen and personal friends have related to me, with enthusiasm, the kindness and protection which they have received at his hands, boons which are doubly valuable where places of entertainment do not exist, and where security is not very firmly established.

I had the pleasure of seeing Father Peyri on his way to Mexico; and although I had heard much of him before, yet his prepossessing appearance, his activity and knowledge of the world, far above what could have been expected under the circumstances, gave me even a higher opinion of his worth that I before entertained. The excellent climate from which he had come, and his constant employment in the open air, made him look like a robust man of fifty years of age, although he was then sixty-seven; and although his general character and manners were, necessarily, very different from what could be expected from a mere cloistered monk, yet in his grey Franciscan habit, which he always wore, with his jolly figure, bald head, and white looks, he looked the very *beau ideal* of a friar of the olden time. This worthy man having now entered the cloisters of a convent, may be considered as dead to the world; but he will live long in the memory of the inhabitants of California; and of those numerous strangers who have been entertained at his hospitable board at San Luis Rey.

The best and most unequivocal proof of the good conduct of these Fathers, is to be found in the unbounded affection and devotion invariably shown towards them by their Indian subjects. They venerate them not merely as friends and fathers but with a degree of devotedness approaching to adoration. On the occasion of the removals that have taken place of late years, from political causes, the distress of the Indians in parting with their pastors, has been extreme. They have entreated to be allowed to follow them in their exile, with tears and lamentations, and with all the demonstrations of true sorrow and unbounded affection. Indeed, if ever there existed an instance of the perfect justice and propriety of the comparison of the priest and his disciples, to a shepherd and his flock, it is in the case of which we are treating. These poor people may indeed be classed with the "silly sheep" more than with any other animal; and I believe they would, in the words of the poet, even "lick the hand" though it were "raised to shed their blood"—if this were the hand of the friar.[6]

Notes to the Text

1. The position of *Comisario Prefecto* was established in 1812.
2. This was not the case. Neophytes were normally expected to "persevere at the catechism for two or three months with the same determination, and if they have acquired sufficient knowledge, then they are baptized." See *Diary of Fray Pedro Font* in the Santa Barbara Mission Archives, entry for January 5th, 1776.
3. The author probably is here referring to Benediction of the Blessed Sacrament, rather than Mass. Evening Masses were not allowed during those times.
4. The author might have noted that the natives were free from this dread malady until the arrival of the Europeans.
5. Antonio Peyri (1769-1835) was the founder of Mission San Luis Rey where he labored for thirty-four years before retiring to his native Spain.
6. An interesting commentary on the entire Forbes account is that of Joachim Adam, entitled "A Defense of the Missionary Establishments of Alta California." See *Historical Society of Southern California Annual* III (1896), 35-39.

19

Richard Henry Dana
(1815-1882)

It was a youthful Richard Henry Dana who penned the "most popular work on California ever written"[1] in 1835-1836. The author "possessed not only extraordinarily keen powers of observation but a fine facility for expressing his ideas in writing."[2] His narrative "had all the fascination of [James Fenimore] Cooper's and [Frederick] Marryatt's sea-stories, and it was doubtless this charm mainly that caused its immense popularity; yet it was instructive no less than fascinating, as it contained the most realistic picture extant of sailors' life and treatment in American trading vessels, with intelligent observations on the countries visited."[3]

"Dana was perhaps more or less prepossessed as a New England American against the Mexican character"[4] and his views on California reflect a definite "bias against a Hispanic society."[5] One authority cautions that "anti-Catholic prejudices enter...his expressed judgments, and must, in fairness, be allowed for."[6]

The Boston-born adventurer "exhibits almost unpardonable ignorance of the history"[7] of the missionary endeavors. Nonetheless, apart from his personal convictions, he admitted that "the dynasty of the priests was much more acceptable to the people of the country, and, indeed, to everyone concerned with the country, by trade or otherwise, than that of the administradores.*"[8]*

Dana's recollections, initially appearing as Volume CVI of "Harpers Family Library," were published at New York in 1840, under the title, Two Years Before the Mast. *The book was regarded as a "classic"[9] and over the succeeding years this "literary masterpiece - the first in the annals of California literature,"[10] was issued in no fewer than ninety-one editions in the United States alone. The original and complete text was published for the first time, in two volumes, under the editorship of John Haskell Kemble, in 1964.*

References

1. Charles E. Chapman, *A History of California: The Spanish Period* (New York, 1923), p. 495.
2. Leslie E. Bliss in *The Zamorano 80* (Los Angeles, 1945), p. 20.
3. Hubert Howe Bancroft, *History of California* (San Francisco, 1886), III, 413.
4. Theodore H. Hittell, *History of California* (San Francisco, 1898), II, 291.
5. Andrew F. Rolle, *California* (New York, 1963), p. 264.
6. Bryan J. Clinch, *California and Its Missions* (San Francisco, 1904), II, 454.
7. John J. Bodkin, *The Tidings*, May 26, 1905.
8. This excerpt is from the 1840 edition, published at New York as volume CVI of "Harpers Family Library."
9. Abraham P. Nasatir, "Book Review," *California Historical Society Quarterly* XLIV (December, 1965), 349.
10. Dorothy Bowen, *A Century of California Literature* (San Marino, 1950), p. 2.

1835-1836

California was first discovered in 1536,[1] by Cortes, and was subsequently visited by numerous other adventurers, as well as commissioned voyagers of the crown. It was found to be inhabited by numerous tribes of Indians, and to be in many parts extremely fertile; to which, of course, was added rumors of gold mines, pearl fishery, &c. No sooner was the importance of the country known, than the Jesuits obtained leave to establish themselves in it,[2] to Christianize and enlighten the Indians. They established missions in various parts of the country toward the close of the seventeenth century, and collected the natives about them, baptizing them into the church, and teaching them the arts of civilized life. To protect the Jesuits[3] in their missions, and at the same time to support the power of the crown over the civilized Indians, two forts were erected and garrisoned, one at San Diego, and the other at Monterey. These were called Presidios, and divided the command of the whole country between them. Presidios have since been established at Santa Barbara and San Francisco; thus dividing the country into four large districts, each with its presidio and governed by the commandant. The soldiers, for the most part, were married civilized Indians; and thus, in the vicinity of each presidio, sprung up, gradually, small towns. In the course of time, vessels began to come into the ports to trade with the missions, and received hides in return; and thus began the great trade of California. Nearly all the cattle in the country belonged to the missions, and they employed their Indians, who became, in fact, their slaves, in tending their vast herds. In the year 1793, when Vancouver visited San Diego, the missions had obtained great wealth and power, and are accused of having depreciated the country with the sovereign, that they might be allowed to retain their possessions. On the expulsion of the

171

Jesuits from the Spanish dominious, the missions passed into the hands of the Franciscans, though without any essential change in their management. Ever since the independence of Mexico, the missions have been going down; until, at last, a law was passed, stripping them of all their possessions and confining the priests to their spiritual duties; and at the same time declaring all the Indians free and independent *Rancheros*. The change in the condition of the Indians was, as may be supposed, only nominal: they are virtually slaves, as much as they ever were. But in the missions, the change was complete. The priests have now no power, except in their religious characters and the great possessions of the missions are given over to be preyed upon by the harpies of the civil power, who are sent there in the capacity of *adminstradores*, to settle up the concerns; and who usually end, in a few years, by making themselves fortunes, and leaving their stewardships worse than they found them. The dynasty of the priests was much more acceptable to the people of the country, and, indeed, to every one concerned with the country, by trade or otherwise, than that of the *administradores*. The priests were attached perpetually to one mission, and felt the necessity of keeping up its credit. Accordingly, their debts were regularly paid, and the people were, in the main, well treated, and attached to those who had spent their whole lives among them. But the *administradores* are strangers sent from Mexico, having no interest in the country; not identified in any way with their charge, and, for the most part, men of desperate fortunes—broken down politicians and soldiers—whose only object is to retrieve their condition in as short a time as possible. The change had been made but a few years before our arrival upon the coast, yet, in that short time, the trade was much diminished, credit impaired, and the venerable missions going rapidly to decay. The external arrangements remain the same. There are four presidios, having under their protection the various missions, and pueblos, which are towns formed by the civil power, and containing no mission or presidio. The most northerly presidio is San Francisco; the next Monterey; the next Santa Barbara, including the mission of the same, St. Louis Obispo, and St. Buenaventura, which is the finest mission in the whole country, having very fertile soil and rich vineyards. The last, and most southerly, is San Diego, including the mission of the same, San Juan Campestrano (*sic*), Pueblo de los Angelos, the largest town in California, with the neighboring mission of San Gabriel. The priests in spiritual matters are the Archbishop of Mexico,[4] and in temporal matters to the governor-general, who is the great civil and military head of the country.

Notes to the Text

1. Mariano Cuevas gives the distinction of the first visit to Marcos Ruiz de Rojas and Melchior de Alarcon in 1529. See "The Missions of Lower California," *Mid-America* XVI (October, 1933), 73.
2. The Jesuits were not represented on the peninsula until 1631 with the arrival of Father Roque de Vega and the Ortega expeditionary force.
3. Dana's "ignorance of geography" beyond those places he personally visited are obvious. See the John Haskell Kemble edition of *Two Years Before the Mast* (Los Angeles, 1964), I, 169 n. Here the author has confused Alta and Baja California. The Society of Jesus never worked in the missions of Upper California.
4. Not so. The friars were subject to their own Apostolic Colleges, either that of San Fernando in Mexico City or Nuestra Señora de Guadalupe in Zacatecas. In the New World, special papal directives gave broad jurisdiction to Apostolic Colleges independent of episcopal interference.

20

Faxon Dean Atherton
(1815-1877)

axon Dean Atherton was an eyewitness to the turbulent years of mush-rooming trade, political unrest and discontent, secularization, revolution and the expansion of foreign penetration that confronted California in provincial times. A sensitive and enterprising business-man, Atherton "had the dreamer's eye; the realist's wisdom."[1] His carefully kept diary, in which he recorded the experiences and impressions during the Mexican regime, clearly reflects the momentous atmosphere of contemporary society. Though not considered as gifted a writer as Richard Henry Dana, the father-in-law of novelist Gertrude Atherton extended the record an additional three years.

Atherton's account "contains significant new material on many aspects of the history of California in the period which it covers."[2] His observations of the mission system were recorded as those foundations were struggling through the final throes of secularization. While "on a number of occasions he shows a misunderstanding and misinterpretation of Catholic practices," he did "add greatly to the day by day scene as he encountered it and balances the more optimistic viewpoints of other visitors to the territory."[3]

The daily record of the travels, experiences and impressions of the Massachusetts-born merchant were published at San Francisco, under the editorship of Doyce B. Nunis, Jr., only in 1964, as The California Diary of Faxon Dean Atherton, 1836-1839. *Had the volume been available to earlier chroniclers, much of the provincial era's history would have carried its imprint.*

References

1. Doyce B. Nunis, Jr. Ed., *The California Diary of Faxon Dean Atherton 1836-1839* (San Francisco, 1964), p. xiii.
2. John H. Kemble, "Book Review," *Southern California Quarterly* XLVII (March, 1965), 115.
3. Maynard J. Geiger, O.F.M., "Book Review," *California Historical Society Quarterly* XLIII (December, 1964), 345.

1836-1839

This Mission[1] is one of those that have been taken from the management of the priests and put under that of an *Administrador*.[2] It appears to be going to ruin as fast as the elements, and the inordinate desires of the Administrador for gain, can make it. Formerly it had 2000 Indians attached to it, church, dwelling houses for the Indians, and large store houses in good repair. Now both church and dwelling houses are in ruins; store houses fallen to pieces, and not more than 50 or 60 Indians belonging to it. Supped with the Padre[3] who has been very unwell but is now better.

For the last two years there has been little or no rain in Upper Californias and in consequence the crops have been so short, last year especially, that grain which should have been reserved for seed has been almost entirely eaten up so that there is, in proportion to what is required for sowing, little or none to be had at any price. Those in favor of taking the Missions from the hands of the Padres say that it is owing to the want of water, whilst those who are opposed to it say that it is because the Indians will not work for any one but the Padres, and that in former years when there was a scarcity of rain there was no scarcity of grain. However, this year there has an immense quantity of rain fallen, and the Indians having been so hard pushed for a subsistence these last two years have turned to with a will, and have already sown in the vicinity of this Mission 500 and odd *fanegas* of wheat besides beans and other seeds in proportion, so that if there is not too much rain there will probably be an abundance of every thing. The cattle as we rode along look remarkably well and good judges say that this will be the greatest year for tallow that has ever been known in California. If so, well and good; so much the better both for inhabitants and foreign merchants.

Saturday, May 7. At 7 a.m. started for Santa Clara after taking a cup of what appears to be called tea in this country but should not know it either by taste or colour from common warm water. However, as it cost nothing but *gracias* (thanks), suppose I must not complain. I would rather pay a pretty sound price and have some good, as I know by experience that it is confounded unpleasant to start at this time in the morning on a journey of 60 miles with nothing but warm water to keep your bowels distended. For about 5 miles we rode over a beautifully cultivated plain the wheat being about 6 inches high and in fine condition. We then came to a low marshy spot at the foot of some hills, and, on crossing a muddy ditch, my horse went into it up to head but managed to keep out of it myself by crossing my legs over his neck. The *barquaro*, horse, and all went into head and heels, and came out in a pretty plight. After a good laugh at him for his good horsemanship, we continued on and arrived at a small stream. After crossing it, our road for at least 10 miles was along the banks of the stream and the foot of some hills, and being confounded rough and slippery, we made but little headway. On passing the hills we came to a plain that extends as far as the eye can reach. About twenty miles of our road through this plain lay through the "Rancho de los Castros"[4] which a few years since, before the death of the father of the family, was said to contain about 20,000 head of cattle besides horses in great numbers. From present appearances it does not contain 200.

We stopped at a Rancho about 12 o'clock and obtained some eggs and milk. Had a bit of a blow out on some whiskey given us by a Mr. Gulnack[5] who has a distillery near the Pueblo of San Jose, but now owing to the scarcity of grain, is at a standstill. Judging from the present sample, the liquor made by him is very good. At least it has a peculiar smack to it which suited my palate very well. At 5 p.m. arrived at the Pueblo of San Jose. Should think that there might be 50 houses. Land appears very rich and well cultivated. Have seen few or no women thus far and in fact there appear to be very few inhabitants, male or female, black or white. From the Pueblo, after stopping a few moments, we continued our journey for the Mission of Santa Clara (through an avenue of willows about 6 miles long planted by the old priests) and arrived there at 6 p.m.

Sunday, May 8. Remained in the Mission until past 12 o'clock owing to the rain. There were a great number of people in church in the morning, some of whom came from more than 15 miles. There are very few at home that would go that far, although it is not required of them there to attend church so strictly as it is here as there each one can pray for himself. Besides, it may be asking a few blessings on the "Girl that's not beside him," while it requires the assistance of a Padre to enable the petitions of a "*Catolico Apostolico Romano*" to seek beyond the influence of the airy stratum that keeps mankind in existence. Rather doubt my ever being made a believer in a creed that rouses one from his bed at daylight and sends him 15 miles to church through a drenching rain, and rain too that comes down with a will, regular double headed drops, a dozen of which would fill a moderate sized bucket. I am too fond of ease and sunshine for that, and besides, I am not fond of troubling priests or anyone else to ask favours for me, whilst I am blessed with health and strength enough to do it myself, as I have yet to learn how it is that the prayers of a priest can have any more efficacy than my own humble petitions.

This is one of the Missions, the very few, that remain under the hands of the priests, and certainly if the great comparison that exists between this Mission and that of St. Johns (San Juan Bautista) is anything by which a person may judge of the comparative advantages of priest or Administrador, I should say the Administradors are the ruin of a Mision, while under the hands of the priests, they flourish and increase not very fast it may be, but still are daily becoming better. In the church of the Mision of S(an)ta Clara, the priest has lately added a tower in which there are 4 bells. He has also refitted, overhauled and cleaned all parts of the church, and other buildings attached to the Mision. The houses of Indians are generally in very good order and the men are all comfortably clothed in good blankets made in the Mision and the women and girls very prettily dressed in fancy calico gowns, and some one or two even sported muslin and silk dresses. There is a fine large orchard attached to the Mision in which there are pears, apples, apricots, etc., in great abundance, and although last year was very unproductive of all kinds of fruits still we found quite an abundant supply at the Padres' table. I am beginning to believe in the old adage that priests consume the best produce of the land. The Padre of this Mision, Padre Moreno,[6] is a devilish shrewd kind of a character, and understands buying and selling as well as most anyone I have fallen in with.

After blowing our pipes out on a regular good dinner, for which fasting since 10 o'clock the night before had given us a good appetite, we started for the Mision of San Jose over a low plain full of mustard as high as a person's head when sitting on horseback. The ground, owing to the rain, was very slippery, and my horse stumbled a number of times but managed to keep from tumbling off. The plain extends for about 10 miles. Then we came to the foot of some hills, wound around them, and then crossed over 3 or 4 small ones, being a distance of about 5 miles, when we arrived in sight of the Mision which does not appear so well at first view of it from this road as you can only see one end and some of the outbuildings. But on coming in front of it, and amongst the different buildings, it looks very well. We found the Padre, Jose Jesus Gonzales, to be in appearance and manners very much of a gentleman and should infer from his way of conducting the affairs of the Mission that he was a very capable man. We also found here the Padre Quijas[7] of the Mision of San Rafael, who it is said, commenced his career as a muleteer then turned soldier and from soldier became priest, and has now charge of the above named Mision. But, owing to the extreme scarcity of provisions, has been starved out and is now here blowing his pipes out on the good things he can fall in with.

In the evening we went to a play performed by the Indian boys and girls of the Mision, being taught by the schoolmaster who appears to be a person of considerable information. They have a band of about 20 pieces of music, and I should think some pieces were executed very well. However, I am no great judge in those matters. After the play was ended, about 11 o'clock, we sat down to a good supper. Although I am no judge of music, I profess to be no bad one of the manner of preparing "Belly Timber" which, when well done, I can discourse the subject as long as most any one. And our supper this night I can truly say was most essentially so, and I also *feel* certain that I have made good stowage of no small portion of what was before me. What greater blessing than a good appetite, especially when the luscious wherewithal to appease it is placed before one.

Monday, May 9. Rose at 6 a.m. Feel rather unwell. Have taken a walk round the orchard, and mechanicks shops of the place, and am much pleased with the well regulated manner of conducting the work. In one part is a blacksmiths shop, in another a carpenters, a card makers, a saddle makers, wool carders, spinners, weavers, dyers, etc., etc. Farther back is the slaughter house, some are killing, some trying out tallow (rendering), some spreading hides, all appear to be busy about something. There are also gangs of men in the fields sowing, some ploughing, some attending the cattle. In front of the Mision, and between that and the houses inhabited by the Indians, is a large fountain at which there are some 20 or 30 women washing, laughing and joking. All the young girls of the Mision are kept locked up nights by themselves, to keep them from mischievous pranks. They are under the charge of a man who is called an Alcalde, but I found that he knew the value of a 4 real piece, and perfectly understood what he received it for. There are some pretty fair looking girls amongst them, and what is more, devilish neat and clean. The large ovens for baking they have here are fine handy things.

The land belonging to this M(ission) is said to be the best of any near here. From the M(ission), which is close under the mountains, it gradually slopes down to the head of the Bay of San Francisco, launches from which can go up the different creeks as far as within 3 leagues of the M(ission). This year there has been 196 fanegas of wheat sown and it now looks extremely well and promises abundantly, but they are fearful there will be too much rain. There are about 1500 Indians attached to this Mision and it owns about 15,000 head of cattle and horses.

At 1 p.m. started for S(an)ta Clara and arrived there at 4 having come along rather slowly. The whole of the land belonging to this as well as to the Mision of San Jose, one continued level making the head of one of the bays of San Francisco, and being crossed and recrossed by numbers of creeks which run into it from the Bay, navigable for launches until within 3 miles of the Mision, makes the land very well adapted for pasturage of cattle of which there is an immense number feeding all over the plains. There are a great number of sheep belonging to S(an)ta Clara; they feed in flocks as close together as they can possibly move, each flock is attended by about 10 or 12 dogs.

Tuesday, May 10. Started at 7 a.m. for Yerba Buena, S(an) F(rancisco). Horses were excellent and roads pretty fair. Our course was along the southern side of the Bay and for about 35 miles pretty level. After that it becomes rather broken and in some places marshy. Saw marks of where some bears had been paseando (walking).

At 11 a.m. arrived at the Rancho of the Mision of San Francisco. Is now deserted and in ruins, lies about 25 miles from the Mision. Land around looks remarkably well, but no signs of cultivation. Stopped at.a Rancho of some Indians, had some dried beef broiled on the coals and, after resting a few moments, started again, and after crossing some sandy hills arrived in sight of the wreck of the M(ission) of S(an) F(rancisco), although it never could have been a M(ission) of any great note as the land around it is not capable of supporting a large population. Still it has been a small but well conducted M(ission) until it was placed under the charge of an Administrador, since which time it has been going to ruins and is now literally a *wreck*, and not an Indian to be seen. We stopped for a few moments, obtained a drink of milk from a devilish pretty young girl, and continued on over a road so sandy the horses sank up to their middles.

In about an hour, however, on emerging from a thicket of bushes, bastard oaks, etc., we arrived in sight of the Pride of the Ocean, the Brig

Bolivar Liberator, anchored close under our feet. Immediately went on board and had a cup of tea and good dinner, and then commenced selling. The water here is as smooth as possible, scarcely a ripple breaking on the shore, caused it is said by the extreme narrowness of the channel, which makes the tide run so very fast that it entirely destroys and smooths down the swell of the ocean. It is said by the old Indians that this Bay was formerly an inland lake connected with the sea only by a small stream that served to empty it in seasons of heavy rain, and that a great many years ago there was a tremendous earthquake which opened the stream to such a width and depth that it let in the water of the ocean, and what seems to corroborate this statement is that the mouth of the Bay is yearly growing wider, and it is now about as wide again as it was 20 years since. The bar across the entrance is at times very dangerous, especially after a heavy blow from the S.E. and on the ebb tide, about two months since the Sch(ooner) *Pero es Nada* was turned over and over and entirely lost by a heavy *Boar* that struck them while crossing the bar.[8]

The Mission has an exceedingly pretty appearance from the anchorage and is said to look equally well on closer inspection, being kept very neat and in good repair under the management of the Padre. This year they have lost all the grain they sowed, and the poor Redskins appear to fare hard, living on beef alone. The country is all parched up, scarcely a spear of grass to be seen. From appearances should suppose there was about 500 inhabitants in this place, who are now all or nearly all suffering extremely for want of provisions. With one or two exceptions, they are now subsisting entirely on beef, and it is feared the cattle will all die off as there is but very little water and not a spear of grass and all that has been sown by them has been lost.

Saturday, June 25. Brig got underway at daylight for the Port of San Luis Obispo. Mr. Thompson[9] and myself started at 9 a.m. by land with an Indian boy for a guide. Road pretty good for about 10 miles; then struck on to the beach for about 5 miles. From thence-crossed a small hill and came on to a small beach by which is an entrance to a deep gully up which we turned, and came after riding about two miles to the "Rancho de los Ortegas," where we found them all busy—men, women, children killing cattle, trying out tallow, jerking beef, etc., being what is here called "making a *matanza*" (slaughter). After taking a bight (bite) of jerked beef we continued on and in about an hour arrived at the top of the *cuesta* "de Sta. Iness" (hill of Santa Ines). We found it in some places almost impossible to descend, being in some places literally perpendicular. The distance from top to bottom in a straight line might be about 1 mile, but the only possible way of descending is by a zigzag course of about 4, and as rocky and uneven as can well be imagined. We found the road at the foot to be very good, in fact any thing almost would appear good to us in comparison. About 2 miles from the foot of the hill we arrived to the bed of a river about two hundred rods wide from bank to bank. It is now entirely dried up except about 10 feet wide on its right bank. The country we have passed through in this day's journey looks miserable being entirely parched up, and as dusty as can well be imagined.

At 5 p.m. arrived at the Mision of Santa Iness (Ines) situated on a high bank about 30 feet above the bed of the river, seen from which it has a fine appearance. We found it a small but very neat, clean, and apparently well regulated Mision, being under the hands of Padre Jimeno.[10] At the supper table found Padre Arroyo[11] of the (Mission) Purisima who had been sent for in great haste this morning by the Padre of this Mision stating that Padre Victoria[12] (a very old man and an invalid) was at the point of death and that he was wanted to confess him. Padre Arroyo arrives and find P(adre) Victoria in better than usual health, and that it was all a bit of joke to get the Padre here on a Sunday spree and they appeared to enjoy with as much spirit as any I have ever met with, notwithstanding their sackcloth dresses and shaved heads. I shall soon believe, "More of the Priests more of the Devil."

Padre Arroyo is a very talkative old man and appears to be possessed of good information. He kept me listening to his yarns for about two hours, and most of the time was endeavoring to make me understand *his* theory of the motion of the Planets, he believing or pretending to believe the Earth to be a plane and that the Sun revolves around it.

This Mision has sown about 37 *fanegas* of wheat from which, notwithstanding the dryness of the season, they expect to obtain about half a common crop. The Indians of this and as well as most of the Misions round have at present rather hard fare, and the prospect is that they will fare worse before they fare better. They are now out among the hills in immense numbers gathering wild oats of which there is great quantities growing all over the country. After *Misa* we started for "La Purisima," the road being over a level plain. For about 5 miles from the M(ission), (the land is) burnt and parched up as dry as the deserts of Arabia. After passing that (burnt land), we came among some hills equally dry, the roads leading right across the bottom of a pond entirely dried up.

At 2 p.m. arrived in sight of the "Mision de La Purisima." Passed a tremendous large bear that was killed the night before, the vultures already having made sad havoc amongst his flesh and bones. The Mision is small but appears to be in pretty good order for one in the hands of an Administrador.[13] He is, however, a young man of pretty good talent and should think of very good ideas about the management of Misions in general. We were treated to a good dinner immediately on arrival and as may be supposed was not at all unpleasant. We found Mr. J. McKinley here from the Pueblo do Los Angeles.

Monday, June 27. At 8 a.m. started for the Mision on San Luis about 50 miles from this. We rode from the Mision about 3 miles up a beautiful cañada, then up a very high and rugged hill, the opposite side of which is very precipitous and sandy, in some places almost perpendicular. Notwithstanding, our *baquero* rode down it at full gallop, while we could hardly hold on to our horses in walking. About three miles from the foot of the hill we came to a rancho of the Mision. Exchanged *baqueros* and continued over a fine plain, having few or no cattle and less appearance of anything to maintain them, the ground being as bare and dried up as can possibly be imagined. About 15 miles was of the same, when we came to some sandy barren wastes which continued for 10 miles or more, occasionally interspersed with a spot that appeared to produce something green in the rainy season. At the end of this we crossed the dry bed of a river which had some appearance of vegetation springing out every 8 or 10 steps. We then came on to the land known by the name of "*Oso flaco*" or "poor lean bear," which is covered with wood and low under brush, the soil sandy and barren. From this we came to some high sand hills of about a mile in width, crossed them and came on to the beach of the Bay of San Luis (Obispo). I have never met with anything so dreary as the sand hills, heaped up as they are in all directions, they appear like waves of the ocean stopped in their wild career by some superhuman power. There is no sign of a road or anything to guide a traveller. Occasionally you will meet with where a bear has been taking a *pasear* (walk) in pursuit of game. It reminds me of what I have read of the desert of Arabia. We rode along the beach for about 8 miles, came to where a creek was running into the sea, and there being a heavy sea on it had deepened the channel so much that it was impossible to cross. We then had to turn again among the sand hills to endeavour to find a road whereby we might cross the creek. After about two hours hard riding, sometimes our horses were sinking up to their knees in the sand, we managed to cross and then had fine riding for some miles, the country on our right being all full of smoke and fire from the wild oats and brush that was burning. We now came to a fine cañada and the land began to look green. At about 6 p.m. arrived at the Mision of San Luis Obispo. This Mision is under the management of an Administrador lately appointed by the new General, his name is Manuel Truxillo,[15] a Mexican but a short time in the country. (He) is a pretty good man, apparently not of very extensive information. In fact all he appears to know is about the City of Mexico and his yellow, fat, cigar smoking, squab built wife is of the same stamp. However, we were very hospitably received by them, treated I believe with the best the M(ission) afforded. This Mision is now in a most miserable, dirty condition. Apparently in a short time it will be tumbling about the ears of its inmates if not repaired. Its situation is most beautiful and the lands belonging to it exceedingly rich and well watered. Formerly it was famous for its beautiful mules and horses which were raised in great numbers and although at present it has an immense number of both, still nothing in comparison to what it formerly possessed. The Padre whose name is Ramon[16] is without exception the most dirty brutish looking person I ever met with. His hands are so covered with a crust of dirt that I question whether a sharp knife would cut through it without their being first soaked some hours in water. His nostrils and the corners of his mouth are filled with snuff which he is continually taking and by continually rubbing his eyes with his dirty hands they have become inflamed and are complete running sores. And I should suppose that his dress has never been changed since it was first put on some years since.

Tuesday, June 28. Mr. T(hompson) left to meet the Padre of the Mision of San Miguel.[17] In the afternoon I rode down to the beach a distance of about 10 miles through a beautiful cañada to see if the Brig had arrived; found she had not and returned rather disconsolate to the Mision. On passing through the woods saw Mr. Bruin taking siesta about 5 rods ahead of me. My horse started, snorted and refused to proceed and whilst we were fighting to see who would be master, Bruin waked up and made a spring into the bushes, much to my satisfaction, as they will sometimes attack a man on horseback especially if they should commence running and are hotly pursued.

Notes to the Text

1. *I.e.* San Juan Bautista, founded June 24, 1797.
2. Jose Tiburcio Castro served as administrator in 1835 and 1836. He "is not mentioned with respect by those who know his record." See Zephyrin Engelhardt, O.F.M., *Mission San Juan Bautista* (Santa Barbara, 1931), p. 62.
3. *I.e.* Father Jose Antonio Anzar (1793-1874) who had served at the mission since 1833.
4. The former Rancho Vega del Rio de Pajaro was near Santa Clara and San Jose.

5. William Gulnac (1801-1851) had lived in Peninsular California before coming north in 1833. He was a blacksmith by trade.

6. Father Rafael Moreno (1795-1839) died shortly after Atherton's visit.

7. Father Lorenzo Quijas came to California early in 1833.

8. See Bailey Millard, *History of the San Francisco Bay Region* (Chicago, 1924), I, 5-6.

9. Maine-born Alpheus B. Thompson (1795-1869), *supercargo* on the ship *Bolivar*, was a well-known and prosperous smuggler.

10. *Viz.*, Father Jose Joaquin Jimeno (1804-1856) who was *Presidente* of the Fernandino friars between 1839 and 1846.

11. *Viz.*, Father Felipe Arroyo de la Cuesta (1780-1840) who was then nearing the end of his thirty-two years of service in the mission system.

12. *Viz.*, Father Marcos Antonio Vitoria (1760-1836) who had served in California since 1805.

13. *Viz.*, Joaquin Carrillo (c.1811-1868), the son of Domingo Antonio Carrillo and Concepcion Pico, sister of California's one-time governor, served for many years as a district judge. He was a man of high reputation.

14. James McKinley (d.1875) was a Scottish sailor who arrived in 1824. At the time of Atherton's visit he was owner of the *Ayacucho* and engaged in commercial trading.

15. *Viz.*, Manuel Trujillo who was associated with the administration of Governor Carlos Carrillo (1783-1852) in 1837-1838.

16. *Viz.*, Ramon Abella (1764-1842), a native of the Kingdom of Aragon and for many years the only survivor of those friars who came to California before 1800.

17. *Viz.*, Father Juan Moreno (1799-1845).

21

Abel Aubert Du Petit-Thouars
(1793-1864)

*T*he French frigate Venus, *manned by a force of over 300 men, arrived at Monterey in October, 1837. Its navigator, Abel Aubert Du Petit-Thouars, a keen observer and a man of considerable intelligence, kept a careful account of the three year, world-wide voyage, whose purpose was "the accumulation of data which might be of use to French foreign commerce,"¹ especially the whaling industry.*

Du Petit-Thouars was the first of the visitors to collect those original documents so useful to later writers. His journal, probably the "most important on California during its Mexican regime,"² contains "not only valuable information concerning the history of people and institutions" but also "an accurate, fairly detailed account of the actual conditions in California as they existed during that troublesome revolutionary time."³

Though he viewed the overall missionary program initiated by the Spaniards with skepticism, Du Petit-Thouars admitted that the missions were well cared for in pre-secularization days. "The friars of the Franciscan order who administered the twenty-one missions of Upper California enjoyed," in his view, "a great reputation for piety, regularity of conduct and honesty."⁴

After his return to Europe, the versatile observer devoted several years to correlating his copious notes. His Voyage autour du monde sur la frégate Vénus *pendant les années 1836-1839 was published at Paris between 1840 and 1855 in eleven volumes of text and four beautiful folio atlases. Excerpts from Du Petit-Thouars' "excellent sketch of Californian history for the ten years preceding his visit"⁵ were translated and issued for the first time in English by Charles N. Rudkin for the* Early California Travel Series. *That edition was released at Los Angeles in 1956, as the* Voyage of the Venus: Sojourn in California.

References

1. Charles N. Rudkin (Trans.), *Voyage of the Venus: Sojourn in California* (Los Angeles, 1956), p. ix.
2. Wright Howes, *U.S. Iana* (1650-1950) (New York, 1963), p. 451.
3. Abraham P. Nasatir, *French Activities in California. An Archival Calendar-Guide* (Stanford, 1945), p. 5.
4. The excerpts here cited are from the 1956 edition.
5. Hubert Howe Bancroft, *History of California* (San Francisco, 1886), IV 149.

1837

According to the laws under which the missions of California were founded the Indian, after a stay of ten years in these establishments, was to receive title to a piece of land sufficient for his needs and for those of his family, as well as the seed and agricultural implements indispensable to the cultivation of this land. Furthermore they were to receive from the mission food for the first year of their occupancy. But whether the Franciscans who managed the Upper California establishments did not approve the views of the government in this connection or whether for some reasons of community interest they did not favor the system, or finally whether, as they claimed, the Indians were incapable of appreciating the benefits of this civilization, they made few attempts to carry this out and the greater part of these were unsuccessful. The Indians thus emancipated, after abandoning themselves to unreserved laziness, giving themselves over to drunkenness and shameful debauch, at last, having dissipated all they owned by gambling, which they loved passionately, returned to their missions to ask for a subsistence which they were incapable of getting by their work and by their domestic economy.

The heads of the missions employed the Indians, and still employ them in those missions which still exist, at heavy labor, irrigation, as herdsmen, at tanning, gardening, in fact at all the work of an extensive agricultural exploitation. Another part of the community was kept busy in the interior of the establishments and charged with the housekeeping. Some missions, among them the most flourishing, had shops for weaving coarse cloths used to clothe their neophytes, in addition to carpenter shops, cabinet shops, forges and other trades common to all. There were also numerous leather-working shops. All of the missions also hired out Indians for domestic and personal service to the *gente de razon*. These domestics were not skilled but they were faithful, for punishment quickly followed any misdeed. When they were guilty of any fault or grave misdemeanor they were sent back to the mission to be punished or exchanged, as the employer might request.

Many of the Indians who lived at the missions had been brought in by stratagems; very few had been brought in by persuasion and, to tell the truth, in general they were treated rather as slaves than as neophytes. Nevertheless the Fathers, while laboring for their salvation whether they wished it or not, did not neglect their temporal well-being. Children were brought up separately and the young girls were cloistered until marriage. It does not appear that Indians have been actively recruited since the emancipation of the Californias but it is a very remarkable fact that as soon as constraint ceased many natives belonging to the *gentiles* class have come in to be baptized and then have gone back to their tribes. In spite of their conversion these Indians still retain all the superstitions of their early education. They believe in the devil, in magic, in witches, and have priests who make themselves feared as oracles.

Several missions had considerable revenues. Almost all were well administered and the priests who managed them showed a generous hospitality toward strangers. Now the time of decadence has come, very few missions have kept their revenues intact, many are badly managed, and if the government does not stop the progress of this decay by giving the temporal management of the missions back to the churchmen who used to manage them, re-establishing them in all their rights by efficient protection, soon not a single one will be inhabited.

The friars of the Franciscan order who administered the twenty-one missions of Upper California enjoyed a great reputation for piety, regularity of conduct and honesty. Their conduct was the more praiseworthy in that all the orders scattered throughout the two Americas, subject to no restraint, far from acting for the edification of their neighbors and the improvement of customs, almost always gave an example of the loosest living and abandoned themselves in general to all the licentiousness that could be imagined. The fifteen missions of Lower California were, and still are, managed by Dominicans. In the exercise of their ministry and in their administration they have not acquired as much reputation for regularity, capacity, and generosity as their colleagues of Upper California.

Since the revolution of 1836 all the Indians of San Carlos mission, set at liberty, have returned to their tribes in the interior and resumed their nomadic life. A very few who were in the service of the *gente de razon* at Monterey have remained there. In the early days of this desertion the people found themselves greatly inconvenienced since they were not accustomed to labor nor to serving themselves. This sharply felt privation lasted up to the time of our visit but the number of Indians returning to offer their services was already increasing day by day.

Now that the natives who formerly occupied the missions have returned to their wandering life they are neighbors no less disagreeable than dangerous. They kill cattle for their needs, and this without any care for the future, sometimes without any necessity or even often in a spirit of malice. This magnificent and fertile country endowed with an excellent climate still cannot fail to prosper and flourish as soon as the population, increasing in numbers, is placed under a good administration, especially a strong and just government.

22

Cyrille Pierre Theodore Laplace (1793-1873)

*C*aptain *Cyrille Pierre Theodore Laplace arrived in California in August, 1839, flying the colorful flag of Orleanist France. Though ostensibly on a research tour, local officials "shrewdly conjectured that the Frenchman's 'scientific observations' were closely related to French colonial possibilities in the Pacific world."[1] The political overtones were later confirmed when it was disclosed that Laplace had discussed, on a strictly informal basis, the possibility of establishing "a protectorate over California."[2]*

For a man of such obvious literary ability, Laplace's observations are considerably impaired "by his habit of drifting constantly into the by-ways of long and fanciful speculations."[3] One authority contends that the French naval officer "is an active competitor with his compeer, Dr. John Coulter, for the laurels of the California Munchhausen."[4]

In his general survey of the missions, Laplace "gives no flattering account"[5] though he visited only two of the foundations at the very most. While speaking of the "eminent services" of the Franciscans, he felt that "they did not sufficiently exert themselves to develop in these unfortunates, the moral feelings and at the same time the taste for work and the love of the family."[6]

Upon concluding his four year, round-the-world voyage, Laplace, by then a rear-admiral, compiled his recollections into a six volume opus published at Paris between 1841 and 1854 as Campagne de circumnavigation de la frégate l'Artémise, pendant les années 1837, 1838, 1839, et 1840.[7] *It was translated in part by H. A. van Coenen Torchiana for his* Story of the Mission Santa Cruz *which appeared at San Francisco in 1933.[8]*

References

1. Rufus Kay Wyllys, "French Imperialists in California," *California Historical Society Quarterly* VIII (June, 1929), 116.
2. Abraham P. Nasatir, *French Activities in California. An Archival Calendar-Guide* (Stanford, 1945), p. 6.
3. Hubert Howe Bancroft, *History of California* (San Francisco, 1886), IV, 155.
4. H.A. van Coenen Torchiana, *Story of the Mission Santa Cruz* (San Francisco, 1933), p. 364.
5. Willard O. Waters, *Franciscan Missions of Upper California as seen by Foreign Visitors and Residents* (Los Angeles, 1954), Entry 28.
6. The excerpts here cited are from the van Coenen Torchiana translation.
7. George Verne Blue, "the Report of Captain Laplace on his Voyage to the Northwest Coast and California in 1839," *California Historical Society Quarterly* XVIII (December, 1939), 316.
8. *Op. cit.*, pp. 438-443.

1839

The missions were multiplied everywhere where the fertility of the soil, a favorable location, or the vicinity of a good anchorage seemed to promise a future. They had generally prospered, but principally in those districts to the North, of which Monterey was the main one, and whose roadstead was so to say the boundary to the South. The largest ones developed on the shore of the ocean; the mission and presidio of San Francisco, both situated on the magnificent bay of the same name, those of Santa Cruz, San Carlos, Santa Barbara, where the travellers, tired from their long voyages, always found a hospitality as generous as insistent, and also provisions in abundance, derived from the towns of San Jose, San Raphael, San Solano, and many others less important, all more or less removed from the shore of the sea.

...after a very peaceful night, during which we profited by all the little variations of the breeze to skirt the shore at a short distance, the frigate arrived at break of day in the vicinity of the mission of Santa Cruz, only a few leagues distant from Monterey to the north, and we let the anchor drop in the afternoon on a good bottom, near two islets only about a mile from a favorable small cove of white sand, where a small river flowed.

This anchorage, which awakened a desire to procure for the crew, for the ship's officers and myself a provision of fresh vegetables, before leaving California for Peru, is frequented during the summer by the merchant ships and coasters. Many famous explorers have put into port here during the last century; amongst them our illustrious compatriate de la Perouse, who, in the account of his voyages made mention of the reception, equally pressing as generous, which he as well as his companions received from the monks of this missions then the finest, the richest, the best administered of all those in California. The good priests heaped up their cares and the most delicate attentions, and even wanted to furnish *gratis* all the provisions which they needed to the crews of the two ships of the expedition. It was under the gentle influence of such recollections, the same, however, which had occurred to me when arriving at San Francisco and which had been so painfully dispelled, that I disembarked on the shore near where the frigate had dropped anchor. I was quite enchanted by the lovely views which we had at intervals of the mission with its little white houses and red tiled roofs, its church surmounted by a little steeple, which seemed to appear suddenly from the bosom of a magnificent stretch of green, at the end of which it arose. At the same first view of the picture, there unrolled before our eyes, the fields, which with their color of emerald, one could believe to be cultivated with care, so rich was the vegetation, the charm of which was enhanced anew by the clusters of fruit trees, distributed here and there. Further on and closing the perspective on that side, there arose a ridge of higher elevation, covered from the foot to the summit with a forest of large pines with dark foliage, contrasting in an agreeable manner with the warm colors of the plain, which bordered on the sea. All that was delicious; and yet deceptions awaited me there also and still more painful, for after having completed a walk, quite prolonged under a burning sun, although the afternoon was advanced a spectacle of misery and of desertion offered itself to my eyes.

The buildings, which from afar had a good appearance, were in ruin and abandoned by their former inhabitants. In vain I searched for some human being in the courtyards surrounded by wills, which we crossed before arriving at the principal part of the lodgings, occupied in former times by Franciscan monks; everywhere a profound silence reigned, in the very places where some years ago a thousand converted Indians, maintained through their agricultural and manufacturing activities an abundance and life and progress. All of that indigenous population has disappeared, decimated by misery, sickness and desertion. The main building, where de la Perouse had found such a noble and kindly hospitality, did not show a vestige of its former splendor,[1] if I may so express myself. On every side a picture of disorder; and even the apartment of the administrator of the mission was stripped of necessities, bordering on uncleanliness. However, I was agreeably surprised when I discovered in the master of the dwelling, manners and a figure prepossessing, even distinguished, which contrasted singularly with the forbidding aspect of everything surrounding him. He made excuses in very good terms for his destitution, which prevented him from receiving us as he would have desired, and he offered in an amiable way, but not without a certain embarrassment, of which I soon understood the cause, to conduct is through the different parts of the establishment.

In fact with every step we encountered objects of sadness and disgust; the long rows of little huts made of sun-dried bricks, lately occupied by the neophytes of the monks, had no doors or windows and were covered in part by their debris; in a court adjoining the lodging of our guide and contaminated by a thousand sweepings which gave off an abominable odor, we saw several individuals occupied rather in tearing to pieces than in properly cutting up the cadavre of a steer, still palpitant, of which the blood and the entrails lay about upon the ground, and where they would remain until the birds of prey devoured them. The kitchen garden, into which we had entered by a gate half in ruins, the sill of which was covered by rubbish and filth, offered scarcely a space for our feet; it did not have any less repulsive aspect; in a corner were lying several carrion, covered by a myriad of winged insects; the borders—walks of that sort of field—found themselves encroached upon equally by weeds, to which some cabbages, half nibbled by the caterpillars, gave a desperate resistance; the fruit trees, poor exiles of our southern provinces, left to themselves, were exhausted by a mass of tall sprouts and bore only poor fruit. But in the midst of that chaos, nature showing itself always beautiful, always disposed to repair the damage caused by the errors of man, endeavored to hide miserable results of the California carelessness and heedlessness under a magnificent cover of verdure, which had already invaded almost all of the ruins and the surrounding fields.

That reflection, not very flattering to our poor humanity, and which unfortunately I have made only too often in the course of my long role of observer, seems to me even more justified, if possible, when walking over all the parts of the deserted mission, I thought of what it had been and of the state in which I found it now. How many mistakes must have been committed by the men charged with the destinies of that country, before they succeeded in destroying an institution, the creation of which had demanded so much care and so many years of work! On which side lies the blame? Is it on the side of the founders, or is it necessary to blame only the present masters? The monks without doubt were somewhat to blame, they showed themselves too convinced that in their hands the temporal power should be inherent to the spiritual power. They considered their neophytes perhaps too much as the instruments of fortune and well being; as unintelligent beings, big children; and in these diverse convictions, equally unfounded, they did not sufficiently exert themselves to develop in these unfortunates, the moral feelings and at the same time the taste for work and the love of the family. The result was that instead of these Indian converts becoming civilized and better, they were completely brutalized, thus justifying the profound contempt in which the whites held them.

The adversaries of the Fathers have equal wrongs to reproach themselves with on this account. They should be taxed with injustice, even with ingratitude, not only because of the prompt forgetfulness with which they have repaid the eminent services rendered to the country by the Franciscans, but even with having made the latter miserable by persecution, by abandonment of the establishments which gave them a living as well as a prosperity which they enjoyed. Nevertheless, let us admit that the Mexican government has, as far as it was able on account of the incessant revolutions with which it has had to battle since the commencement of the century, made efforts to pull the converted indigenes out of the profound degradation in which they were. For a long time it has shown itself their protectors by its orders, the Indians of the missions who conducted themselves well and who showed some aptitude for agriculture or the mechanical arts, obtained concessions of land, cattle, implements of irrigation, assistance of all kinds, to exercise their industry; and where more of their kind were aggregated they were aided to form villages under the direction of curates and magistrates. Other advantages were accorded them by the same government, which unfortunately had no more favorable results than the first ones.

The new citizens gave themselves up to idleness and debauchery, in spite of all that could be done to restrain them; some returned to the forests, their primitive residence; others retired to the little villages along the sea, where they found more opportunity to follow their evil inclinations. Is it for this that the severe judgment held against them by their former pastors and adopted a little blindly by the white population, should be considered as just and as applying to the whole race? I do not think so. In the first place, I have heard it said generally, that the Indians, once converted, showed much less cleverness than their free compatriots belonging to the same tribes, who proved in the chase, in war, even in their relations with the colonists, as well as in their industries, coarse as they were, to have a skill, an intelligence, one would almost say a spirit, of which the poor Californian serfs seem to have been entirely deprived. On the other hand, the commandant general of the troops, Vallejo,[2] a resolute man of means, first nephew of Governor Alvarado,[3] seeing that it would be impossible for him to persuade his fellow citizens to take

195

arms to repulse the most audacious assaults of the hordes of savages on the inhabited districts, concluded, as I said above, to form a corps of infantry from the Indians of the missions, to whom he accorded a good pay and whom he treated like Spanish soldiers. The men, seeing themselves so raised in their own eyes, entrusted to carry arms and wear a respected uniform, well nourished, cared for when ill, in fact, loved by their chiefs, have given incontestable proofs of courage, moral capacity and devotion.

I confess, that seeing in that desolate place which I traversed, those few neophytes who were still confined there, so ugly, so dirty, so badly dressed, with such a brutal air, I felt myself quite disposed to range myself amongst their detractors. In fact, they resembled beasts more than human beings; and if the women, instead of the chemise of thick cotton cloth and the covering of wool, which composed the clothing of the men, had not worn a camisole and a short petticoat of a coarse kind of flannel, of reddish color, I would have found it impossible to distinguish between the individuals of the two sexes. Still it was said that occasionally some rather pretty girls were found amongst the families of the indigenes, either amongst the Christians or the independents; but I am forced to confess that, despite my most determined researches to verify the truth of such assertions, I did not find anything to justify this contention. I have reason to believe, on the contrary, that the complaints were well founded, which the ships captains expressed generally, when putting into ports of California, regarding the fatal consequences which the debauches of the sailors had with these ugly creatures, a very great many of them being prey to shameful diseases, developed to a really frightful point. No wonder many of the individuals belonging to that unhappy race died from it; and when abortion was added to these guilty and destructuve practices, which caused inflammatory fevers, lung and bowel infections, misery naturally followed such misconduct, in fact, such frightful deprivation preyed upon the former subjects of the monks that one is not astonished that they diminished so rapidly since the destruction of the missions.

As the administrator[4] at the Mission of Santa Cruz, knowing that I desired to buy fresh vegetables and fruits for our crew, had warned the proprietors of neighboring farms, we found when we came back to the house several of them awaiting our return. Amongst them was a signora, who, by her fine features, dignified air and gracious figure attracted my attention immediately, although she was no longer very young. Our merchants, showing too exaggerated pretentions, we soon left them, but not without our having sworn many times that in no part of the country, not even at Monterey, had we found any better conditions. Nevertheless, we did not fail to remain to talk to our pretty farmerette, and to speak truthfully, we showed ourselves generally willing to make to her better terms than to her competitors; unfortunately, she was able to satisfy only a small part of our needs; and it is easy to believe that she promised more than her resources permitted, for on the morrow, at the time fixed for the delivery of the commodities, she did not put in appearance.

Notwithstanding we parted on the best possible terms, and the meeting was an agreeable diversion to the painful impressions which I had experienced shortly before, by that certain attraction which women, if gracious and good, always spread about them, and which makes men gentle, influences them, subdues them even often in spite of themselves. What an immense power, what a source of great benefit to society, when exercised with gentleness, good-will and chastity!

At the moment when we were leaving the enchantress, the monk of the mission arrived,[5] whom we had seen on landing, crouching close to the earth, hunting in the fields, and whose presence, I think, hastened the departure of our California dove. Really it was no wonder that she was frightened, because it would be difficult to find anyone with a more cynical expression, with a more brutal appearance than this unkempt Mexican priest, with his burned face, great black eyes, the whites yellowed, his head covered with a large wide-brimmed hat, the crown dented in the center, his Franciscan robes, formerly white,[6] now covered with a thousand spots, and without a cowl, but raised almost as high as his waist, in order to give sufficient liberty to his lower limbs; and finally with a carabine and a shoulder strap which contrived to make his costume somewhat picturesque, recalling to my mind the tableaux in which modern painters have retraced some of the episodes of the Spanish war, where monks, escaped from the monasteries, took up the calling of brigands and guerilla soldiers. Such a one had replaced the old Spanish padre, chief of Santa Cruz, an old man very much venerated,[7] loved in the countryside; and who having founded this mission, was able to raise it to remarkable prosperity which it enjoyed before the several revolutions had commenced, of which Mexico had been the theatre for so long a time. Instead of this prosperity I found ruins, the most profound misery, a priest, unworthy from all reports to fill the so noble and important functions of priesthood. How could a society, so unique, so little advanced in civilizations be able to progress under the direction of such ministers of religion, men as generally disreputable as their predecessors were respectable! Otherwise our new acquaintance soon made himself at home with us and acted as a good companion. Having taken us along to his abode, the same which had been occupied by his venerable predecess-dor, and which we found abandoned to disorder and the most sordid uncleanliness, our host took from the cupboards and placed on the dirty, wobbly table, nearly the only piece of furniture in the apartment, a demi-john of native wine, bread and fruit, and then invited us to partake of his improvised meal; and upon our refusal, he took long drafts, without his head seeming in the least affected.

The sun having set, and since such society did not attract us suffi-ciently for us to remain longer, I made my adieus to the two authorities of the establishment, thanking the administrator for his friendly recep-tion, and retraced the route which led us to the place on the shore where my captain's gig awaited me.

The evening was lovely; the moon gently lighted the countryside, the heavens scintillated with stars, a light breeze from the land refreshed the atmosphere, still warm from the heat of the day, and brought to us the distant sound of the clock of the mission sounding the Angelus. The path which we followed wound sometimes across a cluster of large trees, under which a superb greensward unrolled, sometimes in the midst of fields covered with a rich vegetation, from which we exhaled sweet aromatic odors.

Each of us, feeling the influence of such a lovely moment and of the memories which that enchanted spectacle awoke in his soul, marched quietly along, wholly absorbed in his own reflections. I enjoyed one of those moments so rare for a man who has reached the autumn of his life, when the imagination, left to itself, once more beautifies his future, tears away all difficulties, makes us dream again of pleasures which fate often has not reserved for us, or by which perhaps we would not be at all bene-fited. But these dreams, are they not happiness, compared with the reali-ty of life, so full of deceptions, compared with the satiety of joy, which, like the harpies of Virgil, spoil all that they touch and which impose once more the chances of war and the perils of long sea voyages, upon the very navigator who during previous expeditions has sworn a thousand times that he would never again abandon the dear beings amongst whom he so often had desired to return and pass his life?

Notes to the Text

1. The author apparently confused San Carlos Borromeo and Santa Cruz for La Perouse visited California prior to the founding of the latter mission.

2. Mariano Guadalupe Vallejo (1808-1890) a "generous and valiant Californian," was one of the west's most fascinating personalities. See Myrtle M. McKittrick, *Vallejo, Son of California* (Portland, 1944).

3. Juan Bautista Alvarado (1800-1882) served as governor between 1836 and 1842. He has been described as a "well formed, fullblooded, Californian Spaniard" with "the clearly marked mien of a pompous coward, clad in broad cloth and whiskers of a gentleman." See Thomas J Farnham, *Life, Adventures, and Travels in California* (New York, 1850), p. 54.

4. There is no record of an administrator prior to 1840. See H.A. van Coenen Torchiana, *Story of the Mission Santa Cruz* (San Francisco, 1933), p. 359.

5. *Viz.*, Father Antonio Suarez de Real (1804-1850), a Mexican-born friar who served three missions during his eighteen years in California.

6. The friars in California never wore white habits. To a person unfamiliar with their clothings the gray garment may have given the appearance of a "spotted" white.

7. Here the author compares the founder of the Mission, Father Fermin Francisco de Lasuen with the resident friar, Antonio Suarez de Real.

23

Thomas Jefferson Farnham
(1804-1848)

The once-popular recollections of Thomas Jefferson Farnham, based "partly on his own observations and partly on older printed sources,"[1] "have not withstood the tests of time."[2] Indeed one reputable authority felt, from the very outset, that the American lawyer's estimates and descriptions about Californians, "against whom he conceived a bitter prejudice, are as a rule absurdly false."[3]

Farnham harbored a deep-seated admiration for the accomplishments of the early Franciscans, noting that he "could not forbear a degree of veneration for those ancient closets of devotion; those resting-places of the wayfarer from the desert; those temples of hospitality and prayer, erected by that band of excellent and daring men, who founded the California missions, and engraved on the heart of that remote wilderness, the features of civilization and the name of God."[4]

Nonetheless, even though the Maine-born author "was not hostile to Catholic missionaries,"[5] his style "had in it too much of the 'spread eagle' to be particularly attractive"[6] to the unbiased observer.

Farnham's Travels in the Californias, and Scenes in the Pacific Ocean, "in which his own exploits and experiences are described in most exaggerated language,"[7] was published by Saxton & Miles at New York in 1844. Subsequent editions have appeared under variant titles.

References

1. *California. The Centennial of the Gold Rush and the First State Constitution. An. Exhibit in the Library of Congress* (Washington, 1949), p. 25.
2. Carl I. Wheat, *Books of the California Gold Rush* (San Francisco, 1949), Entry 73.
3. Hubert Howe Bancroft, *History of California* (San Francisco, 1886), IV, 157.
4. This excerpt is cited from Farnham's edition of 1844.

5. Zephyrin Engelhardt, O.F.M., *The Missions and Missionaries of California* (San Francisco, 1915), IV, 814.
6. Robert Glass Cleland, *A History of California: The American Period* (New York, 1927), p. 98.
7. Zoeth Skinner Eldredge (Ed.), *History of California* (New York, 1915), II, 379n.

1840

The mission buildings are situated on the north side of the valley near the sea.[1] They stand on elevated ground, which overlooks the bay and seven or eight miles of the vale. They were inhabited by a family of half-breeds, who kept the keys of the church. The edifices are built around a square area of half an acre. On the west, south, and east sides of it, are the Indian houses with their ruined walls, scalloped tile roofs, clay floors and open unglazed windows. On the north side are the church, the cells and dining hall of the Padres. The latter is about forty feet by twenty, lighted by open spaces in the outer wall, grated with handsomely turned wooden bars, and guarded by plank shutters, swinging inside. At the west end of this room is a small opening through which the food was passed from the kitchen. On the north side and east end are four doors opening into the cells of the friars. Everything appeared forsaken and undesirable. And yet I could not forbear a degree of veneration for those ancient closets of devotion; those resting-places of the wayfarer from the desert; those temples of hospitality and prayer, erected by that band of excellent and daring men, who founded the Californian missions, and engraved on the heart of that remote wilderness, the features of civilisation and the name of God.

There was an outside stairway to the tower of the church. We ascended it and beheld the broken hills, the vales and the great heaving sea, with its monsters diving and blowing; and heard it sounding loudly far and near. We saw the ruined mission of San Carmelo, and the forsaken Indians strolling over its grounds! On the timbers over head, hung six bells of different sizes—three of them cracked and toneless. Formerly one of these rang to meals, to work, and rest; and the others to the various services of the Catholic faith. Dr. Bale[2] informed us, such was the regularity of these establishments that the laboring animals stopped in the road or furrow, whenever the belle called the Indian to his duties. But prayers are no longer heard in San Carmelo; the tower no longer commands obedience to God; the buildings are crumbling to dust; the rank grass is crowding its courts; the low moss is creeping over its gaping walls; and the ox and mule are running wild on its hills.

The walls of the church are of stone masonry; the roof of brick tiles. The whole structure is somewhat lofty, and looks down upon the surrounding scenery, like an old baronial castle, from which the chase, the tournaments and the reign of beauty have departed. An oaken arm-chair, brown and marred with age, stood on the piazza, proclaiming to our lady of Guadalupe and a group of saints rudely sketched upon the walls, that Carmelo was deserted by living men. There is an old Catholic mission, one mile and three quarters above the town, called El Mission de Santa Barbara. The church itself is a stone edifice, with two towers on the end towards the town, and a high gable between them. The friars complimented Father Time, by painting on the latter something in the shape of a clock dial. In the towers are hung a number of rich toned bells, brought from old Spain nearly a hundred years ago. The roof is covered with burnt clay tiles, laid in cement. The residence of the Padres, also built of stone, forms a wing with the church towards the sea. The prisons form another, towards the highlands. Hard by are clusters of Indian huts, constructed of adobes and tile, standing in rows, with streets between.

The old Padres seem to have united with their missionary zeal a strong sense of comfort and taste. They laid off a beautiful garden, a few rods from the church, surrounded it with a high substantial fence of stone laid in Roman cement, and planted it with limes, almonds, apricots, peaches, apples, pears, quinces, &c., which are now annually yielding their several fruits in abundance. Before the church they erected a series of concentric urn fountains, ten feet in height, from the top of which the pure liquid bursts, and falls from one to another till it reaches a large pool at the base; from this it is led off a short distance to the statue of a grisly bear, from whose mouth it is ejected into a reservoir of solid masonry, six feet wide and seventy long. From the pool at the base of the urn fountains water is taken for drinking and household use. The long reservoir is the theatre of the battling, plashing, laughing and scolding of the washing-day. Around these fountains are solid, cemented stone pavements, and ducts to carry off the surplus water. Nothing of the kind can be in better taste, more substantial, or useful.

About the church and its cloisters, they brought the water around the brow of a green hill, in an open stone aqueduct, a rapid, noisy rivulet, to a square reservoir of beautiful masonry. Below, and adjoining this, are the ruins of the Padres' grist-mill. Nothing is left of its interior structure, but the large oaken ridgepole. Near the aqueduct which carries the water into the reservoir of the mills, stands a small stone edifice ten feet in length by six in width. This is the bath. Over the door, outside, is the representation of a lion's head, from which pours a beautiful jet of water. This little structure is in a good state of preservation. A cross surmounts it, as, indeed, it does everything used by the Catholic missionaries of these wilderness regions. Below the ruins of the grist-mill is another tank one hundred and twenty-feet square, by twenty deep, constructed like the one above. In this was collected water for supplying the fountains, irrigating the grounds below, and for the propulsion of different kinds of machinery. Below the mission was the tan-yard, to which the water was carried in an aqueduct, built on the top of a stone wall, from four to six feet high. Here was manufactured the leather used in making harnesses, saddles, bridles, and Indian clothing. They cultivated large tracts of land with maize, wheat, oats, peas, potatoes, beans, and grapes. Their old vineyards still cover the hill-sides. When the mission was at the height of its prosperity, there were several hundred Indians laboring in its fields, and many thousands of cattle and horses grazing in its pastures.

But its splendor has departed and with it its usefulness. The Indians who were made comfortable on these premises, are now squalid and miserable. The fields are a waste! Nothing but the church retains its ancient appearance. We will enter and describe its interior. It is one hundred and sixty feet long by sixty in width. Its walls are eight feet in thickness. The height of the nave is forty feet. On the wall, to the right, hangs a picture representing a king and a monk up to their middle in the flames of purgatory. Their posture is that of prayer and penitence; but their faces do not indicate any decided consciousness of the blistering foothold on which they stand. On the contrary, they wear rather the quiet aspect of persons who love their ease, and have an indolent kind of pleasure in the scenes around them. On the other side, near the door of the confessional, is a picture of Hell. The Devil and his staff are represented in active service. The flames of his furnace are curling around his victims, with a broad red glare, that would have driven Titian to madness. The old Monarch himself appears hotly engaged in wrapping serpents of fire around a beautiful female figure, and his subalterns, with flaming tridents, are casting torments on others, whose sins are worthy of less honorable notice. Immediately before the altar is a trap-door, opening into the vaults, where are buried the missionary Padres. Over the altar are many rich images of the saints. Among them is that of San Francisco, the patron of the missions of Upper California. Three silver candlesticks, six feet high, and a silver crucifix of the same height, with a golden image of the Saviour suspended on it, stand within the chancel. To the left of the altar is the sacristy, or priest's dressing-room. It is eighteen feet square, splendidly carpeted, and furnished with a wardrobe, chairs, mirrors, tables, ottoman, &c.

In an adjoining room of the same size are kept the paraphernalia of worship. Among these are a receptacle of the host, of massive gold in pyramidal form, and weighing at least ten pounds *avoirdupois*, and a convex lens set in a block of gold, weighing a number of pounds, through which, on certain occasions, the light is thrown so as to give the appearance of an eye of consuming fire.

A door in the eastern wall of the church leads from the foot of the chancel to the cemetery. It is a small piece of ground enclosed by a high wall, and consecrated to the burial of those Indians who die in the faith of the Catholic Church. It is curiously arranged. Walls of solid masonry, six feet apart, are sunk six feet in depth, and to a level with the surface. Between these the dead are buried in such manner that their feet touch one wall and their heads the other. These grounds have been long since filled. In order, however, that no Christian Indian may be buried in a less holy place, the bones, after the flesh has decayed, are exhumed and deposited in a little building on one corner of the premises. I entered this. Three or four cart-loads of skulls, ribs, spines, leg-bones, arm-bones &c., lay in one corner. Beside them stood two hand-hearses with a small cross attached to each. About the walls hung the mould of death!

***

Each of the missions had allotted to it by the old Spanish Government fifteen square miles of ground; and the priests having the right of choosing the sites, selected the very best soil, and in other respects the finest locations in the country. On these have been erected buildings of various plans and sizes, according to the taste of the priests and the number of Indians to be accommodated. Some are built around a square; the buildings themselves forming an enclosing wall on three sides, and a wall and gateway supplying the other side: the church, the priest's house, and Indian dwellings, workshops, granaries, and prisons, all fronting upon the enclosed area. Others are surrounded by a high wall; others are built on the open plain, the church in the centre, and the Indian huts leading off from it in rows, forming streets. And still others have the church, the granaries, magazines, jail, &c., enclosed with a wall, while the huts of the Indians stand unprotected outside.

They are generally constructed of large unburnt bricks, and roofed with tiles. Some of the churches and priests' houses are of stone; and being whitewashed by way of preeminence among the Indian dwellings, make an imposing appearance upon the lofty hills, on the borders of the sea, or the rich spreading plains among the green highlands.

Each of the establishments is designed to have two priests. This intention, however, is not always carried out. More commonly one priest, with his major-domo, and several subordinate officers to overlook the labor of the Indians, constitute the official court of a Mission.

The married Indians, and the officers and priests of the Missions, occupy houses. The unmarried Indians of all ages are put into large rooms at nights which are well grated and locked, to prevent them from escaping to the wilderness and their former habits of life. The unmarried females and males thus imprisoned in their separate apartments at night, and kept separate at their duties during the day, never associate much together until they are married. This is deemed necessary to preserve their virtue.

The churches of these missions are well supplied with the paraphernalia of the Roman Catholic worship, the altar, the receptacle of the host, the censer, the cross, the images of the Saviour and the Saints, pictures of Paradise and Hell. These, the costly dresses of the priests, and the imposing processions and ceremonies of the church, were well calculated to arrest the attention of those most stupid of all the North American Indians; and give them their first impulses toward the paths of moral virtue.

The religious exercises of the Missions are those common to Catholic churches throughout the world. Morning and evening Mass; the commemoration of the Patron Saints; High Mass on extraordinary occasions; religious processions on Corpus Christi and other great festal occasions; at which times the young Indian girls are dressed in scarlet skirts and white bodices, or other colors suitable to the occasion. Every Indian, male and female, is obliged to attend the worship; and if they lag behind, a large leathern thong, at the end of a heavy whip-staff, is applied to their naked backs, that the pain of disobedience may be contrasted with the pleasures of the opposite course.

In church, the males and females occupy different sides, with a broad aisle between them. In this aisle are stationed men with whips and goads to enforce order and silence and keep them in a kneeling posture. By this arrangements the untamed and vicious are generally made willing to comply with the forms of the service. In addition to these restraints, a guard of soldiers with fixed bayonets occupies one end of the church, who may suppress by their more powerful weapons and strong demonstrations against this comfortable mode of worshipping God. The choirs of the churches are composed of Indians, who perform quite well upon various kinds of instruments, and chant with considerable musical accuracy. It is due to the Padres to say, that they devote nearly all their time to the good of the converts; and, bating the objections which we have to the manner of conversion, and of sustaining them in the way of grace, no fault can be found with them. They treat them like children, and appear to have a sincere concern that they should live and die in the arms of that faith, which they believe to be the only guide of the soul in its way to Heaven.

Notes to the Text

1. The author is referring to San Carlos Borromeo Mission.
2. Edward Turner Bale (1808-1849) was an English surgeon then practicing at Monterey.

24

Eugene Duflot de Mofras
(1810-1884)

Eugene Duflot de Mofras, a young attache at the French embassy in Mexico City, came to California, in 1841, "to examine and report on the country, its institutions, resources, history and prospects."[1] An advance agent of King Louis Philippe, Duflot de Mofras was a "gentleman of learning and culture"[2] who recorded his observations and later published "a complete description of the country, its past history and present condition."[3]

The diplomat's account, "superior to any issued within that decade,"[4] was compiled from the principal works that had been published on the subject, and supplemented by his own researches."[5] Presumably intended as a continuation of Friedrich H.A. Humboldt's description of California, "it would be difficult to find a more complete account of any comparatively unknown country."[6]

Duflot de Mofras was sharply critical of such foreign visitors as Frederick William Beechey and Alexander Forbes who slandered "the Spanish clergy from whom they have received the most generous hospitality," maintaining that facts "clearly disprove their contentions." Concerning the missions, every one of which he apparently visited, Duflot de Mofras was astonished "to see with what scanty resources they have achieved amazing results."[7] While speaking reverentially of the friars and their works, he unfortunately swallowed, in good faith, "the extravagant stories [about mission finances] and published them to the world which stood gasping in amazement at the immense wealth of the missionaries."[8]

Published at Paris under the editorship of Arthus Bertrand by the French government, the two volume Exploration du Territoire de l'Orégon des California et de la Mer Vermeille, exécutée pendant les années 1840, 1841 et 1842 was "the only early illustrated work on the Pacific coast comparable in beauty to the Voyage pittoresque of [Louis] Choris or to [Frederic B.] Litké's account of the Russian survey of the northwest coast."[9] The 1844 edition *was reproduced a number of times. In 1937, Marguerite Eyer Wilbur provided an English translation which was released in twin volumes at Santa Ana as* Duflot de Mofras' Travels on the Pacific Coast.

References

1. Francis Price and William H. Ellison, (Trans.) *Occurrences in Hispanic California by Angustias de la Guerra Ord* (Washington, 1956), p. 89.
2. Theodore H. Hittell, *History of California* (San Francisco, 1898), II, 291.
3. Robert J. Woods in *The Zamorano 80* (Los Angeles, 1945), p. 23.
4. Robert E. Cowan, *A Bibliography of the History of California and the Pacific West, 1510-1906* (San Francisco, 1914), p. 74
5. Hubert Howe Bancroft, *History of California* (San Francisco, 1886), IV, 253.
6. Theodore H. Hittell, *op. cit.*, II, 292.
7. The quotation here cited is from the 1937 edition.
8. Zephyrin Engelhardt, O.F.M., *San Gabriel Mission* (San Gabriel, 1927), p. 197.
9. Wright Howes, *U.S. Iana (1650-1950)* (New York, 1963), p. 174.

1841-1842

While the Fathers were thus building missions to civilize the Indians, the governors were establishing military posts, called presidios, and pueblos or villages composed of married soldiers and white settlers who had been brought up from Sonora, Sinaloa, and Lower California. Since these three types of establishments, missions, presidios, and pueblos, are somewhat similar, a description of one will indicate in a general way their main characteristics. By way of illustration, the mission dedicated to St. Louis, King of France, one of the finest and architecturally the most symmetrical, will be chosen.

Mission San Luís Rey de Francia is built in the form of a quadrangle, 150 meters in width, with a chapel occupying one of the wings. Along the facade extends an ornamental cloister. The building, which is one story high, is raised a few feet above the ground. The interior, in the form of a court, is adorned with fountains and planted with trees. Off the surrounding cloister open doors lead into rooms occupied by priests, majordomos, and travelers, as well as the main rooms, schools, and shops. Infirmaries for men and women are placed in a secluded corner of the mission. Nearby the school is situated. Young Indian women live in what is known as the monestary, *el monjerío*, and are called nuns or *monjas*, for the Fathers are forced to lock them up to protect them from the brutality of the Indians. Placed under the surveillance of faithful Indian matrons, these young women are taught to weave wool, cotton, and flax, and do not leave the monastery until old enough to marry. Indian children are educated in the schools together with the children of the white colonists. A limited number, selected from pupils who display the most intelligence, study music—elementary singing, the violin, flute, horn, violincello, and other instruments. Those who show ability as carpenters, blacksmiths, or farmers are called *alcaldes*, or chiefs, and are given charge of a group of workers.

In the days before civil authority was substituted for the paternalism of the Fathers, the personnel of each mission consisted of two priests. The elder took charge of administration and religious instruction, the younger of agricultural development. Although the Franciscans wisely mastered several Indian dialects, yet they were often forced to resort to interpreters, because of the variety of idioms in Upper California an inexplicable phenomenon encountered, moreover, throughout America. The Fathers employed only what white men were strictly necessary to keep order and discipline in the missions, for they realized how the latter corrupted the natives and how contact with them only developed in the Indians habits of gambling and drunkenness for which unfortunately, they had a natural taste.

To encourage the Indians to work, the Fathers often labored with them. Only a few years ago Father Caballero,[1] head of the Dominican Order, died at the plow, where he was working among his neophytes at the Mission of Nuestra Señora de Guadalupe. Necessity forced them to be industrious; and it is astonishing to see with what scanty resources they have achieved amazing results. Frequently without the aid of European workmen and with the assistance merely of unintelligent and often hostile natives, they have found time, in addition to their cultural achievements, to construct buildings of considerable architectural merit, and devices requiring mechanical knowledge such as windmills, machines, weavers' looms, bridges, roads, and irrigation ditches. To construct the majority of the missions it has been necessary to carry stone or timber that was cut up in the mountains for 8 or 10 leagues to the site selected and to teach the Indians to make lime, cut stone, and lay adobes.

Surrounding the mission are the workshops, the huts of the neophytes, and the houses of a few white settlers. In addition to the main buildings, 15 or 20 subsidiary farms and some auxiliary chapels lie within a radius of 30 or 40 square leagues. Across from the mission are the quarters of the priests' bodyguard, an escort consisting of four cavalrymen and a sergeant. This guard is also used to relay messages and dispatches from mission to mission, and to repulse Indian raids which, in the early days of the conquest, threatened the settlements.

A uniform regime was followed in each community. For convenience the Indians were divided into working units. At sunrise, as the bells tolled the angelus, all assembled at the church. After mass came breakfast; then the daily tasks began. Luncheon was served at eleven. A period of rest lasting for two hours followed, then work was resumed until the evening angelus, an hour before sunset. After prayers and the rosary, the Indians dined, danced, and played games. Food consisted of fresh beef or mutton and wheat or corn cakes, as well as stews called *atóle* and *pinóle*. The natives also received peas and beans to the amount of an *almud*, or one-twelfth of a *fanega* each week; that is, approximately one hectoliter a month. Clothing consisted of a linen shirt, trousers, and a woolen blanket; however, the alcaldes and best workers wore the Spanish costume. Once a year the women received two chemises, a dress, and a wrap.

Whenever hides, tallow, cereals, wine, and oil were sold at a profit to foreign ships, the Fathers distributed handkerchiefs, clothes, tobacco, rosaries, and glass beads to the Indians, reserving the surplus to embellish the churches by the purchase of musical instruments, tablets, and sacerdotal ornaments. Part of the harvest, however, was always stored in the granaries to be used during years when the crops were poor.

Especially notable in the organization of these missions is the fact that no assistance was received from the government. In the original establishments of Lower California the viceroys, on the other hand, supplied some assistance. In the early years of his reign, Philip V granted the missions the sum of 30,000 *piasters*. But by 1735, the Jesuits, who had received a considerable number of donations which they had managed successfully, were able not only to support their own missions but also to branch out into new territory. In 1767 a resident of Guadalajara, Doña Josefa de Miranda,[2] left to the college of the Company in her city a legacy exceeding 100,000 *piasters* in currency, which the Jesuits, already embroiled in European scandals, had the delicacy to refuse.

At the present day the properties owned by the Pious Fund of California, with their subsequent increases, are: The lands or *haciendas* of San Pedro, Torreón, Rincón, and Las Golondrinas, as well as several mines, freight boats, immense herds, and lands that include more than 500 square leagues, all situated in the new principality of Leon, or the province of Tamaulipas. These properties were donated to the Company on June 8, 1735, by the Marquis de Villa Puente,[3] grand chancellor of New Spain, and by his wife, the Marquise de las Torres.[4] Other legacies that have materially enriched the properties of the Society of Jesus are situated near San Luís de Potosí, Guanajuato, and Guadalajara.

The estate known as the Hacienda de la Cienaga del Pastor, which lies near the latter village, still brings in annually, despite its dilapidated condition and poor management, more than 24,000 piasters. Another property owned by the company, the Hacienda de Chalco, belongs to the

Pious Fund which also possesses a large number of houses and other buildings situated in the cities, especially Mexico City.

In 1827 the government confiscated the sum of 78,000 *piasters in specie* that had been deposited in the bank at the capital, which represented the profits from the sale of Arroyo Zarco, a property of the Company. The Pious Fund also had extensive lands confiscated by the Congress of Jalisco and, as has already been said, President Santa Anna sold the entire Pious Fund to the firms of Barrio and Rubio frères.

During the Spanish régime revenues amounted approximately to 50,000 piastres. These were adequate to pay the stipend or *sinodo*, made to the Fathers—15 Dominicans at 600 piasters and 40 Franciscans at 400 piasters. After subtracting this total of 25,000 piasters, the balance was used to purchase materials, machinery, tools, and sacred ornaments for the faith. The government in turn reimbursed the procurator of the missions in Mexico for various kinds of furniture made by the missions for the companies at the presidios. The procurator then converted this money into merchandise which he shipped at his own expense overland to the port of San Blas. From there frigates transported this twice a year gratuitously to the various ports of California.

During the prosperous reign of Charles III the port and arsenal of San Blas achieved considerable importance. At the instigation of the Spanish government, an intelligent agent came out to show the Fathers how to handle hemp; and, since the land belonging to the missions offered conditions favorable to its cultivation, the priests raised crops with such success that they were able to send out large shipments annually to the boatswain's warehouse at San Blas. An amount equal to the value of these products was then paid from the royal treasury to the procurator of missions in Mexico City. For the last twenty years this valuable industry has been inactive and at all the ports along the west coast of Mexico ships can procure rope made only in Europe or the United States at exorbitant prices.

From 1811 to 1818, and from 1823 to January 1831, the missionaries, owing to the political troubles which at this time were rife in Spain and Mexico, failed to receive their regular salaries. Thus, by adding the amounts due Franciscans in Upper California alone, and increasing by 192,000 *piasters*, the 78,000 taken forcibly from the Order, there remain 270,000 *piasters* which the missions of Upper California should recover for furniture made at the presidios. This, together with the revenues derived from the Pious Fund properties for a period of ten years or more, makes a total in excess of 1,000,000 piasters which the Mexican government has confiscated from the various missions in open defiance of the wishes of the donors.

On May 25, 1832, the Mexican Congress handed down a decree whereby the executors were ordered to consolidate the properties held by the Pious Fund for seven years and impound its revenue in the national treasury. A second decree of Congress, enacted September 19, 1836, ordered the Pious Fund to be placed once more at the disposal of the new bishop of California and his successors.[5] This was to enable the prelates, to whom its administration had been entrusted, to use this revenue to develop missions or similar enterprises in conformity with the wishes of its founders.

On February 8, 1842, General Santa Anna,[6] acting president, by virtue of his discretional power received[7] from the bishop of California, in the face of his protests, the administration of the Pious Fund. By a decree of the 21st of that same month, this was entrusted to General Valencia,[8] commander-in-chief of the army. To those familiar with this country, the true significance of the term administrator is obvious. This was the last blow before the final sale, directed against an organization built by the Jesuits. In all fairness, however, the fact should be mentioned that up to the present time the few Franciscans remaining in California have received an annual subsidy of 400 *piasters*, but in merchandise quoted at exorbitant prices.

So long as the Fathers retained complete control both of temporal and spiritual matters at the missions, an annual report was made of the births, marriages, and deaths of the Indians, the amount of grain planted, harvests, and the increase in live stock. The Fathers were not compelled, however, to give a minute account of their products, for they were known to be devoted to the interests of their neophytes who were as dear to them as if they had been their own children. These reports, sent to the apostolic prefect, were dispatched to the governor of the province who transmitted them to the viceroy of Mexico and the king of Spain, and, later, to the Mexican Government. A copy of these documents was also sent to the Royal College of San Fernando and through this channel finally reached Madrid and the Commissioner for the Indies,[9] who was head of the Franciscans in America. From there these reports were sent to the general of the Order at Rome.

While the Mexican Government was thus absorbing the Pious Fund and removing from the Fathers the temporal administration of the missions, their agents were working diligently to pillage these same establishments and destroy their live stock which was worth a fortune. Already by 1822, the fatal year of separation from Spain, a few partisans of the new régime were advocating the idea of secularization.

Notwithstanding, until 1830 the Spanish missionaries were able to retain control. But in 1831, the Reverend Father President Sánchez,[10] who had courageously opposed the advent of civil control, had died of grief and the majority of the Fathers who had been harshly treated decided to leave the country. And so these men who had consecrated thirty or forty years of their lives to enlightening and civilizing the Indians, who had succeeded by their efforts in turning them from their heathen ways, who had acquired agricultural properties and live stock of considerable value, who had administered immense sums, amounting at one time to more than 500,000 francs, these venerable Fathers departed from a land they had civilized by their own labors and apostolic teachings, carrying with them as their entire capital only a few coarse woolen garments!

A fundamental principle in the establishment of the Spanish mission system was that the fruit of their labors and the soil itself belonged to the Indians, the Fathers being merely administrators and directors. The sacred precept, *Pater est tutor ad bona Indiorum*,[11] was carefully followed, and the prelates watched to see that the priests took from the revenues only what was needed for food and clothing. Furthermore, the Franciscans observed the vow of poverty, and could own no personal property.

During the Spanish régime, the priests were under the control of a president or apostolic prefect, a member like themselves of the Royal College of San Fernando in Mexico City. In Lower California the Dominicans also had their local president.

In 1833 the ranks of the Spanish Franciscans were materially reduced by the departure, or death, of several of their members, and as the College at Mexico City could not replace them, the government appealed to the College of Nuestra Señora de Guadalupe, at Zacatecas, which sent ten of its members to New California.[12] The Mexican clergy soon met opposition from the older Spanish Fathers who by their exemplary conduct and austere morals formed a striking contrast to the lax habits of the creoles. To avoid difficulties the two Orders separated; and as a milder climate proved more suitable to the aged Franciscans, they withdrew to the southern missions, while Mexican priests took charge of administrating those in the northern territory.

Prior to that time the popes, by a series of bulls, had accorded the apostolic prefect various ecclesiastical powers. Finally, on April 27, 1840, Gregory XVI established the bishopric of the Californias and appointed to this seat the Reverend Father Francisco García Diego, a Franciscan from Mexico, who had served many years as a missionary, designating

San Diego, the most central point in these two provinces, as his place of residence. In the meanwhile the bishop for various reasons failed to reach California before January, 1842.[13] Since the mission at San Diego is extremely poor, and since he was receiving only a small subsidy from the government, he decided to take up his residence at the mission that afforded the most resources, and so located temporarily at the pueblo of Santa Barbara.

The influence of the bishop, under these circumstances, will not be widespread; his advanced age and his Mexican education will not permit him to take part in any spiritual conquests, nor augment the imposing foundations that are the glory of the Spanish Fathers. To erect new establishments, or to rehabilitate those now in ruins, requires men who are young, ardent, and of pure morals, men who are imbued with high ideals and undaunted by hardship or danger. Only by their religious proselytising did the early Fathers succeed in winning over the Indians, for the latter seldom understood Spanish and the Fathers did not always know the local dialects. In this task of conversion, even though religion was their aim, material considerations proved the means to this goal. The Fathers also solved the important problem of how to make work attractive. They also led the Indians to believe that by living near the missions they would be sheltered from the attacks of hostile tribes, and could more readily find a livelihood by taking part in the simple and varied tasks at the mission rather than by seeking it in the dangerous and uncertain manner afforded by hunting and plunder.

At certain seasons when agricultural work was suspended, many neophytes returned to their own tribes. The tales they invariably told of the kind treatment received at the missions encouraged their friends to visit the nearest settlements where they were regally received by the Fathers, who showered them with gifts. From time to time the latter also went out on scouting trips of exploration among the native tribes, where they succeeded, both by persuasion as well as by the distribution of trinkets, in winning over Indian converts. That they ever used force to attain this end is entirely false.

For foreign writers to slander the Spanish clergy from whom they have received the most generous hospitality is indeed deplorable. With typical English coldness, Captain Beechey and Mr. Forbes, men imbued with the intolerance of Protestantism, are inclined to ridicule and cast insinuations on the activities of the Fathers. Facts, however, clearly disprove their contentions.

What has become, moreover, of the population of the Tahitian Islands

216

under the tutelage of the Methodists, Anabaptists, and other sects? They now number scarcely 6,000 inhabitants! And what has happened in the Sandwich Islands, where Captain Cook found 400,000 natives, and where at the present there are fewer than 100,000? When the English colonists settled along the New England coast and in Pennsylvania, these lands were occupied by large and powerful Indian tribes. Yet, with the exception of the unfortunate Seminoles whom the government at Washington has already spent over $6,000,000 in an attempt to exterminate, not a single Indian is found along the coast of the United States. In the Spanish possessions, on the other hand—Mexico, New Granada, Chile, Buenos Aires, and even in the Philippines, all lands where Catholicism has extended its benign influence—there exist entire tribes of Indians who have retained their own manners, customs, and traditions under the paternal care of the Fathers. Travelers are invariably impressed to discover near Indian villages where the lands are carefully cultivated and where irrigation is highly developed, colonies of white settlers living in abject misery, who rank as freemen under so-called republics.

While the inferior intelligence of the Indians did not permit them fully to understand the mysteries of the faith, yet the Fathers, with the aid of the sign language, usually succeeded in making them understand its main truths. They attempted especially to develop in them moral instincts and sound habits. Their relationship with the Indians was primarily paternal, being not unlike that of father and son. When a Father met an Indian, he greeted him with the words, "Love God, my son!" "Love God, Father," was the reply.

Although instances are not unknown where Indians, instigated by the medicine men and sorcerers of their tribes who were jealous of the influence of the Fathers have massacred the latter, yet they usually revered them as supernatural beings. This was especially pronounced after they watched the Californian missions which had been erected by their own hands, and the cattle which had been raised with infinite care by their own efforts, being destroyed and confiscated by Mexican agents. For after they themselves were forced to submit to harsh treatment, they thought with regret of the ways of these charitable men who knew how to temper rigid justice with kindliness, men to whom they could always turn for help in times of need and for consolation in times of sorrow.

At this time[14] the Spanish monarch created the office of captain general of the internal provinces which was independent of the viceroyalty in Mexico City, and which included New Mexico, Sonora, and the Californias. To this office, Teodoro de Croix was appointed.[15] De Croix, while en route to his port, stopped on August 15 at Queretaro, where he gave orders for the Franciscans of the local Santa Cruz College to found two missions on tho banks of the Colorado River. These were needed to facilitate the trip from Sonora to California, by affording a place of rest and a means of protection to trains coming overland.

Unfortunately, these two missions were established under a new system. They had no presidios for their support, although each had a guard of eight soldiers in charge of an ensign for its defense. Eight colonists and their families who had charge of the live stock lived near the mission. The Fathers, four in number,[16] had charge only of the spiritual life of the community. The Indians continued to live among their own tribesmen beyond the jurisdiction of the Fathers, instead of being grouped around the missions as they were in Upper California. The two missions were established on the right bank of the Colorado above its mouth. The first was dedicated to San Pedro y San Pablo; the second, established three leagues farther south, was called Purísima Concepción. These lay about 60 leagues east of the port of San Diego, and approximately 80 from Mission San Gabriel.

Later, in 1781, De Croix sent Captain Don Fernando Rivera,[17] in command of a company of 75 cavalrymen, with approximately 100 colonists and their families and 2,000 animals, to found the presidio, pueblo, and three missions planned along the Santa Barbara channel, as well as the pueblo of Nuestra Señora de los Angeles on the tiny Porciúncula River. Having reached the Colorado, Captain Rivera sent his train on toward Monterey, then stopped with seven soldiers on the banks of this river to give his animals time to rest. The Yuma Indians, who lived nearby, had been watching the founding of new colonies with some displeasure, for the colonists seized what little fertile land lay along the river banks and prevented the Indians from planting their usual crop of corn, beans, melons, and gourds. Their live stock also destroyed the pastures where the Indians formerly found abundant game, as well as several kinds of barley and wild oats whose kernels when boiled afforded an agreeable diet. To these grievances the Spanish soldiers added further insults by abusing several Indians and their wives. As the missionaries, stripped of temporal authority, were unable to restrain them, the tribes began to hate the white settlers, and resolved to exterminate them. The Fathers, aware of this situation, tried to persuade the soldiers to be more moderate and prudent, but the latter paid no heed to their sage counsel.

Vengeance came swiftly. One Sunday in July[18] several thousand Indians attacked the two missions simultaneously after Mass, set them on

218

fire, killed Captain Rivera, his soldiers, most of the colonists, and the four Franciscan Fathers who, as soon as the massacre commenced, began to exercise their saintly calling. The Indians then pillaged the houses, carried off all the animals, and took prisoners of all whom they could find. A lone soldier,[19] stationed on the left bank of the Colorado River, escaped and carried this sad news to the nearest presidio in Sonora. Almost simultaneously an ensign and a few soldiers who arrived from Lower California where they had met some frontier Indians, communicated the news to the Governor of California; Don Felipe de Neve, who at the time was at Mission San Gabriel. The governor immediately sent an ensign and nine veterans down to the missions that had been destroyed. Upon arriving at the scene of the Massacre they found the buildings in ashes and the bodies unburied.

Attacked shortly after by the Yumas, who killed two men, they were obliged to withdraw in haste to San Gabriel. Informed of this calamity, the captain general of the internal provinces then ordered Colonel Don Pedro Fages[20] to march down with a detachment of Catalonian dragoons and leather-jacket soldiers to avenge their countrymen. These troops crossed the Colorado, reached the scene of the disaster, collected the bodies of their Fathers, and succeeded in rescuing all those taken captive. They were unable, however, to punish the Indians, who cautiously carried on all transactions from a safe distance by signals, and kept well beyond the range of firearms.

This tragic experience revealed to the Marquis de Croix that the original plan adopted for the foundation of the missions, which placed in the hands of the Fathers full spiritual and temporal control, alone could succeed. As a result he now directed his attention solely to the founding of pueblos and the organization of presidios. This led to the development of the triple system which has proved so admirable a phase of the Spanish colonization policy: religious control of the missions; civil control for the pueblos; and military control for the presidios.

Notes to the Text

1. Father Felix Caballero, O.P., the next-to-last *Presidente* of the Baja California missions succumbed at his post on July 11, 1840.
2. The wealthy Mexican dowager, Josefa de Arguellas y Miranda (d.1767). had willed her entire fortune to the Jesuit missions. Growing criticism of the Society's financial entanglements probably accounts for their renouncing of the estate.
3. Jose de la Puente Peña Castrejon y Salzines, Marques de Villapuente (d. Feb. 13,

1739), was probably the largest single donor to the Pious Fund of the Californias. See Nicholas de Segura, S.J., *Platicas Panegyricas, y Morales, sobre et cantico del Magnificat* (Mexico, 1742). Volume IX.

4. The marquise was a daughter of Andres de Rada, Provincial of New Spain.

5. See Francis J. Weber, "The Pious Fund of the Californias," *Hispanic American Historical Review* XLIII (February, 1963), 80.

6. Antonio Lopez de Santa Anna (1794-1876), a native of Jalapa in the State of Vera Cruz, was a "mere political weathercock" according to Hubert Howe Bancroft. See *Chronicles of the Builders* (San Francisco, 1892), II, 99.

7. A more descriptive and accurate term than "received" would be "seized."

8. General Gabriel Valencia (1799-1848) later gained momentary prominence under Santa Anna when he was entrusted with administration of the Pious Fund of the Californias.

9. The Commissariate of the Indies, to which the Apostolic College of San Fernando was directly subject, operated under provisions of Royal Patronage. See Francis J. Weber, "Real Patronato de Indias," *Historical Society of Southern California* XLIII (June, 1961), 215-219.

10. Father Jose Bernardo Sanchez (1778-1833) was *Presidente* between 1827 and 1830.

11. *I.e.* "the friars are the guardians of the natives."

12. The Zacatecans arrived in California in 1833, under the leadership of Fray Francisco Garcia Diego y Moreno.

13. Although it was only in January that California's first bishop took up residence in Santa Barbara, he had arrived at his diocesan seat of San Diego on December 10, 1841.

14. *I.e.* in 1777.

15. Teodoro de Croix (1730-1791) was appointed *Comandante General* with vice-regal authority of the new territorial division on May 16, 1776. See Alfred Barnaby Thomas, *Teodoro de Croix and the Northern Frontier of New Spain*, 1776-1783 (Oklahoma, 1941).

16. *Viz.*, Juan Antonio Barreneche (1749-1781), Juan Diaz (1736-1781), Matías Moreno (1744-1781) and Francisco Hermenegildo Garces (1738-1781).

17. Fernando Javier Rivera y Moncada had come from Peninsular California where he had been governor. Though not as forceful as Fages and Neve, Rivera "was popular and left among the old Californian soldiers a better reputation probably than any of his contemporaries." See Hubert Howe Bancroft, *History of California* (San Francisco, 1884), I, 363.

18. The uprising took place on July 18-19, 1781.

19. As a matter of fact, in addition to women and children, others escaped the holocaust.

20. Pedro Fages (1730-1796) came to California in 1769. He was named governor in September of 1782.